APACHE VOICES

SHERRY ROBINSON

Apache
Voices

THEIR STORIES OF SURVIVAL AS TOLD TO EVE BALL

University of New Mexico Press   Albuquerque

Library of Congress Cataloging-in-Publication Data

Robinson, Sherry.
   Apache voices : their stories of survival as told to Eve Ball / Sherry
K. Robinson —
1st ed.
      p.   cm.
Includes bibliographical references and index.
   ISBN 0-8263-2162-3 (cloth : alk. paper)
   1. Apache Indians—History. 2. Apache Indians—Interviews. I. Ball,
Eve. II. Title.
   E99.A6 R59 2000
   979´.004972—dc21   99-05069

This book is dedicated to

Eve Ball, a noble lady,

and the Apache people.

Contents

Acknowledgments

When I showed up at Brigham Young University in 1995, I was a stranger to curator Dennis Rowley. And yet he and his staff, which included Susan Thompson, treated me like visiting royalty. Without their help and cooperation, this book would not have been possible. I regret that he didn't live to see the results of that friendship.

Writers often complain of their isolation. I was much less isolated on this trip because of Jo Martín, then working on her master's thesis on Apache women. In months of long weekly phone calls, we visited, commiserated, and exchanged information. I'm indebted to Jo for some of my critical information, as well as for her encouragement and support. Similarly, researcher Alicia Delgadillo, whom I met after completing the work, helped fill in some gaps and provided support.

And I thank Ed Sweeney for his information, his interest, and for keeping me honest.

Introduction

In one of my first jobs, I worked for a mining tycoon who had made his fortune reprocessing tailings piles from the last century. He figured the old technology had left gold behind in the rust-colored mounds that dotted Colorado's mountains, and he was right. I've thought a lot about him in the years spent on this work.

I did the scholarly equivalent in mining the raw data of historian Eve Ball. She had interviewed the elderly survivors of the Apache wars and written In the Days of Victorio and Indeh: An Apache Odyssey. Like others who read the books, I wanted to write about Victorio's sister Lozen, the woman warrior. Seeking more information, I tracked Eve's papers to Brigham Young University in Provo, Utah. There I prowled page by page through seventeen boxes of stuff that hadn't been sorted, much less archived. It was still in the same state in which Eve had shipped it years earlier. This is no criticism of BYU; Dennis Rowley, curator of special collections, intended to archive the papers, but cancer would see that he didn't. Still, Dennis and his staff were enormously helpful to me.

It quickly became clear that this wouldn't be the usual research project. As I sat in the library, sneezing and blowing my nose from years-old dust and pollen in the files, my search became more personal. The boxes yielded portions of transcripts, manuscripts, notes to clerical help—sometimes held together with Eve's bobby pins—along with letters to friends and fellow writers, written in large script, describing her deteriorating vision and repeated cataract operations. At one point, I found the magnifying screen she used to see her own work.

Eve wasn't a young woman when she began interviewing Apache elders in the 1940s, and it took her decades to gather information and run hurdles with skeptical publishers. By the time she was finishing Indeh, her health and eyesight were failing. It was humbling to grasp the enormity of her obstacles. At the same time I realized that not only were the old Apaches, Eve's subjects, long gone, but so too were the people who knew most about them—Eve, Angie Debo, and Dan Thrapp.

Paging through reams of paper, I began to suspect that Eve hadn't used all her material. With a mixed sense of excitement and trepidation, I felt obliged to mine these tailings as my old boss had, tell the untold stories, and be as faithful as possible to Eve's purpose and that of her Apache friends.

I returned home with a box of photocopies and spent six months organizing it. Nothing was in its proper file, the result of use by someone who couldn't see. And because Eve had cut her transcripts to pieces in the course of writing stories for western magazines, a whole transcript was rare. I literally had to piece transcripts and manuscripts back together, attempting to match typeface or even wrinkles and tears in the paper.

It seemed I had some interesting bits and pieces, but whether there was enough to justify a book, I didn't know. I began keyboarding my precious bits. In another six months, I decided I did have enough to knit together some accounts—not the revelations of Indeh and Victorio, but some darn good stories.

And I had something else—some needed corrections, clarifications, and reinterpretation. I have the greatest respect for Eve and the work she did, but it doesn't mean I've set aside my objectivity. Anyone manipulating that much information, no matter how careful, will make some mistakes and I found some. I also believe that she was impartial, but given her close relationship to some of her informants, she couldn't help but take up their point of view. And finally, there is the matter of style.

Eve's good friends and fellow Apache scholars Dan Thrapp and Angie Debo supported her work and defended her presentation of the Apache side of the story when others didn't. But her style—first person and somewhat fictionalized—was problematic. Eve was a regular contributor to western magazines and carried that style of writing into Victorio. Fellow historians urged her to write in third person, quoting from her Apache sources, but as she wrote Dan Thrapp in 1967, she felt strongly that "people of ordinary reading ability and interests might get some history without encountering what is to them forbidding in the way of scholarly concepts of writing history."

To such arguments, Angie Debo responded, "You are entirely right in saying that history should be interesting. There is no excuse for bad writing, either in history or any other non-fiction. But when you are writing history, you cannot invent, say conversation, facial expression, weather — not anything. If you do, this is not history, but excellent historical fiction."

As a journalist, I certainly understood and sympathized with Eve's passionate desire for history to be understandable to everyone. And I enjoyed Victorio because it gave me a more personal view of the Apaches than the usual statistical tallies of battles and casualties. However, as a journalist, I was uncomfortable with this dramatized history and preferred to hear people's own words.

This is how I've presented this information: To give readers a flavor of these original accounts, I've included several in their original, unvarnished form, even though they introduce no new information. In all the accounts, I retained information relevant to the subject. Ellipses reflect instances when the speaker went off on a tangent, where the account didn't make sense or was inaccurate, or where the transcript was unreadable. They also indicate a change in sequence. Anybody who has interviewed people, as I have, knows that all reminiscences jump forward and backward in time, and I reordered some statements so the story follows chronologically.

In relating information, I relied as much as possible on transcripts, but when there were gaps I turned next to Eve's manuscripts because they contained much unused information, and lastly, to her books and published articles. I checked information to the extent possible with other sources.

A second issue I encountered was Eve's penchant for sprucing up her friends' speech, something else that earned criticism from academics. She wrote Thrapp that Asa Daklugie (Geronimo's chosen successor) "was a very remarkable character. I have been criticized for putting into his mouth good English. But I took his dictation in shorthand and wrote it as he spoke.. . . I can't help it if the learned doctors think the Apaches say 'plenty guns' and 'heap game.' They just don't do it. I doubt very much that they ever did. A certain pattern has emerged and writers attempt to make the Indians conform to it."

There is merit to both sides of this argument. Comparing transcripts with the written version in her books, it's clear Eve cleaned up the dialogue. Not only did she object to the "heap-big" vernacular attributed to Indians, but translations of Apache statements reveal that they were articulate and even poetic in their own language. Eve was trying to capture that. Another significant factor is that most of her primary sources were educated at Carlisle Indian School and spoke good English, so they were leagues beyond the usual trading-post-Indian parlance. But it was their second language, so it wasn't exactly the Queen's English. Nowadays, we're open-minded about such things and would expect to see their words exactly as they were spoken.

A third issue was Eve's mixing of history and anthropology; it annoys the academics. I am also guilty as charged. To understand people, you must learn their history and their culture.

In my view, these are small complaints. Eve has an important place in history as the courageous and stubborn woman who earned the Apaches' trust, persuaded them to tell their side of the story, and then got that story into print—significant accomplishments on all counts. She also deserves credit as the first historian to introduce us in a meaningful way to Apache women and family life; I've noticed that subsequent books and articles on Indian women and Apache women rely heavily on Eve's work.

Completing this project, I find that I've loved this work so much that I'm sad to have it end. I've spent four years hearing Apache voices in my head and sometimes in my dreams. Now it's time for others to hear them too.

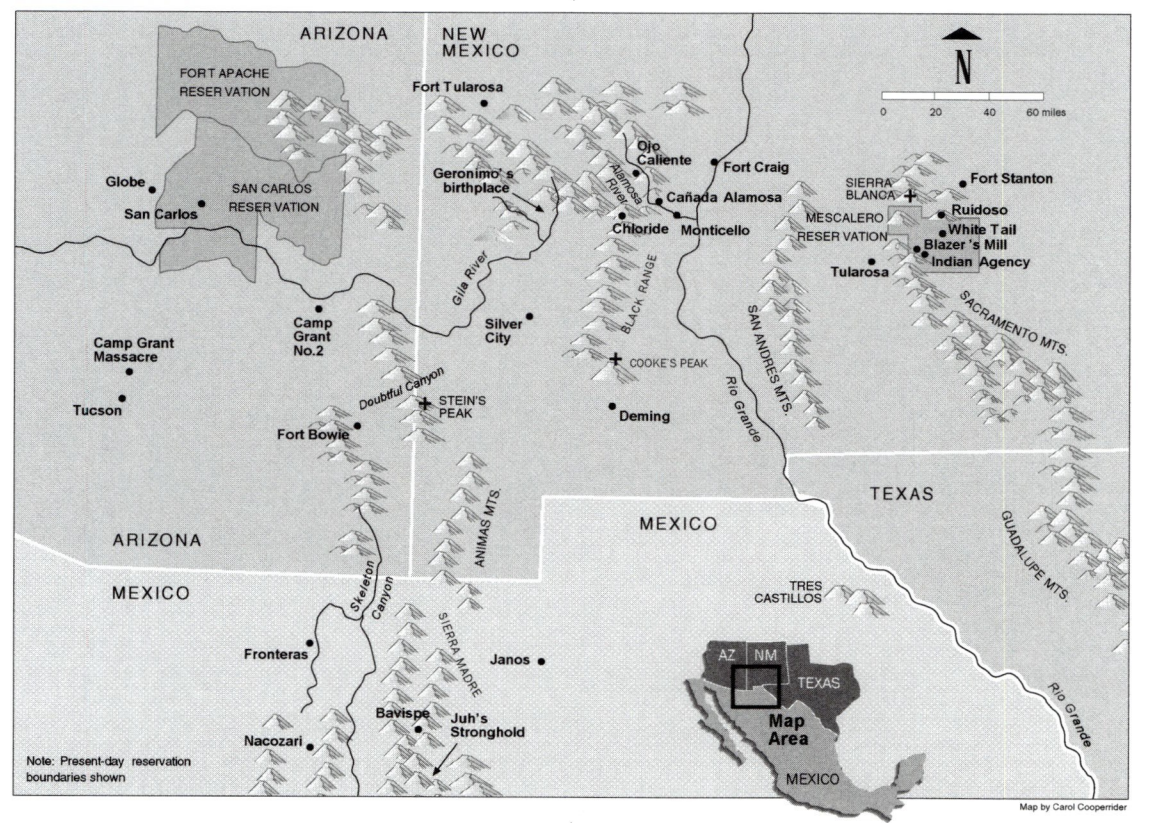

Map 1
Apaches in Southern
New Mexico and
Arizona. (Map by
Carol Cooperrider.)

Part I.

The Warm Springs, Chiricahuas, and Nednhis

Fig. 1. The only known photo of Lozen (*center*), shown here in 1886 when the Southern Pacific train carrying her people to prison in Florida stopped in Texas. To her right is Dahteste. There is some conflict, however, over whether Lozen was on this train. (A. J. McDonald, courtesy National Archives.)

ONE

Lozen

Victorio's sister Lozen, a female warrior and medicine woman, was a remarkable person in any time and any culture. As a result, she's been the subject of speculation and dubious scholarship. And because Lozen was unknown until Eve Ball revealed her in 1970 with publication of In the Days of Victorio, *other historians are skeptical. Some have called Lozen a myth.[1] This would make her the first myth to die as a prisoner of war. A few wonder aloud if Eve invented her. Doubts are such that one respected historian suggested that I drop this chapter from my book unless I had solid evidence.*

Their skepticism and caution noted, I say this: Lozen was real. Along with comments about her in transcripts, I found two pieces of information that settled the question for me. One was James Kaywaykla's handwritten note describing Lozen, who was his aunt. The other was Eve's note to herself on a Kaywaykla transcript: "Find out more about Lozen." These are hardly the words of someone in the process of making up a character.

"I have frequently been asked why nobody but Kaywaykla mentioned Lozen," Eve wrote. Apaches, who observed a moral code more strict in many ways than the Victorians who sought to "civilize" them, told Eve they didn't want it known that an unmarried woman went on raids with the men, nor did they want to subject her to criticism.[2]

Other factors weigh in. Kaywaykla, the narrator of Victorio, *had become a Christian and revealed much that was previously unknown, probably because he no longer felt constrained to keep old secrets. Once Eve knew of Lozen, she asked others, who then confirmed Kaywaykla's account.*

Kaywaykla himself reviewed much, if not all, of what Eve wrote; I found his corrections on drafts, which leads me to believe that Eve couldn't stray far from his recollections. However, Kaywaykla died before the manuscript was published, so he may not have seen everything.

One argument posed by skeptics is that the esteemed Apache scholar Morris Opler never wrote of this woman warrior or recalled that his informants had mentioned her. This may be, but I don't accept it as a reason to doubt Eve Ball. Opler no doubt maintained a researcher's distance from his Apache subjects, who in turn were circumspect in what they told him. Eve not only earned the trust of her Apache subjects, she was their dear friend and neighbor. They confided in her. (See chapter 27, "Eve Ball.")

Eve herself struggled with how to explain Lozen. Called upon to justify her Lozen story to a questioning editor, Eve wrote:

"Lozen was no ordinary woman and the Warm Springs regarded her, Kaywaykla says, as a holy woman because of the Power she had of locating the enemy and of healing. Many women had the latter and . . . wives of warriors (Ace [Asa Daklugie] said, if they really loved their husbands) went on the warpath with them. But Lozen was not married and so is the exception. I've queried the women and some of the men. They are sensitive on the subject, said they had not wanted Lozen criticized and that ordinarily an unmarried woman would not have been with the warriors. Much latitude of conduct, sexually, was permitted the widow. But Lozen had never married, and the unmarried girls (they usually married very young and Lozen did not) required that they be protected. They regarded her much as I think Catholics might a nun — one to be respected."[3,4]

It's my judgment, after living with Eve's papers these months and years, that Eve may have exaggerated some traits or attributed another woman's acts to Lozen, but she wouldn't have invented her.

Geronimo's people called her Woman Warrior. Her own Warm Springs Apaches called her Little Sister and revered her as a holy person.

Lozen, the sister of Victorio, was the only unmarried woman who joined the men on raids. An accomplished warrior and medicine woman, she was a respected member of her brother's band and, after his death, of Nana's and Geronimo's stubborn groups.

"She could ride, shoot, and fight like a man; and I think she had more ability in planning military strategy than did Victorio."[5] Victorio and Lozen both knew childhoods of constant warfare. Lozen was born in the 1840s,[6] probably in southwestern New Mexico in the Warm Springs homeland, and was about twenty years younger than Victorio.[7] Her people called her a name meaning "little sister."[8] Victorio and Lozen had three sisters. Gouyen married the son of Sanchez; Kaywaykla was their child.[9] Another married Kayitah, one of the scouts who persuaded Geronimo to surrender. A third married Nana.[10]

Like all Apache girls, Lozen trained along with the boys. Apaches encouraged their daughters to develop their physical strength. Children learned to mount an unsaddled horse without help. Boys and girls learned archery skills and pretended to hunt and stalk game. Many girls rivaled the fastest boys in foot races and the swiftest participated in rabbit hunts.[11] Girls and young women were expected to guard the camp and fight off attackers when the men were gone. They also learned different ways to escape and evade the enemy, which included camouflage and riding skills. Their teachers were usually women but fathers, grandfathers and married brothers might also step in. On occasion, whole groups of girls would be trained in combat along with boys, and the better fighters could keep training as long as they wished, but they sometimes lacked for sparring partners because boys were constantly told they couldn't strike a woman.[12]

"Much has been written of the low regard in which Indian women were held," Kaywaykla said. "Among my people that was not true. Instead they were respected, protected and cherished."

As a girl the athletic Lozen could outrun the men and ride like the wind. She was also handy with bow and rifle, but the men didn't resent her. "They were frankly proud of her and her ability. Above all they respected her integrity," Kaywaykla said.[13]

At her puberty feast, she earned her Power. Apaches of both sexes had gifts and abilities their people called Power. Lozen's was her ability to divine the location of the enemy. She would stand with outstretched arms, palms up, and pray. While turning slowly, her hands would tingle and the palms change color when they pointed toward the foe. The closer the adversary, the more vivid the feeling.[14]

Many young men sent emissaries to Victorio asking his permission to marry her[15] but Lozen begged her brother not to order her to marry and said she never would take a husband. Victorio assumed she hadn't met the man of her choice.[16]

At this point, Lozen's story wanders into fiction.

Eve's good friend Del Barton, a Seneca woman then living in El Paso, claimed that when Lozen was about sixteen, a tall, middle-aged Seneca chief called Gray Ghost, Barton's alleged grandfather, visited the tribe.[17] The story goes that after seeing the handsome and mysterious Gray Ghost (also called Gray Wolf), Lozen asked her brother to negotiate a marriage. Gray Ghost declined and left. From then on Lozen became a more serious woman, spending time with elders, especially medicine men, rather than with those of her age. No other man ever interested her. She rode beside her brother, living solely to serve him and her people.[18] Barton also wrote a novel[19] of the heaving bosom variety in which she paired the same chief with Lozen.

Eve wrote, "I have talked with Del Barton (a Seneca Indian) about Lozen, and she got the story of the woman warrior partly from her grandfather, Gray Wolf, Seneca chief. He was the man with whom Lozen was said to have been in love but who rejected the suggestion of Victorio that his sister might marry the Seneca. They think that is why she did not marry."[20]

What, you might ask, was a Seneca chief doing in New Mexico? Eve's answer: He had left New York seeking a home for his people in the Northwest Territory. "Why he made the trip alone to New Mexico no one knows."[21] In fact, before Lozen's birth the Senecas took an interest in relocation as their own land base eroded. Some settled in Canada, some in Ohio, and some in Oklahoma.[22] A few settled on a Kansas reservation. Nowhere is New Mexico mentioned, nor could I find a reference to anyone named Gray Ghost or Gray Wolf.

Whatever her level of romantic interest or disinterest, Lozen became a respected fighter, medicine woman, healer, and midwife. Warm Springs people gave her their complete attention when she spoke: "What do you think, Little Sister?"[23]

"Lozen was spiritual. She was magnificent on a horse. She could handle her rifle as well as any man, most of whom she could outrun on foot. She wielded her knife with utmost skill," said a relative.[24]

"She was a tall, broad-shouldered woman and very athletic. Could ride and rope and shoot like a man. Could mount without putting her foot in the stirrup," said Kaywaykla.[25]

Like other Apache women, she wore a long, full calico skirt and a long blouse over the skirt. The moccasin extended to the knee, with a fold or flap where weapons or implements could be concealed. All women wore knives and some, like Lozen and Kaywaykla's mother, had ammunition belts and rifles.

Warm Springs people take their name from their favorite campsite, Ojo Caliente (Warm Springs), located on the east side of New Mexico's Black Range. Here, at an open grassy meadow surrounded by piñon-dotted hills, the Rio Cañada Alamosa carved a box canyon on its way to the Rio Grande. It was their deep love for this place and their wish to live here that drove

Victorio and his people into conflict with the whites. The government's muddled attempts to deal with Apaches was a welter of ill-conceived policy, conflict between Indian agents and the military, incompetent or corrupt officials, and hopeless bureaucracy.

For two decades, beginning in the 1860s, Victorio asked repeatedly to be allowed to live at Ojo Caliente. Instead, the government moved them first to Tularosa in 1872 and five years later to San Carlos in Arizona. In both places disease and starvation consumed lives. The band escaped again and again. Denied refuge at the Mescalero Apache reservation and threatened with a return to the moonscape of San Carlos, Victorio gave up attempting to treat with a people who seemed, to the Apaches, to be habitual liars.

From 1878 to 1880, two regiments chased Victorio and his people all over southern New Mexico. When pressed they took refuge in Mexico, where the Mexican cavalry took up pursuit. In this period, Victorio would gain the respect of soldiers then and now as America's greatest guerrilla fighter. Eve wrote that he never went on a raid without Lozen.[26] Lozen was invited to sit at the councils and was probably a participant in many of the Warm Springs or Chiricahua conflicts during the 1870s and 1880s.

"Lozen is as my right hand," Victorio said. "Strong as a man, braver than most and cunning in strategy. Lozen is a shield to her people. . . . I depend upon Lozen as I do Nana."[27]

While their relentless pursuers had a steady supply of fresh horses, food, water, and reinforcements, the band of some 400 men, women, and children lived off the desert. Victorio knew where every water hole held a bit of moisture; women harvested mescal to bake and eat. They cached weapons and supplies in caves. Children went to sleep at night with food pouches tied to their belts in case they had to flee. When they needed horses, livestock, or ammunition, the warriors raided ranches, supply trains, and the U.S. and Mexican armies themselves.

Lozen wasn't the only woman along on raids. "Dahteste told me that when on the warpath all Apaches were under strict rules not enforced at any other time: Women did not live with their husbands but accompanied them to cook, do the camp work, care for horses, and if attacked, do actual fighting."[28]

During a fight in May 1880 when soldiers surrounded Victorio's group in a narrow canyon and shot the Warm Springs chief in the leg, Army scouts shouted to the women that if they surrendered they wouldn't be hurt. An unidentified woman shouted that if Victorio died, "they would eat him, so that no white man should see his body."[29]

Apaches recall similar acts of female defiance.

"Before they went to Florida the Chiricahuas used to go to a mountain south of Deming to hold the dances," said Eustace Fatty. "There is a canyon and a spring. Once they were all around the mountain and one lady and a boy went out on a plain to get seeds for food far from the mountain. . . . They did not know it [but] soldiers circled around. The little boy looked up and there was soldiers all around.

"'Look, Mama, the soldiers all around us.'

"An army scout told them, 'Look at the sun. You are going to die. . . . Watch that sun today and see how far you are going to go.'

"She challenged him to come over to her so she could cut his throat. The soldiers moved across the mountain."[30]

It's been reported that Lozen was able to ride with the men because she didn't have to perform traditional women's work[31] of preparing food, tanning hides, making clothing, and building shelters.[32] But that's not true. "Between battles, when in camp, she did routine women's chores," said a descendant of Victorio.[33] She was also skilled in dressing wounds.

It was a traditional female duty, midwifery, which took Lozen from her brother's side as he and most of the Warm Springs people rode to their deaths.

In *Victorio*, Eve tells how, during Victorio's last break, when the band was a few miles from the Rio Grande, a young woman told Lozen she was about to have her baby. Victorio ordered the group to go on because they were in danger from the Mexican cavalry. They proceeded to Tres Castillos, a low mountain range near a lake, where Joaquín Terrazas and his troops would find them. Lozen stayed behind, attended the birth, and stole two horses so they could make their way to the girl's people on the Mescalero Apache reservation.

Kaywaykla's original account varies from this story:

"Lozen was middle-aged when I first saw her. It was she who led in the crossing of the Rio Grande; she escaped before Tres Castillos, for she went to look for a young woman who was lost. During our roaming around I don't know what happened. [We were in a] place—something like the White Sands but not white. We were traveling at night and this woman and child disappeared and Lozen went in search of her and the baby—went alone. [They] came to Mescalero and stayed there, but other woman married a Mescalero and stayed with her husband and child. Lozen left Mescalero and went south looking for our people. . . . Down in Mexico she went to a ranch and stole a horse. She took it from a corral at night and roped it and led it off. She rode her horse and led this one and joined us down near Casas Grandes."[34]

At Mescalero Lozen learned of the massacre at Tres Castillos, probably from Mescaleros who had ridden with Victorio.[35] On 14 October 1880, the Mexican cavalry wiped out nearly the entire band—seventy-eight died and sixty-eight were taken prisoner. Only Nana and seventeen people escaped; another fifteen were on a raiding party. Victorio and his warriors fired their last bullets at the enemy and then fell on their own knives. Survivors always believed that if Lozen had been with her people at Tres Castillos, history would have recorded a different ending.[36]

Lozen began the long, sorrowful journey to find her people. It was a joyous day when she rejoined Nana and the Warm Springs remnant camped near Casas Grandes with two other Apache bands—Chiricahuas led by Geronimo, and Nednhi led by Juh.

"She told the story how hard it was to find her people," Kaywaykla wrote in an undated letter. "One night she went to some barn where she found a horse and took it from the stall. She then had [an] extra horse she was leading loaded with supplies. This woman like a man and know how to handle gun."

Nana had become chief of Victorio's remnant and it's probable that Lozen rode with him that fall on raids to avenge her brother's death. It is also likely that Lozen joined the storied Nana's Raid of 1881, a furious sweep in which the old crippled chief and forty warriors covered more than 1,000 miles, killed thirty to fifty people, and captured 200 horses and mules—chased all the while by more than a thousand soldiers and civilians.

Between 1880 and 1886, the Warm Springs band raided and camped often with Chiricahuas led by Geronimo. They called her the Woman Warrior. She became friends with Dahteste, another female fighter who had accompanied her husband, Anandiah.[37] Dahteste would spend three years on the warpath with Geronimo.

"Nobody who knew Geronimo could deny that he was a great fighter and a good leader of men," says Charlie Smith, a Mescalero who was abducted by Geronimo's men with his mother and two other women. "And I think his band was composed of as brave fighting men as ever lived. Nor were the wives of the braves lacking in courage and fighting ability. Especially was that true of Losa [Lozen], the sister of Victorio who was with them. Dahteste too was a very good shot and absolutely unafraid. Even my mother became expert both in dressing wounds and in giving them. Those women fought for the lives of their children and themselves."[38]

The Army seemed largely oblivious to these fighting women, probably because soldiers held "squaws" in the lowest regard. As early as 1868, John C. Cremony had chided fellow officers for failing to recognize their fighting

Fig. 2. Dahteste was a friend to Lozen and a warrior. Both women were Geron-imo's messengers. (F. A. Rinehart photo, courtesy Smithsonian Institution National Anthropological Archives.)

abilities and their numbers. Cremony was inaccurate in much that he wrote about the Apaches, but this point was on the mark:

"Many of the women delight to participate in predatory excursions, urging on the men and actually taking part in conflicts. They ride like centaurs and handle their rifles with deadly skill. I cannot conceive why the bullet sped by a woman should not be quite as much an object of danger as the one shot from the weapon of a man. In the estimate made no account is taken of the fighting women, who are numerous, well trained and desperate, often exhibiting more real courage than the men."[39]

Cremony makes reference to a woman who was most likely Lozen: "There was one who received particular honor from the other sex, but her Apache name has escaped my memory. She was renowned as one of the most dexterous horse thieves and horse breakers in the tribe, and seldom permitted an expedition to go on a raid without her presence. The translation of her Apache title was, the 'Dexterous Horse Thief.'"[40]

Kaywaykla described Lozen as an expert roper who, with the boys, usually rounded up horses along the way. "No man in the tribe was more skillful in stealing horses or stampeding a herd than she," he said.[41] She also cared for them. A relative of Victorio's said, "Warrior Woman was particularly mindful of the horses, their hooves and their legs."[42,43]

In September, Geronimo and Juh fled San Carlos to their hideaways in the impenetrable Sierra Madre of Mexico. The next spring, convinced that Loco and his people would perish if they remained at San Carlos, Geronimo and Juh forced Loco to leave. Attacked across the border by Mexican soldiers, one group took shelter in a deep arroyo. Men and women fired from footholds in the bank and then ducked to reload.

The mule carrying ammunition was shot and lay about fifty feet away. The Apaches were running out of ammunition. As Eve told the story, Lozen ran to the downed mule, cut the heavy ammunition bag loose and dragged it toward the arroyo. Staggering in the sand, she fell but swung her feet over the gully's edge. The men pulled the Woman Warrior and the bag in. However, Kaywaykla said simply that "an old woman" had secured the ammunition.

The Apaches escaped once again to the mountains where they conducted sporadic raids despite pursuit by both American and Mexican troops. By spring of 1883, some of the people, weary of running, were willing to return to the reservation. Geronimo and Nana preferred to fight. General George Crook had sent an expedition into the Sierra Madre. When the chiefs learned that the U.S. Army was nearby, they sent Lozen and Dahteste, at great personal risk, to arrange a meeting.[44]

"Dahteste usually accompanied Lozen when the latter acted as messenger for Geronimo," wrote Eve Ball in a letter. "Even Dahteste could not explain Lozen other than that she had 'great power.' And though Lozen, was (I think) older than she, Dahteste went along as a sort of chaperone."[45]

After agreeing to come in, the various bands straggled in by May 1884 and camped near Fort Apache on Turkey Creek, a place to their liking. It was mountain country with streams, timber, game, and privacy.

A year later, after a dispute with Lieutenant Britton Davis, Geronimo, Nana, and others broke out and headed south. Despite vigorous raiding for supplies, by early 1886, they were suffering from losses and had few weapons. Some of the people wanted to return to Turkey Creek, and Nana wanted all the women and children there.[46]

Lozen and Dahteste approached the camp of Captain Emmett Crawford to arrange a meeting. Scouts recognized the two women and allowed them to pass. The next morning a troop of Mexicans and Tarahumaras confronted the Americans and their scouts, and Crawford was mortally wounded. Lozen saw him fall. The two women then arranged a meeting with Lieutenant Marion P. Maus, Crawford's successor, who in turn arranged for the chiefs to talk to Crook. As a result of those talks, Nana and Chihuahua, a Chiricahua chief, agreed to surrender, but under the influence of a deceitful bootlegger and his wares, Geronimo fled again. A fighter to the end, Lozen parted from Nana and joined Geronimo's party.

After General Nelson A. Miles replaced Crook, he sent Lieutenant Charles B. Gatewood in July 1886 with two scouts to find Geronimo. Gatewood went to Fronteras and learned from another party of American troops that two women, again Lozen and Dahteste, had come to the village with a message that Geronimo was willing to consider a meeting.[47]

The wily medicine man (Geronimo was never a chief) had sent two women as emissaries to the Mexicans to discuss terms and obtain food and liquor. He didn't really want to surrender but was buying time. The women bartered jerky and hides for coffee, sugar, ammunition, and mescal liquor in goatskin bags, which they packed on mules.[48] "To say that this mission on the part of Apache women was courageous is the understatement of all time," wrote Eve Ball. "But they went and they returned."[49]

Eve wrote that the two women were Lozen and Dahteste.[50] However, the two scouts Martine and Kayitah said the women were Dahteste and Dejoneh.[51]

"About the fire at night Geronimo told the story to us at Fort Sill," recalled Eugene Chihuahua. "He said he was going over into Mexico trying to make peace with the Mexicans; that why he was up in that mountain. He sent two women, one of whom could talk good Spanish. He told them to go over there and talk to the big chief of Chihuahua. Geronimo stayed about a week. That woman came back and told Geronimo that the officers say they are going to come after them in a few days. But Martine and Kayitah came there calling them and they went back to the United States."[52]

Gatewood and the scouts Martine and Kayitah picked up the women's trail and followed them for three days to a natural fortress in the Sierra Madre. There the scouts picked their way up the zigzag trail. At the top, they found Geronimo and seventeen warriors, plus Lozen, assembled along the rim.[53] The two scouts persuaded Geronimo to meet with Gatewood. On 3 September 1886, Geronimo surrendered with twenty-four men and fourteen women and children.

A day later, the most defiant people in America boarded a train at Bowie, Arizona, bound for Florida. Lozen appears with Geronimo and Naiche in the famous railroad siding photograph taken on that sad journey. Or does she?

Apache scholar Angie Debo insisted that Lozen wasn't there and that the woman Eve Ball identified as Lozen was Bi-ya-neta, wife of Perico. Her source is Jason Betzinez, a Warm Springs man, who, she admits, "made some errors in identifying the warriors."[54] Eve's sources were Jasper Kanseah and Charlie Smith. Of course, each thought her informants superior to the other's.[55]

In a letter, Kaywaykla too placed Lozen elsewhere: "Yes, Lozen was with our group to Florida but not Geronimo."[56] However, both Dahteste and Kanseah placed Lozen with the last group. "Geronimo take the word of Martine and Kayitah and George Wratten. Perico was with us too. Fun and Eyelash was with them. Lozen was with them," Kanseah said.[57]

We'll never know. The Army identified several of the women only as "wife."[58] I lean towards Kanseah, who was there. The defiant woman in the siding photograph subsequently identified as Lozen is the way I would picture her.

In Florida, Lozen joined the other women and children at Fort Marion in St. Augustine, where crowded, unsanitary conditions and malaria took forty-nine lives. The Apache prisoners of war were moved to swampy, mosquito-infested Mount Vernon Barracks, Alabama, in April 1887. In ramshackle houses with dirt floors, the mountain-and-desert people fared worse. In the next seven years, malaria cut down numbers of people and tuberculosis claimed more. Lozen was one of fifty people to die there of "the coughing sickness." The Woman Warrior, then about fifty, was buried in an unmarked grave.

Dahteste, divorced Apache way from her first husband and remarried to the scout Coonie, eventually settled with other Chiricahuas on the Mescalero Reservation in southern New Mexico. She once said that even in captivity she was happy because they no longer had to run for their lives. She raised six stepchildren and foster children.[59] "Dahteste used to own about twenty beautiful horses. They were very wild but she would get right in between them," said Bessie Big Rope.[60]

As a delicate, white-haired elder, Dahteste verified for Eve Ball her many missions with Lozen for the Apache leaders. "I could hardly believe my good fortune in being permitted to know this courageous woman," Eve wrote.

"Dahteste to the end of her life mourned Lozen. They had been comrades in battle, revered by their people and virtually unknown to the white man."[61]

Del Barton

So, who was Del Barton and why did Eve Ball find her credible? Barton, secretary to the editor of the *El Paso Times* and an aspiring writer, was an activist in Indian causes and Eve's close friend. She died in the 1960s.[62]

A phone conversation confirmed my discomfort with Barton and the Gray Ghost yarn. Over many months, I had compared notes with Jo Martín, who was working on her master's thesis on Apache women. One night Jo asked, "Do you buy the Gray Ghost story?" I had to admit it didn't pass the sniff test. About the same time, I found some curious references to Barton in Eve's letters. A series of events caused Eve to suspend judgment.

"Ace [Asa Daklugie] told me that if it were possible to communicate with me that he would do so because after his death he would have the wisdom and understanding he lacked in this life to guide his people. I listened with respect to him, but had no idea that such a thing was possible. Then people whom I had not seen for twenty years came to visit me. They insisted that a spirit was trying to 'get through' to me. They had a message stating that the Indians would be helped and led by a woman of their race who was to come to me for information and help. And I was to trust her and give her what facts and knowledge I possessed. Within a week Del Barton, daughter of the old chief of the reservation in northern New York, showed up with her husband."

Barton claimed to be guided by Daklugie. Soon after, "the campaign she planned through instructions from Asa Daklugie united the Indians in their getting out the biggest vote ever cast on the reservation. That much is no breach of confidence but is not to be given publicity."[63]

Jo Martín and I reached the same conclusion: The romance was wishful thinking on Barton's part. The usually cautious and skeptical Eve let her guard down for a good friend. Apaches let the story stand because it relieved them of having to explain the unconventional behavior of a beloved figure who might be misunderstood outside their culture.

Fig. 3. History has paid more attention to Victorio's lieutenant, Kaytennae, but at Tres Castillos the boy Kaywaykla and his heroic mother, Gouyen (Kaytennae's wife) were among the few Warm Springs Apaches to escape the ambush. (Ben Wittick, courtesy Museum of New Mexico, #14221.)

TWO

Tres Castillos

When James Kaywaykla described his and his mother's narrow escape from the Mexican ambush at Tres Castillos on 15 October 1880 that wiped out Victorio and most of his band of Warm Springs Apaches, it was a rare first-person account from the Apache perspective. However, Eve Ball presented it, as she did the rest of the Victorio book, in a somewhat fictionalized form.

I've pieced together the story of Tres Castillos and the aftermath from three separate interviews Eve did with Kaywaykla, reproduced here in Kaywaykla's words. Interestingly, the dramatic detail in Victorio *that has a Mexican soldier smoking a cigarette next to Kaywaykla's hiding place never happened. What did happen is actually more exciting.*

In this story, I was awed by Kaywaykla's intrepid mother, Gouyen. Forced to abandon her infant daughter, she scrambled up the hill with her young son, then about four. She saved her life and his but would lose her baby and three brothers within a week. No wonder the Apache women were relieved to surrender!

"I am the only living person of Victorio's band. I was born out here near Ojo Caliente.[1] I don't know my birth date or the exact place, but I am the only survivor of my people, of those who remember Victorio.

"My grandfather's name was Sanchez. Kaytennae was my stepfather. My grandfather's wife and children were captured. He went to Mexico and tried to find them and the Mexicans got him. After that, they used him to hunt

17

the Apaches under Victorio. Finally, he escaped. He came back somewhere near Casas Grandes. That's the last time I ever saw him. Nana was my grandmother's brother . . .

"My father was killed in a battle south of Deming near the Florida Mountains [in 1879]. . . . [2] My father was riding a spotted horse, black and white. He and Kaytennae went behind a mesquite and sand hill. He looked up and was shot in the head . . .

"I remember Ojo Caliente, but it seems much like a dream. And I remember Loco[3] and Victorio. Some said Loco was the proper chief but Loco was sort of feeble-minded. For that, Mexicans call him Apache Loco. Victorio was chief, and the Mexicans called him Capitán Victorio.[4]

"Victorio's men were on a raid. Our people were camping near treeless ridges waiting for men to return. A few days later there was much cattle brought back by the younger men; older men went on making other raids. Cattle were slaughtered and cut into thin slices for drying. After two days, the sliced meat was nearly dry. Indians moved camp about a day's march to Tres Castillos. Many who broke camp and had an early start had already camped; others came later . . .

"We rode down into the camp in the evening. There are two hills close together and very rocky. There was a little timber and scrub trees and very high grass. And lake right there not very far from the two hills. We had come through places where the sand blew into dunes and lots of holes— probably the homes of rattlesnakes. . . . Near sundown, all had camped and turned the horses loose near the big lake close by. We came in just about sundown and [were] still on our horses when the Mexicans coming out from behind a ridge about three-quarters of a mile ahead attacked the camp, fighting through the night. . . . [T]here were some still coming in. As the soldiers came out from behind the ridge, those who saw them turned around and went back, so they escaped . . .

"At dawn Indians run out of ammunition. Nothing could be done except give up and be killed. . . . The Tres Castillos are very rocky. If Indians had plenty of ammunition, they would have wiped out the Mexicans. Indians in hill behind rocks and Mexicans in the open . . .

"Most of the Indians had turned their horses loose and were camping. My mother and I still were on a mule and my mother's sister-in-law [Blanco's wife] rode a cavalry horse. Grandmother rode a gray horse. That's when the soldiers attacked. We saw them coming but they were waiting for the Indians to settle down for the night . . .

"My grandmother said, 'You wait here. I am going to where my granddaughter is, watering the horses . . . '

"My grandmother was close to where Victorio and his men were. They were out of ammunition and he did not want to be taken prisoner . . . so they used their knives on themselves. . . . The story of the Indian who claimed to have killed him is not true. . . . The soldiers burned the bodies.

"Grandmother said that anyone who raised his head from his hiding place was shot down. She saw her granddaughter surrender to the soldiers and just didn't know what to do. 'I was old. My hair was white and I was sure they would shoot me down. I put a cloth on top of my head and they captured me.' There were many women, girls and young boys captured. . . . [Grandmother] was taken first to Chihuahua City and later to Mexico City, she and all the rest. They tell us that those captured during that time were taken as far as Yucatán for slaves . . .

"There were two Lipan [Apache] Indians who spoke Apache who were guides for the soldiers. That's what my grandmother said; she saw them. They told her and other Indians that were captured, 'Why didn't you get away? You had a chance.' The soldiers had been on the march a long time and their horses were given out. 'You made a bad mistake. You should have got away . . .'

"That was a terrible night—a full moon and little chance to get away. Of course, when they were out of ammunition, if ten of them had made an attempt to rush through the line, they might have made an opening through it and got away. Mexicans are very cruel but are not very good soldiers . . .

"Mother told her sister-in-law, 'We better get on our horses and go toward the lake. My mule will follow.' The sister-in-law said nothing. She got off her horse and fastened the rope and went off and left us. So the three of us were there. My poor little sister was still on the ground . . .

"My little sister cried to my mother and [held out] her arms. But my mother could not get the mule close enough to pick her up. . . . There was an Indian man running by who was related to my father. My mother said to him, 'Save my baby!' He swooped down and picked my little sister up from the ground and rode off. And we never saw her again. We think they were both killed. There was no one left but my mother and me. We could not see anyone else. They had all gone to the hills. They were fled to the mountains.

"The sun was just going down. Later a full moon rose . . .

"We did not go very far, less than a mile, before my mother got off the mule at the foot of the mountain and let the mule go on. . . . [We] tried to climb the hill and get away. We came to two big rocks leaning toward each other and touching at the top. We were afoot—no blankets, no food. Part of the way she carried me on her back. We hid between those two rocks in a narrow crack . . .

"We had been there but a short time. It was getting dark. Between the two mountains I could see the soldiers coming. I was too small to know what the danger was. My mother said, 'Somebody is coming. Be very quiet.' Then I heard footsteps. A Mexican soldier came right to the rock and stood there and listened. He stayed just a little while and then he went on. I could see the dark form and the gun sticking up above his shoulder. . . . If I had had a butcher knife I would have got him. I could almost have touched him. . . . We stayed there about a half-hour; maybe longer. We could not see anybody.

"After he went on, we left. We waited 'til we could no longer hear his steps. Then we got out and climbed the hill. . . . Mother said, 'We will go toward that grass ahead of us. You crawl up there and wait by that rock until I come.' And she followed me, crawling a few feet at a time and stopping to listen. Then she started on again. Then she caught up with me. And that night we went up toward the top of the mountain where there were many big rocks.

"She heard a noise and we stopped and lay still. Then we heard a voice — someone that she knew. It was her cousin with a little girl. My mother asked if she knew where Nana was, with the others. 'I think that they are hiding somewhere. We are going to try to get to the top and escape.'

"The four of us went to the top of the hill, following up a little draw. About halfway there was an open plain with very short grass. We crossed this in the moonlight.

"There was a bunch of horses here with soldiers guarding them. The men were smoking. We could see the lights. And on the other side the same. We crept slowly between them. Part of the way mother carried me, part of the time I crawled. We were right between the soldiers. . . . There was not much space between the soldiers, maybe a hundred yards. . . . When we got into the greasewood, we stopped and rested a while 'til she got her breath. Then we noticed that the other woman was not behind us and we never saw her again . . .

"And we had nothing — no blanket, no food, no knife. And we were afoot. We were hidden from the soldiers now, and she stood and took me on her back. She carried me nearly all night. I don't know how far she went — three miles or more, I think. . . . Next morning she looked for something to eat. She found only some kind of little gourds, not bitter but not very good. Still, they could be eaten.

"But we had no water. We looked back at where our people had been surrounded that night and we could see smoke . . .

"[L]ate in the afternoon it was very hot and . . . we reached a mountain, six or seven miles away. A man saw us from the top of the mountain and sent a man to us. He told mother, 'The people up there saw you and sent me. They want you to come up there. I am going farther where the Indians were trapped to see if anyone else escaped during the night. You go up there to your friends.'

"We went on trying to find water. There was a dry creek, no water. When we reached the hole in the rock, there was water there. I don't know how long it had been there; we were glad to have it. . . . We had no way to carry it with us. We drank as much as we could and started on toward the top of the mountain. Halfway up the mountain we met a young woman who knew my mother. She took us to the top and gave us food and a blanket.

"Next morning my two uncles [Blanco and Suldeen], Nana, and Mangus came up there horseback. . . . These men were south to make a raid for cattle and horses . . . . On the way back they brought many things but they heard the firing at night and hurried back to the camp. . . . There they talked over what is best to do, about trying to recapture some of those who were taken. They talked over the trails and they decided to go north on the old wagon trail. They thought maybe the captured ones would be on that road. They left the women and children in the hills and went north on that trail. They did overtake some soldiers and they attacked them. The girl they had captured was riding behind one of the soldiers. She jumped off the horse; she ran to her people. They killed some of the Mexican soldiers. They tried to get away. They did not stop to fight—they ran.

"Nana, who escaped, said that they were out of ammunition and that Victorio could do nothing more for his people and that he would never be captured . . ."

Apaches always dismissed the claim of Maurício Corredo that he killed Victorio, but the two apparently did fight.

"Victorio and the Tarahumara chief, Maurício, fought at Tres Castillos. . . . It was on a plain and Victorio chose the man who fought with him. Then he comes horseback with no escort—only the one man. Then Maurício is separated from the others and advances afoot. And a compadre, Roque. This challenge when they met, they start to fight at the same time. Victorio and Roque fell on his [unreadable]. Victorio fell from his horse. When the old Indians saw that Victorio had fallen, they cry and said, 'No fight more.' And they waited for night to escape, but they could not escape . . .

"From then on there was just a handful of Victorio's people,[5] but we got along very well. We got everything we wanted. The men made raids for horses and cattle. We did not damage them as much before Victorio's death as after. The Indians were willing to fight it out. They felt there was not much use in living, but they had plenty of ammunition all the time and they knew that they would die but it did not matter . . ."

Tissnolthos[6] was a scout after the remnant of Victorio's band. "I saw two hills lying out on the plain. I remember this: That's the place where your people were the time you escaped. We were right behind you—I was with the cavalry. That's where you stopped to eat. Way down there south in the flats where there was mesquite and grass. There was dust in the air and we always watch that. . . . The men wanted to go down there and see if it was troops. They didn't attack civilians unless they started the fight.

"When Victorio died Blanco took over and he was killed near Cook's Peak. After he and Suldeen were killed, Grandfather Nana and Kaytennae took over . . .

"We came back to New Mexico then, across the Rio Grande to the Standing Mountain [Cook's Peak] and that's where Blanco was killed.[7] He was my mother's brother . . .

"We were traveling this road. We didn't care at all whether anybody got us or not. We were driving a bunch of horses. My older uncle [Blanco] rode up to us. . . . 'I am going on ahead. There is always somebody there. . . . I wave to you from the hill to come if it is safe.' So he went on and it was not long until he waved from the hill for us to come. And we came in a hurry. Before we got to the spring, he hollered, 'Troops right behind! Take to the hills! . . . '

"That's what we did. There was some timber. It was not long until we heard shooting. The Indians attacked the soldiers—Negro troops, I think. . . . Then all got off their horses and started firing at the Indians, but we defeated them, and their horses ran away. There was an Indian on top of the hill and he saw two soldiers go down a dry creek. My uncle, the older one, went to follow those two soldiers. . . . Then they shot him. So we lose our head man. That was Blanco. When the Indians knew that he had been killed, they killed the two soldiers. . . . The Indians killed several and wounded others. We did not stop to count as White Eyes do. . . . We had guns and ammunition, plenty. They buried my uncle there in the dry creek.

"They covered him with rocks. And the soldiers did not bother us any more.

"That same afternoon after we came up on a ridge, they looked way down on the plain several times. When we got up there, they saw three tents.[8] 'We must ride to those tents and see who they are—might be miners or cowboys.'

"One man said, 'From this day, on the first battle we fight I will be killed. My life is worthless to me now.'

"That was Suldeen, the other uncle. . . . In about forty minutes to an hour we heard shooting again. I don't know how many were there or who the people were—miners, I think. People were looking for gold and silver. They knew Victorio and his people were at war and they should have known better. They killed them—got them all. They were marching up this dry creek. I was riding behind my mother and looking ahead. I saw part of the body of a man with a hat and a gun.

"'*Indah*! [White man!] I saw somebody going there!' He went back to that camp while the Indians were still there. . . . The Indians were all in a bunch and he killed Suldeen. So we lost two men in one day. . . . Now my mother had only one brother left but I don't know his name. . . . Of course, the Indians got the man who did the shooting. So they were all wiped out. I always thought that the miners had discovered something in that place. I have read of a lost mine nobody has been able to find . . . [9]

"As they were marching they came to an old trail in Old Mexico. They saw a cloud of dust and knew somebody was coming. They told the women and children to stay hidden and the men went to meet the rough men who were hunting the Indians. They were cowboys—Mexicans. They rode over to a little hill, very rocky. They stopped there waiting for the Indians to ambush them, but the Indians saw they had no protection from those hidden behind the rocks. This young uncle who had lost his two brothers did not care whether he lived or not. He wanted to go fight these men but the older men told him he surely would be killed. . . . My younger uncle whose brothers had been killed only a week or so ago went on alone to fight those men and was killed. . . . My young uncle had intended to go to the Navajo country, for he was friendly with them, but after his brothers were killed, he did not care . . .

"Somewhere around Socorro and Magdalena, way off west, there is Horse Springs. What few of us were left, we came there and stopped and there were some who had been left in the mountains when we went from there while the men made a raid northwest. . . . [W]e remain in the mountains for six days. They return with food [and] supplies of things needed. Also brought back two captives, a girl about sixteen years . . . very blonde—German in appearance—and small boy. . . . Few days later they escape during a night march. . . . We did not look for them, did not want to kill them. I often wonder if they got back to their people. They were on the horse they were riding when captured, and he should have taken them home if they knew enough to let him . . .

"From there we went on into Sonora. We rode along the edge of the mountain a while and then turned into the mountains. They tried to raid down in Sonora. It was there they found the big train of mules loaded with silver bars—sixteen or eighteen mules. All the Mexicans were killed. They brought both mules and silver to the camp . . .

"In the mountains down near Casas Grandes they found Geronimo's band and we joined with them. . . . From that time on Geronimo and his people stayed in the mountains of Sonora. We roamed as far south as the land where palm trees and oranges [grew]. There was a big river they called Swift Water. The timber along it was different—thorns, briars, instead of pines. On this side there were pines and on the mountainside lots of fruit and honey . . .

"I was just a small boy to witness a war dance about the year 1882 in the wilds of Mexico. There was war dance of Warm Spring[s] and Chiricahua just before a big war raid to pull off. A certain warrior was killed during a raid. To avenge, the relative of this warrior ask for help to raid on certain towns. So Indians have a war dance, which usually takes place early evening. A big bonfire is built and soon people coming to fire. Warrior usually carried their weapons to be prepared in case called to take part. Now singing is started. There are over hundred songs those days. Today I don't suppose one half dozen songs anyone could sing. The war dance is not really a dance. It is more like a rehearsal of action in tune of real fighting. Great speed of [illegible] and [illegible] or falling flat on the ground and quickly up again. Some time firing their guns and other weapons they use . . .

"My grandmother was in Mexico City about five years.[10] When she came back I was about nine years old. While we were at Fort Apache, my grandmother and those other women were brought back to Fort Apache by the soldiers.

"I think the Apaches were very good people. I will never forget the incident where a couple of middle-aged men and a well-dressed lady—black dress—[and a child]. I will never forget as long as I live how they stoned that woman and little boy. . . . She pleaded to the men. They were going to stone her. The Indians did wrong. Blanco told them that if an enemy laid down his arms they were not to be harmed. These men disobeyed. . . . After this incident Victorio's downfall came."[11]

Eve Ball almost didn't use Kaywaykla's information about Tres Castillos. Comparing notes with fellow Apache scholar Dan Thrapp, she found Kaywaykla's memory of the hills of Tres Castillos flawed enough to cast doubt on his story. Fortunately, Thrapp persuaded her to use it.

In a letter to Thrapp, Eve wrote, "I was surprised to find that Kaywaykla's account of Tres Castillos is erroneous. . . . I am sure he was absolutely honest in thinking he was right, but because he had not been more than four or five at the time it occurred, and that sixty-five years or more before, his impression of the contour of the land may be incorrect. And we must either make this authentic or omit it. I may be able to rewrite it omitting description, for it is a dramatic account, and I think so far as Kaywaykla is concerned, reliable. Of course, no Apache believes that Maurício Corredo killed Victorio, nor that he shot Crawford. I know, of course, the recognition he got in Chihuahua, but they do not accept the account."[12]

Thrapp responded, "Don't, please, omit your Tres Castillos stuff, which is unique as one of the very few—perhaps the only—Apache versions of that affair, or at least [the] Warm Springs version. The main difficulty I saw was that James [Kaywaykla] took part as a little boy, which must have had a bearing on what he remembered. The principle [sic] difficulty was that he saw, or remembered, the Tres Castillos as a range of mountains, when you know and I know that they are scarcely that, except in form. I doubt if the highest is more than 75 feet above the surrounding plain, and the nearest range of mountains to them is 10 or 15 miles. Virtually all of the features are as described, but on a much smaller scale than one would suppose. I do not think it would have been possible for an Apache to have remained on Tres Castillos overnight and not have been killed or captured the next morning when they were out of ammunition, anyway. If the survivors crawled anywhere—and some of them did as you know and I know—they crawled beyond range of the Mexicans and then made for the mountains beyond.

"I could justify the physical features James describes—the small gulch or ditch, the rocks beneath which he and his protectress crouched while the Mexican smoked outside, and all the rest of it. I think you could fit it all into the geography of the place, and I hope you do, rather than giving it up as a bad job. After all, he was there, and the fight did take place, and the site does exist. But you want it to be right, and so do I."[13]

To double-check, Eve consulted a history professor from Mexico, then living in Artesia, who confirmed Kaywaykla's identification of the site. In another letter to Thrapp, she wrote, "Kaywaykla was so very young that it is possible that the distances seemed greater than they are, but he and his mother must have crossed one low divide and toiled up another if his remembrance of that night is accurate. I shall, of course, rewrite it. And I'm very glad that you think it should be included, for I believe that event and the flight from Ojo Caliente were indelibly stamped on his mind because he had a very vivid memory of each . . .

"I shall, of course, attempt to fit Kaywaykla's account of the massacre into the geography of the country. I, like you, should be sorry to omit the story of the attack."[14]

In his own Victorio book, Thrapp theorizes that Gouyen and Kaywaykla and other survivors could not have spent the night climbing the hill but instead struggled through the darkness across the southwestern plains to the Pegajosas or the Escaramuzas, which they climbed to safety. "With this slight modification, however, his recollections fit the geography remarkably well."[15]

THREE

Captives

❖

Some of the Apaches' most heroic stories are about the escapes and cross-country journeys of their people who were captured by Mexicans. The accounts not only remind us of how resilient and resourceful they were, but also how determined they were to return to their families. Even though many were treated kindly by their Mexican captors, they were ever watchful of the momentary lapse that would afford an escape.

❖

Francesca

After raids into Mexico in summer of 1861, during which Geronimo was wounded, his group split up and later gathered in the Santa Rita Mountains of Arizona. There they camped while warriors hunted and traded and Geronimo healed. But three companies of Mexican troops had pursued the group. They surrounded the settlement in the night and opened fire in the morning. People fled in all directions and four women were captured and taken to Sonora.[1] One was Id-is-tah-nah, who would be called by her Mexican name, Francesca.[2] Geronimo recalled that Francesca was then about seventeen and the youngest of the four women taken captive.[3]

They were sold into slavery. Id-is-tah-nah became a housekeeper and nurse for the children of a maguey plantation owner, who called her Francesca. The other three women were sent to the fields where they cut leaves from the maguey, a cactus whose sweet, greenish sap was drinkable.

In their five years on the plantation, they learned to speak Spanish. Francesca "was intelligent, resourceful and courageous. She planned an escape but would not leave until all could go with her." Finally, they had their opportunity. The women got permission to attend an evening religious service at the church just outside the city gate. They kept walking, traveling mostly by night and hiding by day. They timed their escape so that as they made their way north they could eat tunas, the fruit of the prickly pear cactus. When they reached northeastern Chihuahua, they decided to camp two or three days and let their bleeding feet rest.[4]

Eugene Chihuahua said Francesca was "my mother's mother's sister" but, in Apache fashion, always called her Grandmother. He tells this story, which differs in significant details from the account in Eve Ball's *Indeh: An Apache Odyssey*:

"Francesca was captured by the Mexicans when she was a child and kept as a slave. She spoke Spanish well. There were two other women captives with her. They got to talking and planned to escape. She . . . and the other women collected things that they would need for their trip back to their own people . . . [knives and blankets]. And they started out.

"One night they camped and built a little brush arbor by tying some saplings together at the top, cutting brush and weaving it in them. Dug a fire hole in the middle and slept around the fire. Toward morning they let the fire die down low. One woman thought she heard something.

"When that tigre [jaguar] come after them women Francesca tell them to be quiet—maybe it not find them. They hear it walkin'. But it smell them, I think. Then something walking on the top of the arbor and break through. And the tigre attack Francesca. She was pinned down and can't get to her butcher knife. One woman helped her fight but three ran off at first. Just those two to fight that tigre. It dragged Francesca and she got her arm free and reach for her knife. The tigre was tearing her shoulder where it was dragging her. The other woman was running along by her stabbing at its back. Francesca get the knife and she stab at its heart and she kill it.

"She all torn up but they got no bandages. They go back to the brush arbor and build a fire—it gettin' daylight soon. My grandmother, she know how to treat that wound. They rub the tigre's saliva in those wounds. That's all the medicine they got."[5,6]

Geronimo recalled Francesca's struggle this way: "The lion kept trying to catch her by the throat; this she prevented with her hands for a long time. He dragged her for about 300 yards, then she found her strength was failing her from loss of blood, and she called to the other women for help. The lion had been dragging her by one foot, and she had been catching hold of his legs, and of the rocks and underbrush to delay him. Finally he stopped and stood over her. She again called her companions and they attacked him with their knives and killed him. Then they dressed her wounds and nursed her in the mountains for about a month. When she was again able to walk they resumed their journey and reached our tribe in safety."[7]

Francesca was also a medicine woman, and according to Chihuahua, became one of Geronimo's wives. "These horn dances [Dance of the Mountain Spirits] that I have—they belong to her; they are in her honor. She teach them to me. After we go to Florida we dance it in her honor, for she was medicine woman. She was with us in Florida and Alabama and in Fort Sill—that where Geronimo marry her.

"Francesca was terribly scarred and nobody wanted to marry her. Apaches like brave womens, but she have her face tore open and bad scars. So Geronimo, he marry her. He got lots of wives anyway. How many, I don't keep count, but he have plenty wives. And he call me Grandson."[8]

Geronimo said, "Her face was always disfigured with those scars and she never regained perfect use of her hands." She died at Fort Sill in 1892.[9] The dates on her headstone at Fort Sill say 1861–1901.[10] The other women died before the Apaches surrendered.[11]

According to Chihuahua, "The last time she made the dance it was very pretty. She did not like for anyone to see her scarred face and she cover it with a cloth and she sang a beautiful song for the dance. And she teach it to me. And I sing it at the ceremonials for the maidens. She said it was the last time she was going to sing for the dance. And after the dance she pass away—she just go to sleep and don't wake.

"And she call me Grandson and so did Geronimo."[12]

Siki

On 14 October 1880, at Tres Castillos, the Mexican cavalry massacred Victorio and most of his band. Seventy-eight died and sixty-eight were taken to Mexico as prisoners. Two of those prisoners were Kaywaykla's grandmother and his cousin Siki, who was the daughter by a previous husband of Loco's third wife, Clee-hn.

"Among the bunch taken south was my grandmother. She was taken first to Chihuahua City and later to Mexico City. She and all the rest. They tell us that those captured during that time were taken as far as Yucatán for slaves. Maybe some of our people are still living there.

Fig. 4.   Siki, a Warm Springs woman, was captured with her grandmother at Tres Castillos and taken to Mexico. The two women eventually escaped and made their way home. (Courtesy Smithsonian Institution.)

"Six of those women escaped[13] and started from Mexico City to Ojo Caliente and walked all the way. They knew when the cactus fruit was ripe and went then. . . . I think those women traveled at night and hide in the day. This was not the bunch that the mountain lion attacked.

"I judge that they had been coming a long time for it was a long trip. When they reached Warm Spring[s] they went to Monticello, an old town where they used to trade. They knew the Mexicans; they were expecting to be recognized and to be treated well. But the Mexican arrested them. They brought some calico like you buy at the store. The Mexican asked, 'Where did you get these goods?'

"They had found the material in a cave and they wanted to trade it for things they needed. One young girl [Siki] could speak Mexican and she told them how it was. They were held 'til they could notify Fort Wingate and they took these women to Fort Apache in a wagon. That was in 1886, I think."[14] The date was 1885.

"For safety they separated," said Evelyn Gaines. "She [Siki] made most of the trip to Monticello alone and once she was almost dying of thirst and went to the road to see if she could stop somebody and get water. She saw a Mexican with a skin water bag. She was afraid but her need was so great that she stood and spoke when he approached. She spoke good Spanish. She asked for a drink and he gave it to her. The Mexicans called her Juanita but her Apache name was Siki. After she got back to her people the other women with whom she had left called her Juanita and everybody got to calling her that."[15]

After her return, she married the scout Rogers Toclanny in 1885 and they remained together for life. Their sons Lawton and Britton were named after officers he served with.

"Mrs. Rogers Toclanny told a story," recalled Isabel Enjady. "We were taking her to San Carlos, Arizona. When we went through Deming [she said], 'Long years ago four of us passed through here.' She pointed to a mountain. 'There is a cave there. It had mescal stored in it. Our dresses were worn out and our shoes were gone. We stopped there and got some of the dried mescal. There was some meat there too and we stayed long enough to make us some dresses so that we could be decent.'"[16]

Years later the locals were still finding Apache caches in the hills. In 1915 rancher Leo Williams spotted some calico under the edge of a rock in the Goodnight Mountains northeast of Deming. After some digging, Williams and some volunteers unearthed gunnysacks, saddle blankets, Spanish bridle bits, parts of guns, a hatchet, lace, crochet, and numerous bolts of fabric. They believed the loot was taken from a wagon train ambushed by Victorio thirty-five years earlier in Magdalena Canyon. The Apaches had covered their goods with native hay and sotol (plant resembling yucca) and then a foot of dirt, leaving a bit of cloth sticking out to mark the spot. Much of the cache was still in good condition.[17]

Bonsi

One of the more amazing stories is that of Bonsi, the brother of Rogers Toclanny's first wife, Dolores.

George Martine said, "Bonsi was a Nednhi, captured by Mexicans when he was a child but old enough to remember his language. When he was about seventy-five he walked from Lower California to San Carlos," from which he was stolen. And there he learned that his people were at Fort Sill. "So he worked his way and found them in Oklahoma. He knew no English but a man wrote his name and destination on a card and asked that people help him reach his people. I knew him, for he stayed at Ace's [Asa Daklugie] a long time."[18]

Doubtful Adams

On 3 June 1885, the Duncan Militia Company in Arizona got word that Apaches were on the warpath and the militia began trailing them, figuring they were headed toward Stein's Peak on their way to Mexico. Two days later at dusk, they caught up with them at Doubtful Canyon and in a running fight managed to kill a man and a woman.[19]

As the pursuers rode back along the canyon in the dark, their horses shied from some boulders. One man stopped to investigate and found a baby strapped into an Indian cradleboard and figured that when the woman was shot, she threw her child to the side of the trail. (Cradleboards were ingeniously designed so that if they were dropped the child would be unharmed.) The militia members took the child with them.[20]

"Martine's wife lost her child during an attack by soldiers. The Apaches were trying to flee," said George Martine, son of the scout Martine. "Kah-goh-ush-en, Martine's wife, mounted her horse with a baby in a *tsach* [cradleboard] on her back. The tsach got loose and fell off. She tried to turn back to rescue the baby but she couldn't control her horse. It ran with the other horses. It was the child of her first husband, not Martine's. The cavalry rescued the baby and gave him to someone to rear."[21,22]

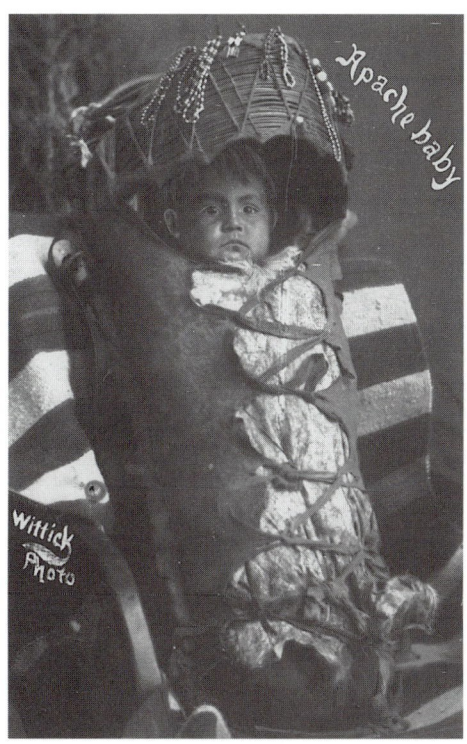

Fig. 5. Apaches constructed their cradleboards to protect infants if they fell or were dropped. Shown here is an Apache baby in 1883. (Ben Wittick, courtesy Museum of New Mexico, #15918.)

Arnold Kinzuma was then a scout and recognized the tsach and the baby and knew whose baby it was.[23] The father was Chin-che, one of few members of Zele's Chiricahua band to flee during the May 1885 outbreak from the San Carlos reservation. Chin-che's wife wasn't with him but was instead with a group at Doubtful Canyon trying to rejoin their relatives in Mexico. Although Chiricahuas from Mexico tried several times to reach the reservation to take their families, they were thwarted by Apache scouts and returned to Sonora. Chin-che died in 1885 during a raid on a northern Sonoran ranch, shot by a rancher named John Hohstadt. That gave him the distinction of being the only man killed by whites during the 1885–1886 campaign.[24]

John Parks and another man took the child, joined a party of New Mexico Rangers, and rode to Lordsburg where they caught a train for Duncan. Word spread about the baby and when they arrived at Duncan, Parks walked home, followed by passengers and crews from two trains plus curious local residents.

"Father took the cradle with the papoose in it into the dining room and leaned it against the wall," said Jennie Parks Ringgold. "People crowded in until the room was packed, and many stood on the outside waiting to get in. The poor little papoose was frightened almost to death and set up a pitiful wail."

Her mother and a neighbor removed two layers of canvas and found that the infant was wearing "a beautiful dress of a white baby." For a month, Louise Parks cared for the child, whom they dubbed "Doubtful" for the canyon where he was found. But, with her own young family to care for, she told her husband the baby needed another home, and they placed him with a family named Adams.

The Adams family lived near Duncan until about 1892 and then moved to Solomonville, where Doubtful went to school until Bill Adams got work at the copper mines near San Carlos. The Adamses always treated Doubtful like one of their own and he returned their affection, although as he grew older he asked to be called Sam. But after a clash with an Adams relative, he lived with John Parks until 1906 when he went to work for a rancher named Bud Ming.

In 1910 Doubtful Adams succumbed to tuberculosis and died in 1912 at a cow camp, where he was buried.[25] In her notes, Eve Ball wrote, "Was this Doubtful Adams—later Sam Adams, then Sam Parks? Yes."

In an interview with Eve Ball, Evelyn Gaines said, "A lady came to San Carlos and told my mother that the boy Martine's wife lost was living in Arizona and it was not far from Mescalero and to go over there and see him but she could not go. I think he died in 1920, about that time. This boy's name was Adams."[26]

George Martine said, "It has been told that he was the Apache Kid, but that is a mistake. . . . He told the people [at San Carlos] just what happened and of how he was lost and was found and cared for. He never came back to our tribe, for we were gone by that time, even though he learned that [his] mother was still living. He got sick at San Carlos, died and was buried there. He never knew his name."[27]

Geronimo and the Arroyo Fight

Geronimo in his time was the most feared and hated leader of a dreaded group; his name alone could panic remote Mexican and American settlements. He made the Army's decorated military strategists look like fools and he could awe his own people with the power of his medicine.

While accounts of his day lionized Geronimo for his villainy and daring, oral history and scholarly work have since revealed that the medicine man who assumed leadership of Cochise's Chiricahuas harbored fears and vulnerabilities. In battle, Geronimo possessed the steely courage of all good Apache warriors—more so because Ussen, as Apaches called God, had told him that bullets wouldn't kill him—but on one occasion he acquitted himself in less than honorable Apache fashion. It was the "arroyo fight," as Eve Ball dubbed it in her notes.

"That story has been told by my people over and over," James Kaywaykla said.[1]

In 1882, the related bands of the Chiricahua, Warm Springs, and Nednhi had gathered in the Nednhi stronghold in the Sierra Madre of Mexico. In council, Juh and Geronimo concluded that Loco and his Warm Springs people would die of disease and starvation in the malaria-ridden waste of the San Carlos reservation. They resolved to remove them, by force, if necessary. On 19 April, Juh[2] led a raid that swept Loco's band from the hated reserve. About a hundred warriors and several hundred women and children began a desperate escape, traveling day and night and stopping to secure horses and livestock from hapless ranchers.[3]

Fig. 6. The Chiricahuas considered Fun one of Geronimo's bravest warriors. He's shown here in 1886 in captivity. (A. J. McDonald, courtesy National Archives.)

Lieutenant Colonel George A. Forsythe caught up with them in a rugged canyon but the Apaches drove him off and continued south. Soldiers pursued and caught them again in a camp on the Janos plains; after a day of fighting the army again withdrew. The Apaches lost fourteen men and most of their horses and supplies and suffered many wounded. They struggled onward through the night, straight into a trap set by Mexico's renowned Indian fighter Colonel Lorenzo García, who had learned their route from two captive raiders.[4]

García, wrote Dan Thrapp, "moved in regimental strength and left the Indians to their mountains, but woe betide them when they rampaged through the lowlands—if he could catch them."[5] García and some 250 soldiers (in the Apache telling there were 600) of the Sixth Mexican Infantry were camped near the Corralitos River when they spotted the fleeing Apaches.[6]

The Apaches approached a dangerous place. "They knew there were usually troops there," Kaywaykla wrote. "Mangus and his band decided that they would cross during the night. They did. The others attempted the crossing before dawn. The column was strung out a long distance [along a dry streambed].

"Kaytennae, Naiche, and Chato were away. They had turned into the hills with their families."[7] At the sound of gunfire, Kaywaykla's mother and Kaytennae fled into an arroyo and then up a mountainside with rocks for cover.[8]

"Those in advance smelled coffee before daylight but they went on [thinking they had reached their own people]," said Kaywaykla. "They felt that they were in no danger. As they approached the dry creek, a shot was fired. The women and children turned back, for the men were in the rear.

"The Mexicans attacked. By daylight they were all mixed up. Indians retreated as best they could."[9]

"They turned back, scattering as they went," Eve wrote. "Those who fled up the arroyo could not get out because of the steepness of the banks. A large group turned into a ditch, perhaps ten feet deep, and the rest went on, pursued by soldiers.

"Indians were strung out for a mile or so and those in the rear took to cover when they heard the first shots. The warriors in the rear heard them also and rode to the rescue. By the time it was light enough to see well, Geronimo, Fun, Loco, and several other men had reached the side arroyo under the overhanging banks of which many women and children had taken shelter."[10]

Jason Betzinez recalled, "When we had gone a few hundred yards we were suddenly attacked by Mexican soldiers who came at us out of the ravine where they had been concealed. The first thing I saw was Mexicans firing at the Apache women who were about a quarter of a mile ahead of where my mother, sister, and I were. Almost immediately Mexicans were right among us all, shooting down women and children right and left. Here and there a few Indian warriors were trying to protect us while the rest of the band were running in all directions. It was a dreadful, pitiful sight, one that I will never forget. People were falling and bleeding, and dying, on all sides of us. Whole families were slaughtered on the spot, wholly unable to defend themselves. . . . Those who could run the fastest and the farthest managed the escape. . . . [M]y mother and sister and I were among them, being excellent runners . . ."[11]

As they sped toward the mountains, Betzinez's mother could hear Geronimo calling to the men to gather around him to protect the women and children who had clustered in the arroyo. Thirty-two warriors heeded his call and with Chihuahua they made their stand.[12]

"It was not a cave but in a deep arroyo with an overhanging bank. They had dug the gravel away and made a big hole for the women and children," Kaywaykla said.[13]

"The Mexicans concentrated their attack at that spot. Others watched from the ridge. Several attempts were made to counter attack."[14]

As the Mexicans charged repeatedly, the women dug holes in the banks to shelter themselves and their children. Scraping at the sand in the arroyo bottom, they had water, which was soon mixed with blood. Men and women quickly carved footholds from which the men could step up and fire, repelling charge after charge by the soldiers.

"This made a good defensive position from which the men began shooting down the Mexican soldiers as fast as they appeared. The Mexicans quickly learned that the Apaches were skilled marksmen," Betzinez said.[15]

"[T]he soldiers were maybe 200 yards or so back on the hillside," Kaywaykla said. "Every now and then they would blow a bugle and the commander would say, 'Go right in there and get Geronimo!' Some of the Apaches understood the [Spanish] language and they told the others, 'They are coming again. Get ready for them.'"[16]

"The Indians got ready and they heard the bugle call to attack. They heard 'adios, adios.' They got some with every shot. Fun was up in front and [with each shot] he gets him a Mexican and drives them back and then he gets up on the side of the bank."[17]

Fun, whose Apache name was Yahe-chul (Smoke Comes Out), became the real hero of this battle and thereafter a hero to his people. He was Perico's half-brother[18]; his mother, Bonita, was Geronimo's first cousin.[19] Kaywaykla remembered Fun as "a big man and very strong. . . . Fun was the man who saved Geronimo."[20] He was about sixteen.

In the heat of battle, as Geronimo cowered under the arroyo overhang, Fun leaped up on the bank and, with cartridges between his fingers, darted in a zigzag toward the Mexicans, reloading after each shot as he ran. He would do this three times as Chihuahua covered him, lying on his side.

"It has been told many ways but this is the way it really happened: That is where Fun got up on the bank and fought the Mexicans," Kaywaykla said.[21]

"They were down in a dry creek and they were close under the bank ready for the Mexican soldiers when they came. This man [Fun]—some had run out of ammunition—he was determined to save his people and the only way he could do it was when the soldiers were ordered to come get Geronimo and started to charge, he gets up on the bank and began shooting. He ran back and forth and every time he fired somebody fell."[22]

"That was where Fun put the bullets between his fingers. The Springfields fired only one shot and had to be reloaded. I often think about that. No ordinary warrior could have done that. We know there is a God who can protect us even against a thousand and if you have sufficient faith, you can be saved.

"I knew Fun well. He was a man of great strength and of great character."[23]

Fun's heroics weren't uncommon in Apache warfare: "You see pictures showing where the Indians attacked the army and got shot. Well, that's not the way it was done. On level ground the Apaches zigzag and shoot fast, for they can move and shoot very quickly. If he was going forward toward the enemy he goes sideways and he stand sideways so that he isn't so big a target—like the edge of my hand. Apaches were fast enough to dodge bullets."[24]

Chihuahua joined Fun in his bold assault. "People told me about my father, that he was the man that helped save the tribe," Eugene Chihuahua said. "He and Fun, they saved the tribe. My father lay on his side firing at the Mexicans. The bullets came so close they pitted his chest by throwing gravel against him—looked like he had had *viruelas* [smallpox]."[25]

"Fun and my father were doing all the fighting—killing all those officers and Geronimo was in a cave with the children," said Eugene Chihuahua. "Fun told him to get out or he would shoot him. Geronimo and his boy got out [and escaped].

"I was not in there in that fight but my father was." Chihuahua's band was in the mountains but Chihuahua was along to help free Loco and his people. "My mother told my father not to go but he felt like he had to."[26]

Loco too fought bravely, even though he was there against his will. The defenders of the arroyo were running out of ammunition but fifty feet away lay a cowhide bag of ammunition, dropped when the mule carrying it was shot.[27] Loco attempted to slip to their rescue.

Fig. 7. Chihuahua, chief of a Chiricahua band that sometimes rode with Geronimo, was one of the heroes of the arroyo fight. (Courtesy Arizona Historical Society, Tucson, #949.)

"Loco was carrying a sack of cartridges," Kaywaykla wrote. "Mexicans were firing while he was in the open. They fired and he dropped [the sack] and joined the rest. How they needed that ammunition! Then a very old woman crawled out of the hole and brought back the ammunition. Soldiers charged on foot."[28]

As the Mexicans charged again, she climbed over the bank and ran, knife in hand, to cut the bag from the packsaddle. Unable to carry the heavy pouch, she dragged it as Fun drew the Mexicans' fire.

"Alone, Fun jumped over the bank and rose to his feet," Eve wrote. "With cartridges between his fingers he fired and loaded, fired and loaded, all the time zigzagging back and forth amid a shower of bullets. . . . Dodging from left to right he managed to delay the charge long enough for the ammunition bag to be grasped by the desperate woman who attempted to drag it to the brink of the arroyo. Unable to make the remaining two or three steps she fell, with her feet toward the ditch and was dragged to safety with the precious supply of bullets."[29]

Toward evening the ammunition was depleted, the warriors exhausted. It was then that Geronimo stunned his men with an uncharacteristic suggestion.

"Geronimo said, 'Let's us men make a break. We could if we leave the women and children.'

"Fun spoke, 'Geronimo, if you say that again I am going to shoot you down right here.'"[30]

Even Geronimo's biographer, Angie Debo, found this exchange hard to explain.[31] Was Geronimo being cowardly or practical? Their situation was certainly critical, maybe enough so to warrant desperate, even unseemly, measures.

"The Mexicans were forming for a last charge before it got too dark," Eve wrote. "The besieged Apaches could hear the commands. They could hear the soldiers saying, 'Adios! Vaya con dios!' The bugle blew the charge and here they came. Even Geronimo rallied to repel this attack. The soldiers got to the very brink of the arroyo and several fell. But Fun shot the officer giving the commands and the soldiers fled out of range."[32]

"At night the Mexicans set fire [to the grass] in a circle around the hole . . . so they could see if the Indians were trying to escape. But they did. It was said that the children did not," Kaywaykla said. About a dozen children were left behind.[33] Geronimo said Apaches set the fire.[34] Fleeing warriors asked the women's permission to strangle their infants "so that they wouldn't give away their movements by crying. Then they all crawled through the fire and got away without being seen."[35]

In a manuscript, Eve wrote, "It was Fun who gave the order to run. It was every person for himself." However, in *Victorio*, she wrote, "Fun fired steadily until the children in his sector had been taken from the arroyo." As they fled, Talbot Gooday and Dexter Loco swept up a child—Loco's youngest son.[36]

"The few survivors assembled at the next water and found that their losses had been heavy. . . . A few at a time, they straggled to the camp. Many women and children had died but Geronimo had lost few warriors."[37]

When Lieutenant Colonel Forsythe reached the bloody site the next day and met García, he counted bodies: 78 Apaches, and 3 Mexican officers and 19 soldiers. The Apache dead included only 11 warriors; most of the Indian casualties occurred in the opening ambush and not during the arroyo stand.[38] Three officers and 13 men were wounded. The Mexicans had captured 33 women and children, including Loco's daughter.[39,40] A year later General George Crook's expedition into the Sierra Madre passed near the site and found "many bleached-out bones, pieces of women's dresses, and lots of beads scattered on the ground," a scout recalled.[41]

The Apaches resumed their journey slowly because of the number of wounded. Three badly hurt people stayed behind—an unknown woman and two men, Tsoe and Kayitah, who would later play major roles in helping the army subdue Geronimo and his warriors. A month later they rejoined their people.[42]

When they reached Juh's stronghold, the devastated survivors were welcomed and given food and blankets. Although their losses were great, the largest number of affiliated Apache groups in some time had gathered and included many seasoned warriors.[43]

Fun would go on to distinguish himself again in battle and at the time of surrender was next in rank to Geronimo.[44] After the Chiricahuas were sent to Mount Vernon Barracks in Alabama, Fun enlisted in Company I, 12th Infantry, and became a corporal. There, suspecting that his wife Belle had been unfaithful, he shot her.

"Fun thought that he had killed his wife," Martine said. "He knew the Apaches would approve but wanted to escape the terrible death and mutilation of hanging. . . . So Fun used his rifle as his means of escaping. He took off his shoes, leaned against a tree and placed the barrel against his head. Unable to reach the trigger with his fingers, he pulled it with his toes."[45]

On 31 March 1892, First Lieutenant W. W. Witherspoon reported to the post adjutant, "Corporal Fun killed himself in a fit of jealous insanity after shooting and slightly wounding his young wife. The excitement amongst the Indians on the occasion of this tragedy was very great, it being the first case of suicide known amongst them; the first thought with some of the men seemed to be to take revenge upon someone, but the prompt action of the officers and noncommissioned officers, both white and Indians, soon quieted them and no trouble arose; the wife has now recovered and is back in the village."[46]

Despite his suicide, Fun remained a hero to his people. "Fun was one of the greatest warriors and the bravest of Geronimo's band," recalled Martine, a brave man himself. "Fun never did get scared no matter what happened."[47]

And what of Geronimo? Was his suggestion to desert the women and children the sign of a coward or Apache survival instinct, the willingness when pressed to sacrifice some lives to allow the band to go on? Apaches themselves were always divided on that question and some, who lost relatives in Loco's forced exodus, never forgave Geronimo.

Sam Kenoi, one of Morris Opler's primary informants, said, "Geronimo was nothing but . . . an old troublemaker. He was a shaman. He was as cowardly as a coyote. You can ask men like Perico what he was like. Perico is a brave man and was one of the best Apache fighters. He is well known for this, as was his brother . . . Fun. Fun was a great fighter. . . . Perico will tell you how he and others did all the fighting while Geronimo stayed behind like a woman . . .

"The Apache were falling right and left. Instead of standing up and fighting, Geronimo got behind the women and children. Women and children were dying right on top of him, with their blood running down over him, and he was under them, burrowing in the sand. One of his soldiers caught him by the feet and pulled him up and said to him, 'Where are you going? You were man enough at the start. Why don't you stand up now and fight like a man?' I know plenty of stories like this about Geronimo."[48]

Solon Sombrero, a Mescalero, tells a similar story, which must have circulated among his people:

"Geronimo was in a hole where he stay and give orders from there. They could not get him out. They were out of ammunition. Everything that moved, they shoot it. . . . They were in a cave and surrounded by the army. And way back in it there was Geronimo and his warriors could not get him out."[49]

Geronimo himself told of fighting from the arroyo: "I gave strict orders to waste no ammunition and keep under cover. We killed many Mexicans that day and in turn lost heavily, for the fight lasted all day. Frequently troops would charge at one point, be repulsed, then rally and charge at another point."[50]

At one point Geronimo crawled close enough to overhear the Mexican general tell his men to "exterminate this band at any cost." Geronimo shot him. "In an instant the ground around me was riddled with bullets, but I was untouched. The Apaches had seen. From all along the ditches arose the fierce war cry of my people. The columns wavered an instant and then swept on; they did not retreat until our fire had destroyed the front ranks."[51]

Jasper Kanseah said, "Some man say about Geronimo such a coward. . . . He was a good fighter."[52]

Asa Daklugie, Geronimo's chosen successor, said, "It is not true that Geronimo was a coward. Geronimo offered his heart to any man in this country."[53]

Streeter

⬚

Western history has taken occasional note of white men who "went Indian," aban-doning their own culture and trappings and becoming members of a tribe. Zebina Nathaniel Streeter was one such renegade. Historian Dan Thrapp described him as "the most intriguing figure of these perilous times." Streeter not only joined Geronimo's band and led raids; he apparently became Geronimo's son-in-law.

A shadowy figure among his own people, Streeter appears in occasional news-paper stories as L. N. or I. N. Streeter, "for no one knew him well," Thrapp wrote.[1] He's rarely mentioned in Apache stories because nobody wanted to embarrass Geronimo.

⬚

Zebina Nathaniel Streeter was born in Genoa, New York in 1838. At eleven, he left for school and went to sea instead, an occupation he continued until he deserted his ship in Panama at eighteen, getting shot, tracked by bloodhounds, and captured. A year later Streeter was serving with the quartermaster during Albert Sidney Johnston's campaign in the Mormon War of 1857 and was nearly captured by hostile Cheyennes.

After a visit to his father, then in California, he served briefly in the 1st Battalion of Native Cavalry during 1864 and 1865, during which time he was court-martialed and thrown for drunkenness. He quickly rejoined as a private in Company C, becoming a sergeant several times before being busted back to private. He mustered out in December 1865. He was then described as five feet, five inches tall, light complected, with gray eyes and auburn hair.

Streeter went to Mexico and, under the name Don Casimero, served under Benito Juárez, reaching the rank of colonel.[2] As an officer in the Mexican forces that ultimately defeated Napoleon's puppet Maximilian in 1867, he became a member of the American Legion of Honor, which gave him honorary Mexican citizenship.[3]

In the next few years his whereabouts are unknown. In the early 1870s, he was at Fort Craig in New Mexico territory. He spoke fluent Spanish and had picked up enough Apache to be an interpreter and scout. Here he became a friend of Tom Jeffords and met Loco, Victorio, Juh, Geronimo, and possibly Cochise. The army sent him on delicate missions with the Apaches, including General Oliver O. Howard's 1872 visit to Cochise.[4]

As a clerk at the San Carlos Apache Agency in Arizona during Governor Anson Safford's administration, Streeter "had some difficulty with officials, caused, it is said, by his giving aid and comfort to hostile Apaches."[5] He fled to the camp of Juh and Geronimo, never to return. The territorial legislature declared him an outlaw and Safford put a $5,000 price on his head. Streeter claimed he had a run-in with the "Indian Ring," the parasites who profited from the army's presence and the Indian wars.

Streeter's new family became Juh's band of Nednhi Apaches, who were closely related to the Chiricahuas. From his days as a Mexican officer, Streeter apparently knew the governor of Sonora, Vicente Mariscal. After the Chiricahua reservation was broken up in 1876, Streeter persuaded Mariscal to permit Juh and Geronimo to live in Sonora if they behaved themselves. The Chiricahuas and Nednhis took refuge in Mexico for three or four years until they joined Victorio in raids.[6] Streeter traveled and raided with them until Juh's death in 1883.[7]

It was during this period that Streeter apparently married a daughter of Geronimo. It was something Apaches discussed reluctantly. Apaches intermarried with other tribes and with Mexicans but considered whites inferior.[8]

"I knew of the white son-in-law of Geronimo and that all Indians were ashamed to admit that Geronimo's daughter married a white man," Eve Ball wrote to Thrapp.[9]

Said Charlie Smith, "Once my father was trying to bring back a white man from Mexico. I do not know this man's name but he was thought to have married a daughter of Geronimo. But it is wrong to tell of such a disgrace of Geronimo."[10]

Interviewed together, James Kaywaykla and Jasper Kanseah recalled that Geronimo's daughter married "a Dutchman" they described as a small white man with reddish hair, which he wore long. He also wore Apache clothing. "He was a good warrior and all the Indians said so. . . . The Indians all respected him."[11]

The daughter in question was most likely Dohn-say (later called Lulu), who around 1881 was considered one of the outstanding young women of the band[12] and old enough to marry.[13]

(Geronimo also had a white father-in-law who was a captive raised as an Apache.[14] "He is known—Chilyeah-kinay—by name. I had seen him once or twice," Kaywaykla wrote in a letter. "About the year 1881 or fore part of 1882 he was killed. He was shot by cowboy from a long range—unexpectedly."[15,16]

In 1965 Thrapp had come across accounts of Streeter and asked Eve about him. She responded: "I've gone over Kaywaykla's and Daklugie's accounts of Geronimo's white son-in-law. Both were with Geronimo's band when it occurred. . . . Neither knew his name." And they wouldn't say the daughter's name.

"I've been thinking about this white man, and while I have no documentary evidence, I think that he is very likely the man Streeter whom you are interested in. If there had been another white member of any of the bands—Chihuahua's, Nana's, Geronimo's, or Mangus's—I think they'd have told me."[17]

There are other descriptions of this white renegade. A scout and guide with the unlikely name of Pauline Weaver heard a story from an Apache friend about a white man directing Indians in a fight with soldiers. The man had come out of the mountains a year before to an Apache camp in the Tonto Basin and wanted to live with them. He claimed to have trouble with the white men and wanted revenge. The Indians had their doubts and kept an eye on him until he proved himself in raids against the whites and the Pimas. The Apaches then came to trust him and valued his knowledge of the ways of whites and soldiers. The Indians called him Cholla. He had light-colored hair and eyes, dressed in buckskin, led raids on camps or ranches, and returned with livestock and occasional firearms and ammunition.[18] The story doesn't provide a name, but it sounds like Streeter.

One newspaper story said Streeter generaled several Apache fights, spoke the language fluently and was said to be influential. Another account reported that "he has taken an active part in every campaign made by Juh in Mexico and Arizona." That means Streeter would have participated in Juh's spectacular raid on the San Carlos Reservation in 1882 to abduct Loco and his band.

As a white renegade, Streeter is the only white man on record to conduct raids with his adopted Apache family against other whites.[19] However, stories circulated of a white man who ran with the Apaches before Streeter appeared at Fort Craig. Was this a white captive raised as an Apache or was it Streeter?

In 1870 a witness described a white man dressed in buckskin coat, canvas, fringed pants, and moccasins, who bought corn at a ranch near Prescott and was thought to be "running with some band of Indians." Another witness was sure he saw a white man directing Indians in a fight, who claimed to have lived with Indians.[20]

This was before Streeter was known to be a renegade but during the period after the Mexican war and before he appeared at Fort Craig. Thrapp wondered aloud how Streeter could have learned enough Apache to be an interpreter at Fort Craig. Thrapp may have answered his own question when he wrote that "there was no one save Streeter on record who, as an adult, became enamored of Apache ways and adopted them, even to fighting his own kind because his new friends did so." It's possible that Streeter rode with Apaches before he hired on with the army.

From 1883 on, Streeter appears sporadically in accounts from Mexico. That year Mexican newspapers report that in leading a band of Apaches, he was wounded in a fight with Mexicans, who captured him, took him to Hermosillo and then released him.[21] A report of the same incident says a white man, misidentified as M. N. Stecker, was "acting as chief in one of the fights" between soldiers and Apaches. "For more than two years he has been a leader of a band of Apaches."[22]

Newspapers in early 1885 reported, "Casimore Streeter, of unsavory reputation in Arizona, because of his affiliation with the Apaches, accidentally wounded himself New Year's night at La Noria, Mexico." The article says Streeter's brother was a store clerk in Silver City.[23] In 1886 he was with Leonard Wood, then searching for Geronimo in northern Mexico. He stayed in Mexico after that.[24]

Streeter's departure from this earthly plane is the subject of some debate. Kaywaykla and Kanseah thought a Nednhi Apache shot him from a distance, assuming him to be an enemy. One newspaper reported Streeter killed in 1879 in Janos but that was mistaken.[25] In fact, he was shot and killed in June 1889 at Nacozari, Sonora, by the brother of a girl who was the subject of his attentions.[26]

Geronimo's Surrender

In the often-told story of Geronimo's final surrender, his warriors and allies played pivotal roles, but we don't know much about them. History might have been different if it hadn't been for Martine and Kayitah, members of Juh's and Geronimo's bands who became army scouts, and Yanosha, one of Geronimo's most seasoned warriors.

Martine, a Nednhi Apache and first cousin of Chiricahua chief Chihuahua, was captured as a child by Mexicans. When he rejoined Juh's band, he was about twelve. At the time, Geronimo and some of his people were with Juh, including the parents of Kayitah. Juh gave Martine to them and the two boys became lifelong friends. When the band spent a winter at San Carlos, Martine met and married Lillian, granddaughter of Victorio and Mangas Coloradas. Kayitah, who occasionally rode with Chihuahua, married a Chiricahua woman, Sahn-uh-shlu, later called Mary.[1] The two men lived near each other.[2]

"Martine wanted to leave peacefully; did not want his wife and children to go on the warpath," said George Martine. "My father never wanted to go. He wished to stay at San Carlos but finally he joined the cavalry as a scout. When General [Nelson A.] Miles got in command, Martine was a scout with the Warm Springs and Chiricahua Apaches. They joined the army and started following Geronimo's band. Kayitah was his pal. General Miles named him Charles, so he was Charles Martine.

Fig. 8.   Geronimo's nephew, Kanseah (left) served as orderly to Yanosha, one of Geronimo's most seasoned warriors. Had Yanosha not confronted Geronimo, history might record a different story of the surrender. (A. J. McDonald, courtesy National Archives.)

"General Miles had two men from the start. When they told them that General Miles wanted two men to go up to Geronimo's hideout, these two went. The soldiers followed and stayed at the foot of the trail . . .

"Kayitah and Martine were always together. General Miles spoke to the Indians, told them, 'You Indian scouts, General Miles calls on you. Geronimo is on the mountain waiting to give us a battle. He is going to be there until I come. I want two men to go to Geronimo early in the morning and tell Geronimo that General Miles wants to see them in a friendly way at Round Mountain.'[3]

"Lots of Indians afraid of Geronimo. . . . Martine and Kayitah got together and my father told me that they talked it over. My father told Kayitah, 'Want to go?'

"'Think we better go?'

"'We got relatives up there,' my father told them. 'We come with General Miles to talk to Geronimo. We want to take our people back so they won't suffer. . . . We tell Geronimo we came to help him and his people. If he kill us that's alright. We got to do something to help our people.'

"Kayitah said, 'It's alright if we never come back.'

"General Miles promised these two men, 'If you come back alive and do what I tell you, the government may take these people away, but you two will stay right here and we will build you a good home for your families with plenty water, grass and everything you need. And they give you seventy thousand dollars from the start and the government will take care of you and your children.'

"These two men did not ask for anything. They wanted to see and to save their relatives. . . . We don't know what money is and they didn't ask for money. But it was promised them and they looked for it 'til they died. But did they get the homes? They were prisoners of war, just like Geronimo's band.

"Father and Kayitah left early in the morning and about daylight the next day got close to Geronimo, who was on the top of the flat mountain. All the warriors were in line waiting."[4,5]

Geronimo's youngest warrior, Kanseah, saw the scouts approach.

"But we in the last hiding place now and I on watch with good field glasses. Way down on the plain, near creek, I see something move. I watch. It something coming up creek. It two. It two men coming up creek—Indians. Scouts. They got something white on stick. That mean they don't want to fight—want to talk maybe. I tell Geronimo.

"'It don't matter who they are. When they get close enough we kill them.'

"I don't say anything; I boy. They come closer. Pretty soon I know them—Kayitah and Martine. Apache scouts—Chiricahuas—and relations to Yanosha[6] and others too. We not have many men—seventeen, I think. Geronimo in middle. Yanosha and his close relatives on one side.

"Scouts keep on coming closer. Geronimo say, 'Let them come on. Pretty soon we shoot them.'

"Yanosha say, 'If anybody shoot them the fight will be right here. I will shoot any man that lifts a gun.'

"Yanosha very brave man. Geronimo know he going to do it. He know, too, that if the scouts don't bring them here white soldiers never find us. He bitter mad toward scouts, even if they his relatives. He think and then say, 'Let them come.'

"Kayitah is carrying a stick with a flour sack tied to it. He don't have a gun. They come on. Then Yanosha call to them, 'Come on in. Nobody going to hurt you.'

"Kayitah was first. He say, 'Geronimo, you might as well give up. There is not any men left, hardly. You not got horses any more. You can't never sleep at night—got to be on watch all the time. Even if you travel at night you likely fall over cliff. Everything your enemy. Soldiers take you to San Carlos.'

"'I don't want to go to San Carlos. They chop my neck off. This my home. I stay here, right here. You chase me. You kill me. Alright. I die right here. I got to die sometime.'

"'You don't have to die now. You come down and talk to soldiers. You come under white flag—they not hurt you.'

"'Mangas Coloradas come under white flag. What they do to him?'

"'These officers will not. You know them. They will do what they promise. You be better off. You got women and children with you. And only a few men—and some of them just boys. You come down, talk to them anyway. It be better for you, better for your families.'

"At last Geronimo said, 'Well, we go, make talk. I will go with you.'

"We went down to camp on the creek and made talk. Geronimo think about it one night. Then he say, 'I will go with you.'

"George Wratten was with the soldiers. He was the interpreter. He had been grown up in the store at San Carlos and speak Apache; speak it well for a white man. He tell Geronimo that Chihuahua already come in with his band and that it was best to give up, for he could not keep running much longer.

"And Geronimo talked with the white soldiers and agreed to quit. They herd us on train and ship us to Florida.

"Just a few days ago Edwin Yanosha die and now I am the only one."[7]

"Geronimo was never captured by anybody. When Kayitah and Martine came to our camp and told him his children and wife were in Florida, he agreed to come in. General Miles did not capture him. Nobody did."[8]

Another factor in the surrender was word that Chihuahua had already gone in.

"When Chihuahua was with Geronimo he had his wife and children along. Everywhere he went, they go too," said Eugene Chihuahua. "Chihuahua was the first to quit and go in. He and Geronimo had no trouble; Chihuahua thought it was the only way to save his family. Chihuahua was a highly respected scout. His own people respected him. If this man wanted plans for his people, he did it with them. He made up his mind to save his family so he went in. . . . Chihuahua would have protected his people. He would come right out and tell them what he thought best for them. He never would have betrayed his people . . .

"So after being wild and free all his life, now my father had to go into captivity. But Apaches love their families and that was the only way he could be with them. He trusted General [George] Crook, though he was his enemy. And he and his band were the first to go into exile in that far away place, Florida.

"Soldiers had my mother and some of us [children] at Fort Bowie. Chihuahua sent Ulzana[9] there and he find everybody except my brother Osolo. Scout say he at Fort Apache. Nantan sent a man and horses to bring him back and he did. So when we start to Florida we got all our family with us.

"It funny riding in that train. Nobody like it. I remember when we coming into El Paso. . . . When we come close to Fort Bliss soldiers fire cannon for salute to general. Scared us, too. Scared us, even if we don't care whether we live or die. Got to die sometime, anyway.

"[T]he [man] my father talked to in Mexico, he promised Chihuahua that if he gives up and quit fighting that we go way off two years but our families be with us. But they were not."[10]

Kanseah and Yanosha

Jasper Kanseah was born on Cochise's reservation near Fort Bowie, Arizona, around 1872. His father died in a battle with Mexicans before he was born. When he was four or five, his mother died as the army drove his band to San Carlos. His grandmother took care of him for three years before she died. Other Apache mothers shared their scant rations with the orphan. He always believed that his small size was the result of poor nutrition in his childhood.[11]

"Geronimo was my uncle. My father died before I remember; he was killed by Mexicans. My grandmother raised me."[12]

When Geronimo, Kanseah's only living relative, broke from San Carlos and returned to the warpath, he took the boy with him.[13]

"I was about fourteen when I went with Geronimo. . . . [14] We live first one place and then another, always in the different place. Sometimes stay anywhere, like a coyote."[15] The first night the group—men, women and children—rode hard, traveling ninety miles and changing horses as Yanosha found fresh horses. They changed mounts three times that night. Kanseah remembered that Victorio's son Istee was in the group.[16]

"When I was a little boy I knew Yanosha; he was about sixteen when I first saw him. . . . When I first went with Geronimo he had only a few— seven or eight—Naiche, Chihuahua, Chato, Massai, Yanosha."[17]

Geronimo assigned Kanseah to Yanosha as a kind of orderly. Yanosha, whose sister was Geronimo's fourth wife,[18] was one of the bravest of a courageous group and was a great warrior. In 1871, when Juh was awaiting the opportunity to kill Lieutenant Howard Cushing,[19] it was Yanosha who reconnoitered and reported to Juh that it was Cushing they trailed. Yanosha had been in the Guadalupes and recognized Cushing.

Yanosha treated the boy well, and Kanseah took care of his horses, cooked his food, and ate what was left, completing his chores without talking, unless Yanosha gave an order or asked a question. Kanseah practiced with bow and arrow, ran long distances, and learned to ride. It took Kanseah about three winters to serve his apprenticeship, participate in four raids, and become a warrior.[20]

"Yanosha was a good runner. . . . These young people today can't do it. I had to run all time . . ."[21]

Kanseah said he didn't know what distance Yanosha was capable of because the Apaches didn't measure distance. He once said Yanosha could run almost as well as the great Hopi Lewis Tewanamo, who won a 45-mile race in Europe. Yanosha was also a sharpshooter who never wasted a bullet.[22]

Kanseah considered Yanosha one of Geronimo's most loyal warriors, but for a time he was a scout. "Yanosha was a U.S. scout at San Carlos and Fort Apache against his own people and his brother-in-law Geronimo." At this time, Yanosha's relatives, Fun, Eyelash, Perico, and another brother, were all scouts at Fort Apache in a company with the Chiricahua Noche as sergeant major and Chato (another former warrior of Geronimo's band) as first sergeant of the company. Crawford and Maus were the officers of that company. "They [Chato] could not turn Yanosha against his own relation." Yanosha, a cousin to Chato, left his troop because Chato treated him badly. Cisna and Fun also returned to Geronimo.[23]

Chihuahua was also a scout at that time. Asa Daklugie said, "That's why Chihuahua always hated Yanosha and those others. . . . When they broke out [from San Carlos] they said goodbye to Chihuahua. Yanosha had said to him, 'If we ever see you up front, just look out!' That's what Yanosha told him." He added that "When Chihuahua led a fight, he led it," meaning, Chihuahua was always in front.[24]

According to army records, Yanosha was thirty-two at the time of capture, his wife twenty.[25,26] When his service as a scout was up, Yanosha should have gotten a pension but the agency's books burned.[27]

Kanseah was about fifteen at the time of surrender. (The army estimated his age at twelve because of his small size.) He was sent to Carlisle with other young people and given the name Jasper. He later married Lucy Gonoltsis, who was also Chiricahua.[28]

For thirty-two years, Kanseah was a respected chief of police on the Mescalero Reservation. He once said he dealt with culprits resisting arrest by shooting them in the arm. He never missed. Like his mentor, Yanosha, Kanseah was a sure shot.

Both men died in the 1950s on the Mescalero Reservation.

SEVEN

Geronimo and Naiche

History tends to remember Geronimo as the white man saw him. Eve Ball, relying on Geronimo's chosen successor, Asa Daklugie, gave him more sympathetic treatment. Among his own people, he was both legend and pariah, credited for heroic deeds or blamed for the Army's persecution of Apaches and twenty-seven years as prisoners of war.

"I know that he and a few others like him were the cause of the death of my mother and many of my relatives who have been pushed around the country as prisoners of war," said Sam Kenoi. "I know we would not be in our present trouble if it was not for men like him . . ."[1]

Kenoi was critical earlier in his life but softened his remarks somewhat in an interview with Eve:

"Lots of Indians say he was afraid, claim that he was a coward. . . . But as I knew him it looked like he had the same virtues and faults of the average person. Charlie Istee said the reason Geronimo led his people away [was] 'cause he was afraid. . . . [2] He believed anything that he was told. . . . I think white people think he was a greater man than we do. . . . To a lot of Apaches he was just another man."[3]

Daklugie and Geronimo's nephew Kanseah defended their relative all their lives. "Geronimo was a good man and kind to his people and take good care of them,"[4] Kanseah insisted.

Fig. 9. Cochise's son Naiche fought bravely under Geronimo's leadership, but it was an uneasy relationship. The two men are shown here around 1885. (Courtesy Museum of New Mexico, #43060.)

Daklugie said, "I am the man who would defend Geronimo. We were punished for his sake but we knew why Geronimo was punished. He was unwilling to give up, and he offered to die fighting for what was his by right—his country. I don't blame him for it. The white people came to this country, pouring out like popcorn. To locate themselves in our country, they treated the Indians bad—tie them together and shoot them, robbed them of everything, take everything they got, shot them, showed them no mercy, killed them like animals, tried to exterminate them. Geronimo was fighting for his own. He tried to win back his country for his people and died a prisoner."[5]

Daklugie may have contributed to Geronimo's legend, but he also debunked stories on occasion: "Geronimo did not tell them he could not be hurt by a bullet but their imagination made them think he could not be hit. But he was meat and bone just like any other man, only he had more courage than others."[6]

Kanseah, Geronimo's youngest warrior, describes his group's loyalty to Geronimo: "After my father died I went with Geronimo, for he was looking after his people. It was because of the relation of the family. After all, if he die, we die. There was none of my family left but me. Kanseah, Yanosha, Massai, Naiche, Fun, and Perico were with Geronimo [sometimes together and sometimes apart] for they separate when hard pressed and reassemble [later at a predetermined place].

"It is not true that Geronimo [forced people to accompany him]. This is not said by those who went with him. They went because they wanted to go. He always knew that there were too many [against him], that they could not win, but people just kept after them so they have to defend themselves. That's how it was. They could not stop. If they go to the reservation, they would be killed."[7]

Naiche, son of Cochise, also followed Geronimo willingly and fought bravely, but his daughter's comments indicate that theirs was a complicated relationship. Cochise had passed on his knowledge and medicine to his oldest son, Taza. When Cochise died,[8] Taza became chief, but Taza died during agent John Clum's ill-conceived trip to Washington D.C., and Naiche was too young and unprepared to be chief. Initially, the Nednhi chief Juh, Daklugie's father, took over. "Naiche was afraid to take his father's place. I don't like to talk, [but] after he refused my father had to act," Daklugie said.[9]

When Juh died, Geronimo stepped in. Geronimo and Cochise had been good friends. "I never heard of them having any disagreement," Kanseah said.[10]

It's revealing that among Eve Ball's sources, Naiche's daughter Amelia was most critical of Geronimo. Even though Eve considered Amelia Naiche one of her most accurate informants, her remarks don't appear in the two books, probably out of deference to Daklugie, who was the primary informant for *Indeh*.

"Asa worked with Geronimo and knew lots of things that Geronimo did and he didn't like for anybody to criticize Geronimo," Amelia said. "No one ever say anything against Geronimo to Ace. He become very angry if they do. He always talked good for Geronimo. But Geronimo was not a great man at all. I never heard any good of him. People never say he is doing good."[11]

Naiche, by all accounts, was a tall, handsome man with a dignified bearing that reflected the Apache equivalent of a royal bloodline as the son of Cochise and Dos-teh-seh, daughter of the great Warm Springs chief Mangas Coloradas.

"Naiche was six feet, two, needless to say strong and agile, and from the Indian point of view, very handsome. Their ideal of beauty was very much that of the Greeks—physical perfection," Eve wrote.[12] "His grandson, Harold Kaywaykla,[13] resembles [him] very closely and but for his long hair, Naiche and he might be mistaken for each other."[14]

Naiche had two wives, Haozinne and Grin-eh-zel-eh-had. "When I think how my mother Haozinne lived in fear, running and hiding from the cavalry, I am thankful that I did not experience those dreadful days," Amelia Naiche said.[15] If there was any doubt about Naiche's willingness to follow Geronimo, he dispelled it by shooting his second wife in the leg when she started to leave with Chihuahua's people, who were surrendering. Naiche had turned back and apparently expected her to follow him.[16] She recovered.

Though Naiche fought bravely alongside Geronimo, "there was resentment."[17] Even in captivity, their relationship continued to be complicated. They maintained a distance, but Geronimo once cured Naiche's ailing daughter.

"Even in Oklahoma, as far as I know, Geronimo never came near our place," Amelia recalled. "They were not good friends. He never visited us. I was born and reared there but I never saw Geronimo close." When Amelia was young, her sister Hazel, then a toddler, got sick. Naiche thought Geronimo had caused this sickness and he told Geronimo to come over, make his daughter well. Geronimo was reluctant, but he came and made medicine.[18]

"My father used to say that Geronimo was a good medicine man. I remember my sister Hazel was sick and my father sent for Geronimo and he sang for her four nights and she got well."[19]

Although it has often been said that Cochise didn't teach his medicine to Naiche, apparently the younger son did practice some medicine.

"My father knew the white people did not believe in ghosts. . . . A white lady brought her little boy to him. He could not open his eyes. He was very sick. She brought him to our camp. Naiche found that the little boy had been scared and that he could not open his eyes. Naiche prayed over him and sang a song. He sang two Apache songs before the child. For two nights he prayed and the fourth night the child spoke and opened his eyes and was alright after that. Even today some of our people know the ghost medicine."[20]

In time, Naiche became a member of the Dutch Reformed Church "because he thought it was a good influence for women and children," Eve wrote.[21] Geronimo maintained his traditional faith until the end. And until the end, he had his regrets. "Geronimo always said he wished he had never given up," Daklugie said, "that it would have been better to die fighting."[22]

"In Oklahoma when he died people took his picture in his coffin," Amelia recalled. "His own people did not have anything to do with him—called him an outcast. . . . Geronimo was with us, of necessity, but we never were friendly with him. He had no friends. The Apaches did not count him a great man at all. I never heard of him being a great man until we came to New Mexico. Then I heard much about him. He did not have any friends among us."[23]

A curious statement from Naiche's son Christian indicates that when people visit Geronimo's grave, it may not be the actual resting place of the old warrior.

"Geronimo died at Fort Sill in January of 1909. I understand his grave was molested and his body took out and somebody else's put in that grave. The Indians did it to prevent his being taken by the white people. They remembered what had happened to Mangas Coloradas. They put Geronimo in a different place. Lots of white people and the army knew it. But he was taken out of there and buried in the grave so that the white people could not find his body. They were afraid somebody would take his body, so a group got together and thought it was better to do it that way. I don't know when this was done but I have always heard it, that he was taken out by the Chiricahua Indians and that another body was substituted for his."[24]

Naiche died at Mescalero.[25] Like Geronimo, Naiche had his regrets. "He was a handsome man in his youth and a tragic figure in his age. He felt that he had failed his people, and grieved over it 'til he died," Eve wrote.[26]

One of history's ironies lives on. In 1981, one of the few people willing to challenge the iron grip Wendell Chino maintained over the Mescalero Tribe was Amelia Naiche's son Silas, who took his great grandfather's name.[27] But Silas Cochise, like his grandfather Naiche, instead became the lieutenant and not the opponent of a strongman.

Amelia Naiche

Eve was particularly close to Amelia Naiche, daughter of Naiche's second wife, Haozinne. One night Amelia and a young grandson showed up at Eve's door after their Model T had stalled. "When I saw the light of your house, I was very much relieved," Amelia said. "I knew you would keep us overnight."

"Any time and with pleasure," Eve said.

Eve took them to see Jeff Chandler's portrayal of Cochise. The critics liked the movie. Amelia said he lacked the dignity and bearing of a chief.

Amelia, who died at Mescalero in 1983, was known to visit prisoners in jail and help the destitute on the reservation. At times of death or tragedy, she returned to Apache traditional religion, as did others, and yet she was also devoted to the reservation's Dutch Reformed Church. The first time Eve met her, she was scrubbing the floor of the church, which Eve said didn't detract a bit from her dignity. "I knew then that I had the honor to meet a great lady," Eve wrote.

It was Amelia who brought James Kaywaykla to Eve's home for the first time. Kaywaykla had married Amelia's half-sister Dorothy. He "began dictating talks that formed the basis of *In the Days of Victorio*."[28]

Fig. 10.   Naiche is said to resemble his father, Cochise. A number of imposters claim to be relatives. (Ben Wittick, courtesy Museum of New Mexico, #16326.)

EIGHT

The Impostors

As her reputation grew along with her knowledge, one of Eve's dubious tasks was to debunk the stories of imaginative folks claiming family ties to Cochise.

One June day Eve got a surprise visit from three Apache friends—the daughter of Daklugie, the son of the scout Martine, and the granddaughter of Mangas Coloradas. The three had seen a letter in *True West* magazine that upset them.

"Saturday about noon Maude Geronimo, George Martine and his wife walked in. They had ridden on a logging truck to the intersection of the reservation road with Highway 70, and then walked eight miles to my place." Several days later Perico's daughter Isabel Enjady, aged and crippled with arthritis, came to visit, and she too wanted to respond to the letter.

The source of their agitation was a letter in *True West* from an alleged grandson of Cochise.

"He came to Mescalero a year or two ago to interview the Naiche men to try to get them to admit that he is a grandson of Cochise. They were not convinced, and would tell him nothing. They say he is an impostor. They think him possibly a Chiricahua, but one who has not lived among his people long enough to know anything of their customs."[1]

Joseph Evans, a California man, claimed to be chief of a White Mountain Apache band and the son of Nantaje, a scout. He said his mother was the granddaughter of Cochise and hinted that his grandmother was one of Cochise's two daughters. He also said he knew Geronimo and was good friends with Geronimo's grandson Chief Silent Dawn.[2] (Besides the fact that Geronimo had no relative by that name, the Hollywood sound of it should have set off warning lights.) He also described Apache dress and customs, and included a photo of himself and an alleged nephew of Geronimo, Joe Sundown, both wearing Plains-style dress, including war bonnets.[3] Apache leaders wore a small but distinctive cap.

Cochise's family is well documented. His principal wife was Dos-teh-seh, daughter of Mangas Coloradas. Their sons were Taza and Naiche. With a second wife, a Chiricahua woman whose name isn't recalled, Cochise had daughters Dash-dan-zhoos and Naithlotonz. "I think there were no other children of Cochise. I don't know of any," said his grandson, Christian Naiche.[4] Dos-teh-seh, Naiche, and Naiche's two half-sisters survived twenty-seven years of internment and spent their last days at Mescalero.

"His mother came here with us and died here. She died three days after we reached Mescalero in 1913. It was too high for her."[5]

Naiche had two wives. With Haozinne, a Nednhi, he had four children who survived—Christian, Amelia, Hazel, and Barney. With E-clah-heh, he had Dorothy. (Angie Debo wrote that Naiche had a third wife, his oldest, named Nah-de-yole, with whom Naiche surrendered with son Paul in 1886. She joined him in Florida and died at Fort Sill.)[6]

Dash-dan-zhoos married Kedizhinne, one of Mangus's warriors, and their daughter was Lena Morgan. Naithlotonz married Gokliz and, after his death, Chiricahua Tom.

"Cochise had no other sons than Naiche and Taza. This is the evidence of Christian Naiche, Amelia Naiche, Lena Morgan, and Eugene Chihuahua," Eve wrote. Jasper Kanseah and Ace Daklugie told Eve the same thing.[7]

That didn't prevent the more enterprising from inventing sons. One of the most convincing pretenders (to whites, anyway) was a man calling himself Niño Cochise. He published two conflicting versions of his story, both challenged by Apaches and historians. In a magazine article, he alleged that in 1873, Cochise's oldest son, Taza, married and in 1874 had a son, Niño, in the Cochise Stronghold of Arizona Territory. After Taza died, his wife and son fled to Mexico, where they remained unknown and uncounted by reservation agents. They returned to the United States when Niño was twelve, and he attended Carlisle Indian School, Haskell Institute, and the University of Washington, where he majored in journalism and English. He also claimed to have toured Europe with Buffalo Bill Cody's Wild West Show and served with the French Air Force. By 1957, Niño was a writer living near Hollywood in the summer and southern Arizona in the winter.[8] In his book he spun an entertaining tale of his life in the wild and told of going to Hollywood in the 1920s, where he became a movie set extra. He opened a western museum in Phoenix briefly, worked for defense contractors during World War II, and flew for a crop duster.[9]

In 1967 Pat Wagner, editor of *True West*, asked Eve to critique an article that carried no byline. Eve quickly identified it as that of Niño Cochise. Initially, she sympathized with the man but her attitude soon changed.

"Now, this man has done a great deal of reading, and has apparently not questioned what he found. If he were half-Apache, he most certainly would not accept all this. The San Carlos Reservation found no record of his having been reared there.

"I have had much sympathy for this man. He has a deep and sincere interest in and sympathy for the Apaches. And there is a possibility—rather remote, I think, after reading this—that his claim to being the descendant of Taza is true. But the Naiches have rejected him and have no hesitancy in saying that he is an impostor. . . . All the older Apaches who knew Taza say he had no children."[10]

"When Pat Wagner sent me a manuscript of a book, writer unidentified, I told her immediately that it was faked and exactly where the writer got his material. . . . In it were statements lifted literally from articles I had published in *True West*, etc."[11]

Besides his "borrowing" of others' work, Niño's own observations were riddled with errors. He referred to blood brothers, an alien concept to Apaches. He also spoke of clans; Western Apaches had clans but Chiricahuas did not. He was ignorant of the unique Apache moccasin with its turned-up toe and unaware that they never smoked pipes or used sign language. Despite flaws that would have been glaring to historians like Eve and Dan Thrapp, the story found its way into print.[12]

"Though I know it is too trivial for anyone's notice, I can't help being annoyed by the ridiculous claims of this so-called Niño Cochise. He may believe his story, but no Apache does. And I'm more annoyed at Western Publications for being took. I do understand that once having won recognition for the Lehmann story,[13] which the Comanches and Kiowas say is untrue, that they naturally wish to affect another startling discovery."[14]

The respected University of Oklahoma Press would have been snookered without the intervention of historian Dan Thrapp.

"First I want to congratulate [you] upon the attempt to prevent this press from being the victim of what I consider a monumental fraud," Eve wrote Thrapp.

"This Niño, as you know, has put one over on many people, including NBC, who uses him as adviser in the 'High Chaparral' series. He doesn't even know Apache customs . . .

"When I think that the High Brass rejected Betzinez' book and James Kaywaykla's (which Arizona U. is to publish for me) and fell for this junk, I am tempted to say that this impostor should be permitted! But there are far too many errors in history without this."[15]

Eve and Dan Thrapp weren't the only historians to take a skeptical view of Niño: Angie Debo wrote that she wouldn't touch the manuscript with a ten-foot pole.[16]

Niño found a publisher and the book appeared in 1971 to enthusiastic reviews that repeated his account without questioning its credibility. Only the *New York Review of Books* paused for a moment of skepticism.[17]

As Niño Cochise was making a name for himself, a Texan named Leroy Yarbrough popped up, also claiming to be a descendant of Cochise. He had an even more incredible yarn. In correspondence with Eve he insisted that Cochise had three sons—Taza, Nachite (Naiche), and Natches. Anyone at all familiar with Apache history knows that the latter two were among many misspellings of Naiche's name by Anglos who didn't know how to pronounce it. However, Yarbrough maintained that after Cochise's death, Taza took one group of their people to the mountains and Natches, the youngest son, took another group to the reservation. He said Nachite had a son with an unknown white woman. (Given the Apaches' contempt for whites, this is highly unlikely.) This son called himself Bud Cole. "Bud was for the new-budding plants in the spring. . . . Cole was for the coals in the campfires of his people." He also said that the son of Natches, called Natchez Cochise, was still living in Tucson in 1965.

As a half-breed among whites, Bud Cole's life was unpleasant, so he set out to find his father, Yarbrough said. When he found him, Nachite ignored him, but Cochise himself ascertained that his story was true and raised the boy himself. Cochise allegedly sent Bud Cole to arrange an alliance with the Sioux. He married Crazy Horse's sister, Running Deer, but then inexplicably decided to live as a white man in a cabin until Crow Indians forced him and his family to leave. They returned to the Chiricahuas and Cochise. After the chief's death, he again took up a white man's life on a farm in west Texas. In a letter to Eve, Yarbrough said, "That is why the blood Apache descendants of Nachite will never recognize me as kin."[18]

Yarbrough presented as evidence of his knowledge some badly rewritten accounts straight out of books Eve recognized. He also visited Mescalero, where the Naiche family, as he expected, dismissed his claims.[19]

Eskiminzin

In Apache history three men are linked by circumstance and the tragedy in their lives: Eskiminzin, persecuted chief of the Aravaipa Apaches; the Apache Kid, who married Eskiminzin's daughter before becoming the territory's most notorious Indian outlaw; and Massai, a Chiricahua who escaped from the moving train carrying his people to captivity and lived as a renegade. Massai rode with the Apache Kid on occasion and was often mistaken for the Kid.

Eskiminzin learned the white man's ways and successfully emulated them but was dogged by unfounded suspicions and the avarice of white settlers.

"If the day ever comes when the white man can find it in his heart to really sympathize with the red man, a volume can be written of Es-ki-mo-tzin and his little band of followers that will excel in pathos and tragedy anything ever conceived by Fenimore Cooper," wrote Lieutenant Britton Davis.[1]

Historian Dan Thrapp called Eskiminzin the "most controversial Apache in border history."[2]

From her notes and correspondence, I believe Eve Ball intended to write Eskiminzin's story but only a fragment ended up in Indeh. *Here is the chief's entire story, including previously unpublished information, which historian Dan Thrapp provided to Eve.*

Eskiminzin was in his twenties when he became chief of the Aravaipa band of Apaches, whose traditional home was along Aravaipa Creek from the San

Fig. 11.   The story of Aravaipa Chief Eskiminzin is one of the more tragic. He's shown here with a daughter and son. (Courtesy Arizona Historical Society, Tucson, #41085.)

Pedro River to the Galiuro Mountains of present-day Arizona.[3] The Aravaipas, who called themselves Tce-jine, or Dark Rocks People, took over the area after 1763 when the Spaniards relocated a Pima group occupying the area. Like other Apaches, Aravaipas were hunters, gatherers, and raiders, but they also farmed and kept cattle and horses. During the eighteenth century, their numbers may have reached one thousand.[4]

Eskiminzin (Hackibanzin, or "Angry Men Stand In Line For Him")[5] "was a determined enemy of the whites and Mexicans," wrote Britton Davis. "With a small band of followers he remained in the mountains refusing all overtures at making peace with him."[6]

One story is that the Aravaipas lived peacefully until a group of band members and prospectors died in a skirmish. Fearing retaliation, the Aravaipas retreated to the mountains but fared badly.

In February 1871, Eskiminzin's mother and four other ragged women ventured to Camp Grant in search of one woman's son. A new officer, First Lieutenant Royal Emerson Whitman, treated them kindly. On a second visit to trade, they were again treated well and Whitman encouraged them to ask the chiefs to come in and talk.[7]

A tall, strongly built man who stood straight as a pine, Eskiminzin was then in his thirties.[8] He told Whitman he was chief of a band of 150 Aravaipa Apaches, that he wanted to live in peace, and that they were weary of running from the cavalry. Whitman suggested they go to the White Mountains.

"That is not our country, neither are they our people," Eskiminzin responded. "Our fathers and their fathers before them have lived in these mountains and have raised corn in this valley. We are taught to make mescal our principal article of food and in summer and winter here we have a never-failing supply. At the White Mountains there is none, and without it we get sick."

Whitman said he had no authority to make a treaty or promise them a permanent home but if Eskiminzin would bring in his band, the officer would feed them and relay his requests to General George Stoneman, the department commander.[9] Stoneman never received his letter.

In March Eskiminzin arrived with his entire band, a miserable-looking 150 people. Other bands followed until 500 people surrounded Camp Grant. "They were nearly naked and needed everything in the way of clothing," Whitman wrote. He arranged a system to pay them for bringing in hay. In two months, the people provided nearly 300,000 pounds. Some gained passes to harvest and bake mescal and others helped nearby ranchers harvest their barley.

"They had so won . . . me that from my first idea of treating them justly and honestly as an officer of the Army, I had come to feel a strong personal interest in helping to show them the way to a higher civilization," Whitman wrote. "I had come to feel respect for men who, ignorant and naked, were still ashamed to lie or steal, and for women who would work cheerfully like slaves to clothe themselves and children, but, untaught, held their virtue above price. Aware of the lies and hints industriously circulated by the puerile press of the Territory, I was content to know I had positive proof they were so."[10]

It was a short-lived peace. What happened next is an often-told tale. Other Apache bands continued to raid in southern Arizona and with each outrage, the Arizona newspapers heaped ridicule on the Army, particularly Whitman. Tucson then was home to a population of profiteers, deserters, gamblers, thieves, and other vultures for whom peace was unwelcome. Many others believed the friendly Indians at Camp Grant were responsible for the attacks.

On 29 April, a mob of Tucson "citizens" and Papago Indians attacked Eskiminzin's ranchería and killed more than 100 defenseless people, all but eight of them women and children. Seven escaped and twenty-seven children were taken captive by the Papago and later sold as slaves in Mexico.[11] At least two women were raped and then shot. The wounded had their brains beaten out with stones. Nearly all the dead were mutilated. Eskiminzin himself lost two wives and five children in the massacre.[12] He managed to save one young daughter when he swept her up as he fled from the massacre.[13] Whitman's soldiers found the camp in flames, the ground strewn with bodies.

President Grant called the attack "purely murder" and told Arizona Governor Safford that if the participants weren't brought to trial he would proclaim martial law. After a half-hearted trial, the jury took nineteen minutes to find the defendants not guilty.[14] Eskiminzin, wrote Woodworth Clum (son of Indian agent John Clum), "was no longer the dominating, good-natured leader of men. His spirit was broken and though he continued as chief, he was morose and cynical. A smile seldom graced his lips."[15]

A month after the massacre, soldiers from the White Mountain reservation fired on Eskiminzin's band. In anger and despair, he found Whitman, renounced his pledge of peace and left Camp Grant. During this outbreak, Eskiminzin reportedly killed Charles McKenney,[16] a rancher who had befriended the Aravaipas. Asked why years later, he told Sam Bowman, an interpreter who was part Choctaw, "To teach my people that there must be no friendship between them and the white men. Anyone can kill an enemy but it takes a strong man to kill a friend."[17]

Returning to the warpath, the Aravaipas left a bloody trail among freighters, miners, and settlers. In one fight with troops, Eskiminzin lost thirteen warriors and he himself was wounded.[18]

With the massacre and its disastrous results, Stoneman was relieved of his duties on 2 May 1871. General George Crook assumed command on 4 June.[19] Soon after, Indian Commissioner Vincent Colyer spent months traveling through Apache country holding councils with Apache leaders in an effort to sell the president's peace program. At Camp Grant he met with several leaders, including Eskiminzin, who again agreed to live in peace.[20]

Riding through the site of the massacre five months later with Eskiminzin, Colyer observed that "some of the skulls of the Indians, with their temple bones beaten in, lay exposed by the washing of the run and the feeding of the wolves. I overtook Es-cim-en-zeen, who had ridden before us, and found him wiping the tears from his eyes when he saw them." And yet Eskiminzin and the other chiefs wanted to stay. They told Colyer that this country had always been their home and the home of their fathers. But they complained that their young men needed to be allowed to hunt and that sometimes the soldiers kick them and throw rocks at them.[21]

In 1872 Brigadier General Oliver O. Howard, a peace commissioner, ordered Apache chiefs to meet with him. The most important was Eskiminzin, who was willing to attend because two trusted officers, Whitman and Crook, would be present. When the religious Howard began to pray, the Apaches scattered like quail. Eskiminzin hid behind a building and demanded of Whitman, "What do you mean bringing that man here to make bad medicine against us?" After Howard's actions were explained, the Indians reassembled. Howard asked if any white man could come into their lodges.[22]

Eskiminzin said, "Yes, so long as there is a man, woman, or child in the Apache nation who remembers the Camp Grant Massacre, so long *that* man [Whitman] can come among us, by day or night, in war or in peace, and not a hair of his head shall be harmed."[23]

The Apaches complained to Howard that Camp Grant was a poor location for a reservation, and in December 1872 he designated a new reservation at San Carlos.[24] Howard "became very much interested in Es-kim-in-zin, and when the general returned to Washington a month later he took with him Chief Santo, Es-kim-in-zin's father-in-law," according to agent John Clum. Howard, in fact, thought so well of the chief that when Clum left Washington for San Carlos, Howard wrote letters of introduction to both Santo and Eskiminzin.[25] We might wonder at letters of introduction to hunters and gatherers, but the Apaches apparently were touched by Howard's remembrance of them.

In 1873 troops removed all the Apaches from Camp Grant to San Carlos, where the army had unwisely amassed the survivors of Crook's campaign on a reservation that one officer described as "rotten to the core," the result of corrupt agents and interpreters. In conflicts over leadership, two factions emerged—one led by Eskiminzin and Chiquito, the other by Chunz, Cochinay, and Bacoon.[26]

Crook ordered a policy of impartial justice, with rewards for those who learned new ways and lived at peace, and punishment to those who crossed the line. Enforcing the directive was newly assigned Major George Randall, a heavy-handed disciplinarian. After a party of Chiricahuas on a *tiswin* (Apache home brew) drunk killed two teamsters,[27] Randall had Eskiminzin arrested. Apparently Crook didn't trust Eskiminzin and implied that he was involved in the teamsters' slayings.[28] Eskiminzin's followers felt the charges were unfair and threatened reprisals.

After three days in the guardhouse, Eskiminzin escaped and fled to the hills with his warriors, which prompted other bands who chafed under Randall's tougher discipline to follow. In the worst weather since American occupation, the Army mounted a brutal chase. Eskiminzin and three other leaders remained at large but after pursuit by their own people and display of severed heads at Fort Apache, Eskiminzin in April 1874 brought in his humbled band.[29]

Eskiminzin told the army surgeon, who was then acting agent, "We did not kill the teamsters. Aravaipas drink very little tiswin. But we were afraid. That is why we ran away. Now we come back. If we stay in the mountains, we will die of hunger and cold-sickness. If American soldiers kill us here, it will be just the same. We will not run away again."

The surgeon told them to return to their old campsite and advised the agent and Randall. Randall again ordered Eskiminzin's arrest with five of his sub-chiefs and sent them in chains to the new Camp Grant, eighty miles away on the New Mexico border. And that's how John Clum met the chief in August 1874, when he stopped at Camp Grant on the way to his new assignment at San Carlos.[30]

"I found several Apache prisoners under a military guard at work making adobes, and among these was Es-kim-in-zin wearing shackles which were riveted to his ankles.

"Little did I dream at that time that a sincere and sympathetic friendship was destined to develop between this shackled Apache chief and myself," Clum wrote. Eskiminzin was the first Apache chief Clum would learn about when he was appointed agent and the first he met face to face in early August 1874 at the new Camp Grant.[31]

Clum asked what the charges were against Eskiminzin, and the post's commanding officer said only, "Major Randall does not like him." No charges had been filed.[32] Clum got Eskiminzin released from Camp Grant and he returned to his family at San Carlos in mid-October 1874. He settled on some vacant land on the Rio San Carlos several miles from the agency and immediately began to clear the land and build an irrigation ditch. Clum got the chief a plow and other farm implements and occasionally loaned him the agency's ox team.[33]

Eskiminzin met often with Clum, who called him "Skimmy,"[34] and he would come to Clum's aid repeatedly. In March 1875, Apaches from the Rio Verde reservation arrived at San Carlos. Eskiminzin not only pacified this otherwise rebellious group but formed a bodyguard to protect Clum. Later that year Clum brought Eskiminzin with him when he took over Camp Apache.[35] "Eskiminzin voluntarily faced the same danger he feared for me, and only a true friend would do that," Clum wrote.[36]

One of Clum's more audacious acts was to organize a trip to the East in which his party of Apaches would stop along the way to perform dramas. "Eskiminzin was the first Indian invited to go. He was greatly pleased and entered into the project with his usual enthusiasm."[37] The chief also proved to be a good actor. This otherwise pleasant trip was darkened by the death from pneumonia of Cochise's son Taza.[38]

After repeated conflicts and confrontations with the military, Clum left San Carlos but returned when the Chiricahuas broke from their agency and began raiding in southern Arizona. During a meeting with San Carlos people Eskiminzin rose and addressed the group at length, declaring that they were good Indians and would not join the Chiricahuas on the warpath. He even offered to fight the fearsome Chiricahuas, if Clum wished. Within hours 250 Apache scouts had volunteered.[39]

Eskiminzin's people may have liked Clum, but in May 1877 Clum earned the undying hatred of the Chiricahuas and Warm Springs people by forcing them from the Warm Springs reservation in New Mexico and removing Geronimo in chains."[40] After hearing about Geronimo and the others, Juh, chief of the Nednhi Apaches, set out for San Carlos, stopping at Eskiminzin's ranchería. Juh knew Eskiminzin well and knew of the Camp Grant Massacre. "Eskiminzin was shrewd enough and was sufficiently concerned for the remnant of his band that he professed great admiration and friendship for Clum."

Eskiminzin and Juh posted scouts at the agency and on the road they expected Clum to take. When they learned that Clum and his captives were near, they rode to the agency and watched the wretched band arrive.

Geronimo and the others had been in the guardhouse for about two weeks when Eskiminzin and Juh met with Clum.[41] Eskiminzin did the talking because of Juh's stutter. Eskiminzin told Clum that if they did not release the prisoners pronto, they would set every Indian on the reservation against him.[42]

"When he [Juh] went to the agency he took his warriors and he told [them] he was going to get Geronimo or else," said Juh's son Asa Daklugie, who heard about Eskiminzin from his father as well as Geronimo, Chihuahua, and Kanseah. "Everybody was waiting. The troops line up but so were the Indians, all ready to attack. My father had to control his people. . . . He had to get Geronimo out. . . . My father said, 'If you want trouble you can get plenty. He got to be released. Release all those men—also Nana and Loco.' They didn't care who they hit either."[43]

Eve Ball wrote that Clum ordered their release[44] and resigned about a month later.[45] Clum, who regarded Geronimo as a "ruthless renegade and multi-murderer," was determined to prosecute Geronimo but he never says he gave such an order,[46] writing only that Geronimo's manacles "were taken off soon after I left the agency in '77."[47] In letters to fellow historian Dan Thrapp, Eve said Daklugie's story about the demand for release of the prisoners was "a very improbable account," but she planned to include it anyway.[48] "As I see it, my obligation is to tell his story but also where I question its accuracy . . . to give that side of the story."[49]

Still, until she heard the story she never questioned Clum's belief in Eskiminzin's loyalty. "I've learned that Apache scouts knew which side of their bread was buttered and acted accordingly."[50]

Daklugie always insisted that Eskiminzin only pretended to be Clum's friend to protect his band. However, Daklugie's people hated Clum and Daklugie himself hated white people. Clum, encumbered by ego and a faulty memory, painted his own picture of life at San Carlos. The truth is probably somewhere in between. Eskiminzin was likely Clum's friend, but possibly not the ardent admirer Clum thought he was.

In July 1877 when Clum resigned a second time and left San Carlos, it was, by his own account, a sorrowful farewell.[51] Eskiminzin decided to leave too, saying, "If there should be trouble here again I will be blamed. I have not made trouble and do not want to make trouble for anyone. I want to live at peace and make my own living and raise things for my family to eat. I can do this and I will do it."

The chief moved to the San Pedro Valley about sixty miles north of Tucson where he established a successful ranch.[52] After he had been there about ten years, Lieutenant Britton Davis visited Eskiminzin and reported,

"What I saw I would not have believed Indians capable of under at least one more generation.

"The little colony of six or eight families might well be mistaken for a colony of prosperous Mexican farmers. They had adobe houses, fields under barbed wire fences, modern [for those days] farming implements, good teams, and cows."

Eskiminzin's family, dressed in their Sunday best, served an appetizing meal on a well-set table covered by a clean white cloth. The chief himself was wearing a suit with a watch and heavy silver chain, "of which he was very proud and by which he had learned to tell the time after a fashion." Later Eskiminzin took Davis to Tucson in his light buggy drawn by a good team of horses and the town's merchants told him that Eskiminzin's credit was good for four to five thousand dollars.[53]

"Seventeen years ago I took up a ranch on the San Pedro, cleared the brush and took out water in a ditch which I made," Eskiminzin would testify later. "I plowed the land and made a fence around it like the Mexicans. When I started I had three horses and 25 head of cattle. I was on the San Pedro ten years; then I had 17 horses, 38 cattle, a large yellow wagon for which I paid $150; four sets of harness for which I paid $40, and another wagon which cost $90, but which I had given to some relatives. I also had many tools.

"For about three years I drew rations from the agent. After that I did not draw any more 'til I was sent to the agency by Lieutenant Watson [seven years later]. I bought all my family clothing and supplies with the money I made."

Again, peace and prosperity were not to be. Not surprisingly, the white rabble in Tucson resented his presence and his prosperity and made frequent threats to attack him at his ranch. After ten years they made good on their threats.[54]

"About four years ago [1888] Lieutenant Watson came to my ranch and gave me a paper from Captain [Frances E.] Pierce, the agent, and told me I had better go to the San Carlos reservation; that citizens would kill me if I did not; that there were about 150 citizens coming with pistols. They came the next day after I left my ranch and they shot at my women, putting bullets through their skirts and drove them off.

"They took 513 sacks of corn, wheat and barley, destroyed 523 pumpkins and took away 32 head of cattle. I took my horses, wagons and harness with me to San Carlos."

Pierce told Eskiminzin he could select a farm on the reservation, so he chose a parcel on the Gila River and started over again, clearing land, and building an irrigation ditch and fencing.[55] Again, peace would remain out of reach.

In 1884 or 1885, the Apache Kid had married Eskiminzin's daughter and they had two children. Five years later the Kid was falsely charged with shooting Al Sieber, chief of scouts. The Kid escaped and from 1889 on became the most feared renegade in Arizona.

At the time Captain John Bullis, then the agent at San Carlos, reported that his reservation Apaches "are gradually, but slowly, yielding to the efforts made to civilize them." But seventeen renegades were still out, including Massai and the Kid, who "made several unfriendly visits to the reservation, killed several married women and [took] girls off with them, terrorized the good Indians and tried to persuade the dissatisfied ones to join them," Bullis wrote in his report for 1890. The military had killed or captured fifteen renegades—all but the Kid and Massai. In March 1890, to prevent an outbreak, Bullis sent to Fort Union seventy-five men, women, and children who were relatives or sympathizers, including Eskiminzin.[56]

Then they were sent as prisoners of war to Mount Vernon Barracks in Alabama, where they joined the Chiricahua, Warm Springs, and Nednhi Apaches interned in the miserable swamps. The group included the Kid's wife and children. He had not wished to subjected them to the trials of the war trail and instead had left them with her family.[57] One of Eskiminzin's wives and their children remained behind to care for the farm.[58]

"There was no doubt in the minds of the prisoners in Alabama as to the reason Eskiminzin came," said Eugene Chihuahua. "Geronimo and all the rest felt sure it was the officers' revenge for Eskiminzin's helping Juh release the ones in that guardhouse."[59]

In 1892 Eskiminzin petitioned for release. "I ask to be sent back with my family to San Carlos and given the land surveyed by Lieutenant Watson; that it may be given to me forever, and I will never ask for rations or anything else for myself or my family from the government. I want to work like a white man and support my family. I can do it and I will always be a good man."[60]

That effort prompted letters from officers who knew him. Captain John L. Bullis, Indian agent at San Carlos from 1888 to 1891: "In regard to the arrest of Eskiminzin, a San Carlos Apache Chief, I would say that he was arrested and sent away at my request, as he was a disturbing and dangerous element on the reservation. At the time of his arrest I had positive proof that he had rendered assistance to renegade Indians [some 16 of them], all of whom were murderers, and who evaded the military authorities by hiding in the mountains of old Mexico and Arizona and some of whom have not even yet been captured. Eskiminzin aided them by furnishing them with food and ammunition. As to his self support; for several years he lived off of the White Mountain Reservation [south of it, on the San Pedro River] where his many crimes caused the people to rise up in arms against him and he for self protection, fled to the Agency, where he and his entire family lived for years supported by the Government Ration.

"Since his removal comparative peace has reigned on the reservation."[61]

Bullis's credibility is suspect. Al Sieber, the Army's chief of scouts, accused Bullis of mistreating the Indians in his care. Apaches were arrested on trumped-up charges and sentenced without trial.[62]

Captain Lewis Johnson, Indian agent at San Carlos, wrote: " . . . I had as [commanding] officer of the Post of San Carlos, frequently urged the apprehension of E. before he was arrested, because it was evident that he was constantly aiding and abetting the Kid and other renegades then at large and committing depredations and outrages in Arizona and New Mexico. Finally the evidence brought to me, besides that obtained by Capt. Bullis, proved conclusively that he had furnished ammunition and other supplies to the Kid and party, for which he was paid in money; it was also ascertained that he had repeatedly harbored the Kid on his premises . . .

"Though formerly a man who had a considerable following among his own people, his greed, unscrupulous and cruel disposition and scheming propensities have caused the great mass of the San Carlos Apaches to look upon him as a bad man, and to feel relieved now that he no longer retards their progress towards civilization."

Brigadier General Alexander McCook, commander of the Department of Arizona wrote: "I know this Indian. He should not be returned to the reservation but held forever in his present condition. He will create trouble at San Carlos should he return there."[63]

Major Russell of Mount Vernon Barracks and General Howard were apparently sympathetic to Eskiminzin. However, the Brigadier General commanding the Department of Arizona replied to them: "When I saw Eskiminzen in the guardhouse at San Carlos, I asked him how long it had been since he saw the Kid. He replied, after counting upon his fingers, 'Last Friday . . . ' When Eskiminzen was sent from the reservation he took his two wives and any children he desired to accompany him. Since his expulsion from the San Carlos Reservation, peace and quiet has reigned there and will in my opinion continue, if such disturbing elements as Eskiminzen be kept out."[64]

And so he stayed. In January 1894, Clum once again found his friend a prisoner. He visited Mount Vernon and encountered Eskiminzin arranging a compost heap with the help of two women. The chief had become head gardener for the Apache camp of some 400 people. Asked why he was there, Eskiminzin said, "Great lies, you know."

In an interview with a *Washington Evening Star* reporter, Clum said, "I believe that Es-kim-in-zin is held a prisoner of war under a misapprehension of the facts, and I am satisfied that Captain Witherspoon shares this opinion with me. Es-kim-in-zin now has charge of the Indians' gardens and their thrifty condition reflects on his intelligence and industry."

Clum decided to campaign for Eskiminzin's release. In letters to various authorities and a visit to the War Department, he tried to determine the charges against Eskiminzin and learned only that Army officers considered him cruel and treacherous. The only crime named was the murder of a white man soon after the Camp Grant massacre. An officer of the War Department could say only that Eskiminzin was being held as a "military precaution."

In a letter to Daniel M. Browning, Commissioner of Indian Affairs," Clum wrote that Eskiminzin "has been condemned, sentenced, and exiled, not only without trial but without the filing of specific charges." Clum then recounted Eskiminzin's tragic history and his good deeds on Clum's behalf at San Carlos.

"Is it not strange that we can pass lightly over the one hundred and twenty-eight treacherous and cowardly murders instigated by white men, while we carefully treasure the memory of a single killing by an Indian . . . without even giving him the benefit of the circumstances which instigated the crime?" Clum continued, "We had many trying times at San Carlos from 1874 to 1877 and not once in all those years was Eskiminzin found wanting in action or advice. I frequently depended upon his support when I felt my life was in danger and he never failed to do his duty well."

Browning responded that he feared for Eskiminzin's safety if he returned to San Carlos.[65]

During a meeting on 29 August 1894 at Mount Vernon, Eskiminzin said, "About twenty-eight years ago I made peace and lived off of what I made with my own hands ever since. I would like to know what I have done, why I cannot go back to my own country. I had horses and other property and do not know what Captain Bullis was thinking about. . . . I had 40 horses, 3 wagons and other property. If I had been on warpath I would not have had these things."

Captain Maus replied, "Were you not accused of giving assistance to renegade Indians?" By this, he meant the Apache Kid.

"That is what Captain Bullis said."

"Didn't you tell General McCook so?"

Eskiminzin responded, "He came in to the guardhouse and General McCook asked me how long I had been in from the mountains and I said seven days. There was a man by the name of Rowdy [an Apache scout] who did not interpret what I said but told Gen. McCook that I had seen [the Apache Kid] seven days before, which was not true. I have a farm on Gila River above San Carlos Agency. I had three wagons, 40 horses and 48 cows. I have since heard that ten of my horses have been stolen. I have a wife and children there and I want to go back. Altogether about 38 people came here with me. They all belong in San Carlos River and have farms there." He said no white man ever told him why he was sent there but an Indian said it was for furnishing the Kid with ammunition. He learned that several officers made charges against him regarding renegades.

"It is false what I have been charged with. I didn't do anything to be sent here and I won't do anything if I go back. I want to go back to San Carlos."

Eskiminzin also found a sympathetic ear in Lieutenant Hugh Lenox Scott, who commanded Fort Sill. The War Department sent Scott to see about relocating the Chiricahuas. The old chief told Scott that he hadn't been at war and that because of some gossip about talking to the Apache Kid, he was imprisoned. He asked to return to Arizona. Scott recommended to General Miles that Eskiminzin and his people be allowed to go home. An angry Miles retorted that Eskiminzin would never set foot in Arizona as long as Miles lived because Eskiminzin had buried a white man up to his neck in an anthill. Scott argued that the deed was twenty-five years earlier and that Miles himself had condoned other tribes' acts of savagery. He reminded Miles of Eskiminzin's productive life off the reservation and added that he thought the general was making a mistake. Then he dropped the subject.

Scott wrote, "There was a vast difference in my mind between him and a criminal who has the advantage of civilization and example. I thought he had already been punished too much. . . ."[66]

On 14 September, Thomas M. Vincent, acting adjutant general, ordered all Indian prisoners except Eskiminzin and his band to be sent to Fort Sill.[67] The Aravaipas were left under guard of Captain Bailey's company of Fifth Infantry while the War Department, increasingly impatient, continued to pester Miles about their disposition. Soon after, Scott learned that Bailey and his soldiers had escorted Eskiminzin and his people to Arizona. "The general had finally come down out of his tree; he had not wanted to do it, but neither had he wanted to put aside my recommendation, and he finally saw it was best."

Years later an officer whose troop had escorted the Aravaipas from the railroad to their agency, said "those Apaches ran far ahead of the wagons, with the tears of joy streaming down their faces as they recognized the land-marks in their old country," Scott wrote. "The agent established them on their reservation, where they proved to be the most industrious, well be-haved and progressive people he had, a notable example to the others. Eskimazin died soon after his return, and I felt glad that I had had some-thing to do with allowing him to die in his own country, for he had been greatly wronged by the people of Arizona."[68]

Eskiminzin died at San Carlos in 1895 or 1896. His descendants contin-ued to farm on their San Pedro land.[69]

TEN

The Apache Kid

The Apache Kid, like his father-in-law, Eskiminzin, successfully learned the white man's ways. He was bright, charming, and earned the trust of the Army's chief of scouts. A series of misunderstandings plus some outright treachery would make him the Southwest's most infamous outlaw, easily blamed for his own and others' misdeeds. Apache scholar Dan Thrapp wrote, "He had greatness within him, and the tragedy of the Kid is that of lost greatness."[1]

The Apache Kid was born around 1860, the oldest son of Togo-de-chuz, a member of Capitán Chiquito's band of Aravaipa Apaches, and he grew up in the canyon of that name.[2] His name was Has-kay-bay-nay-ntayl.[3] In 1875, agent John Clum moved the band to the San Carlos Reservation. The teenager spent time in the mining camp of Globe, where he had various jobs, learned English, and began to wear white men's clothes. That's where he earned his moniker, the Apache Kid. With later jobs, he became a wrangler and marksman and came to the attention of Al Sieber, the Army's chief of scouts.[4]

In 1879 Sieber made the Kid an orderly and cook, and two years later he enlisted as a scout.[5] For the next six years the Kid would distinguish himself as a scout, reaching the rank of first sergeant. "Handsome looking fellow," said Ace Daklugie, who saw the Kid often on the reservation. Then five-feet-nine inches,[6] he had eyesight as keen as his intelligence.[7] The Kid participated in the Battle of the Big Wash against Coyotero and White Mountain Apaches in 1882[8] and in two campaigns against Geronimo, and was standing at Bowie Station the day Geronimo and his band were shipped to Florida.

Between 1884 and 1885 the Kid married the daughter of Aravaipa chief Eskiminzin and had a child.[9]

In the summer of 1887, the Kid's father was murdered by an old rival, who was in turn killed by friends of Togo-de-chuz. Not satisfied that the score was settled, the Kid, accompanied by fellow scouts, killed the man's brother and, while Sieber was away, joined a tiswin party. After five days' AWOL, the Kid and some fellow scouts returned to the reservation to face the music and asked to talk to Sieber as a crowd of armed Apaches gathered to watch. The scouts handed over their weapons and Captain Pierce ordered them to the guardhouse but someone in the crowd began shooting. In the fracas that followed, Sieber was shot in the ankle, crippling him for life.[10] The Kid and the four scouts who had been AWOL with him fled, along with a handful of Apache malcontents. They surrendered on 25 June.[11]

During the court-martial that followed, witnesses and even Sieber himself testified that the Kid wasn't armed, so he couldn't have fired the shot that wounded Sieber.[12] The Kid himself always thought that an old enemy named Curley did the deed but one eyewitness says it was one of the Kid's sidekicks, Paslautau.[13] But Sieber believed the Kid had signaled the others to go for their weapons. The Kid himself said, "If I had made any arrangement before I came in, I would not have given up my arms at Mr. Sieber's tent."[14]

"Al Sieber, he was a Scout captain, chief of scouts and all the Indians hated him," said George Ester, a San Carlos Apache whose father, John Ester, was a scout. "He framed Apache Kid. Said he shot him and nobody knew who shot Sieber. Many shots were fired."[15]

Daklugie said, "Why Sieber framed the Kid I do not know but no Apache doubted that's what he did."[16]

The Kid and the other four scouts were found guilty and sentenced to death. General Miles questioned the verdict, ordered the court to reconsider, and the five were ultimately sentenced to ten years at Alcatraz.[17] Authorities in Washington questioned that sentence and the five were released in 1888.

Returning to San Carlos, he settled in again with his wife six miles below San Carlos on the Gila River, but Arizona civil authorities decided to re-arrest the five men, along with others they considered troublemakers. The list included the renegade Massai, but they never laid eyes on him.[18] During their trial Sieber testified against them.[19] On 30 October 1889, they were sentenced to seven years in the territorial prison at Yuma. Three days later, as Sheriff Glenn Reynolds and a deputy were transporting the Kid and five other Apache prisoners, they were overwhelmed and killed. The stage driver was left for dead and a Mexican prisoner escaped.[20] All but the Apache Kid later surrendered or were killed[21] and the Kid would become the most feared renegade in the territory, never to be apprehended again.

From then on every crime committed on or near San Carlos was blamed on the Apache Kid and the price on his head grew to $6,000.[22]

"It was known that he wore a little mirror on his chest and every time the glint of one was seen it constituted identification, though half the young men on the San Carlos Reservation wore similar ornaments," the late Bert Judia said. He was believed to be in Mexico, raiding on both sides of the border—sometimes with renegade Chiricahuas, sometimes with Massai, sometimes with a woman and at times alone.[23] Massai was often mistaken for the Kid and even the gentle Doubtful Adams (see chapter 3) was described as the Apache Kid.[24]

Stories circulated about the Kid abducting various women, some of whom returned to tell their stories.[25] Dan Williamson, a telegraph operator in those days, says one captive was the sister-in-law of Eskiminzin.[26]

George Ester recalled: "Near Coolidge three women were gathering mesquite. He took the youngest one and made the others go home. He took her over the desert to Wilcox and into Mexico. He had her tied at night and put a sharp rock over his head so that he would wake easily. They got a horse at Wilcox and went on down to the Sierra Madre. . . ." The Apache Kid and his captive traveled farther east and encountered police. "The Apache Kid sure treated her mean. . . ." The police told her to get away "so she took off on the one horse." She eventually returned to her people at San Carlos.

Apaches have told of a cave where the Kid's mother and sister cached food, ammunition, and clothing so that he could return without showing himself. Gladys Scott Cojo, who married the Kid's sister's grandson, heard this from her mother-in-law, who knew the women well.[27]

"In this cave they had cached flour and coffee they got from the settlers mostly, some of it from the reservation," Daklugie said. "In that country they could have something to eat without going to town or spending any money or being recognized. Apache Kid knew where it is and sometimes he stay there."

Hugh Chee and his white brother-in-law knew of the cave in a mountain near Safford.[28] The white man was probably John Forrester, who with his Apache wife, lived at the mouth of Aravaipa Creek.[29]

"White man said, 'I am going to see about my cattle and run those people out of that cave.' Cave had water from a spring and they waited there overnight with their horses staked and supper cooking," Daklugie said. "They took a shot at each other early in the morning, trying to chase them out of the country. White man tell them not to come around any more.

"Apache Kid had the booty in the cave underground and when they left they put a big rock against the door so nobody can get in and can't see it. This white man chased the fellow across the San Carlos River and toward Tucson. . . . He was getting the Indians into trouble all the time. . . . Apache Kid did not really stay at San Carlos. He stayed at Wilcox on the railroad and he never showed himself at San Carlos because it was Indian country and everybody was looking for him to take him."[30]

A bootful of tales linger about how the Kid met his end. In those days, every time somebody shot a renegade Indian he hoped, or claimed, it was the Apache Kid. Bert Judia, a cowboy on the Whitlock Ranch at the time, offered this one[31]: Six years after the Kid escaped, a man, a woman, and their daughter were found murdered and their camp ransacked. Locals, of course, blamed the Kid. "Who could doubt it? I could. I was a boy and I kept still. But it just didn't make sense—shod horses, mules left, and horses taken. The Apaches infinitely prefer mule to horse meat. To me it looked like the work of white outlaws. In 1895 there were many crimes attributed to the Apaches that were committed by white men."

A year later the Duncan postmaster came upon a similar scene, this time a man and his daughter. "The killers made no attempt to hide their trail. Tracks of two unshod horses led south past Ash Peak and close to the Whitlock Cienega. The posse was so close upon its quarry that it did not stop though the horses were ridden down. They kept on 'til they saw a bunch of horses off the trail. They sent two men to rope some out but all were wild. The men found one of Will Park's stallions with a piece of meat cut from his hindquarter.

"They followed the trail leading up a ridge. For a moment they got a glimpse of an Indian on top. The setting sun was reflected by something on his chest; then he disappeared. When they reached the summit he had descended into a canyon and was going up it afoot. He had evidently dropped back to look for pursuers. He was headed for a camp where a woman was broiling meat. Near her stood a black horse. The woman must have sighted the posse for she was packing their gear on another horse. She called to the man, then swerved to the left and began climbing diagonally up the steep wall. He left the trail and used both hands to pull himself onto a ledge. The posse followed slowly because of the steepness of the descent.

They followed down the canyon, shooting as they went. The Indian did not return their fire but continued gaining height. The woman hid behind a rock and fired several times with a small pistol.

"The posse rounded a curve and lost the Apaches. They must have taken cover, for the man opened fire on the party. His bullets struck the opposite wall over their heads. It was so dark in the canyon that he could not see them well but the light was bright on the rim.

"He quit firing. They had no way of knowing whether or not he had been hit, whether he was out of ammunition or whether he had left. And nobody went up to see!

"The posse returned to the camp where the black horse was tied. They found the meat still on the coals. They found a packsaddle made of bear grass and a pair of moccasins. The Apaches usually carried extra ones tied to their belts so that if they were forced to walk they had spares.

"The sheriff left the horse thinking the woman might return for it. They spent the night with us at the Whitlock headquarters. I took their horses, examined their find and heard their story. The next day they circled the canyon and found the woman's trail leaving it. They followed her south to a watering place. From there she had ridden down to Orange Bluff in the San Simon and back to the Whitlock Cienega. She had watered her horse at our trough while we slept. Then she went back to the camp and got the black horse.

"And there the trail ended.

"How her jaded horse had got out of the canyon nobody could understand. After such a trip it could not have traveled far. Had the man left with her? If so the black must have carried both and that seemed improbable. If he had been wounded, could he have made that perilous descent without leaving any traces? Or could this be a trap and tempt the posse to begin the climb and be at his mercy?

"Perhaps his body lay behind the rock from which he'd fired. The sheriff thought so. He thought, too, that he was the Apache Kid, though he was said to hold captive the women he took and to kill those who attempted to escape.

"After that we heard no more of the Apache Kid, for there were no more of the atrocities of the type attributed to him. And that part of Arizona rested secure in the belief that he was dead."[32,33]

One widely accepted account of the Kid's demise is that told by a woman captive who in 1894 said he died in the Sierra Madre of tuberculosis.[34]

Eugene Chihuahua and Ace Daklugie had other stories: Chihuahua said, "Heard the last time he ran off to be outlaw out of jail. The agent came to my father and said to go after the Apache Kid.

"'You can't get him that way. You put up a big dance right here and he will come.' And he did. And they caught him right there just like my father said. He joined in with the crowd and two men caught him. His wife always hide the ammunition and guns different places so he could find them. He would run to the gun and ammunition and fight himself loose. But he could not do it that time. The dancers got him."[35]

"What became of the Apache Kid? All I know," said Daklugie, "is he was killed by getting after another camp of Indians. He came in there for something." He saw a campfire and went off to catch a woman. "When he caught a woman she hollered. They were all sitting together talking and telling stories. These men were camping when a woman wandered outside the camp and [they] ran to her rescue. She hung onto the Apache Kid until the men came and shot him.

"'Is this your leg?' [It was dark.]

"'No.'

"They shot him. Next day they took his head to the agency." This happened in Arizona, near Clifton or Duncan, Daklugie thought, in the mountains.[36]

Chihuahua and Daklugie's stories were not about the Kid but rather Nah-de-ga-ah, a renegade White Mountain Apache who lived in the White Mountains as an outlaw, preying on whites, Mexicans, and other Indians, until the Army announced that it would hold a big dance. A Chiricahua scout nabbed him and the authorities hauled him off to the guardhouse at Fort Apache. He escaped and went back to the hills. He showed up later at an Apache camp where a woman recognized him and held him while her husband got his gun and shot the outlaw.

The Kid's sister (Mrs. Argo Watson, who died at San Carlos around 1955)[37] said that until 1896 her brother visited her infrequently at San Carlos. Then she never heard from him again.[38] When a long time passed and he had not visited, his sister and other family members thought he had died in Mexico and mourned for him. The Kid's mother said that it was not true that he committed all those crimes—no one man could possibly have done all those things.[39]

One plausible story gives the Kid a happily-ever-after ending. Rancher and trapper Jesse Burk, who had befriended the Kid, learned from a passing stranger that the Kid was alive and well in Mexico and owned a well-stocked ranchería.[40] Emilio Kosterlitzky, chief of the Mexican Rurales, said the Kid was living peacefully in the Sierra Madre in 1899.[41] One old-timer who had known the Kid insisted that he'd seen him among Pancho Villa's troops on the border as late as 1915.[42] In 1924 the Kid's nephew said he'd seen the Kid alive in Sonora.[43] Around 1935 the Kid is reported to have visited old friends at San Carlos.[44]

It may be that the Apache Kid eluded the Army, the law, and the best trackers, Indian or white, in the territory until only death itself finally caught up with him.

As for Al Sieber, his demise may have been a delayed bit of Apache revenge. On 19 February 1907, Sieber was supervising an Indian work gang building a road in central Arizona. One sizable boulder had to be moved. The Apaches had labored for a day, scraping below and pushing from above, trying to dislodge the rock so that it would roll downhill. The rock didn't move. Sieber, watching their effort, decided to have a closer look and crawled under the giant stone. Abruptly it moved and then thundered down the slope, crushing Sieber in its path. History called it an accident. Sieber's biographer Dan Thrapp dismissed claims that Apaches pushed the rock down on Sieber.[45] Eve Ball thought otherwise.

"Recently a group discussed the death of Al Sieber. All, including Eugene Chihuahua, were sons of scouts. They knew of the accident—if it were an accident—both through newspaper reports and accounts given by acquaintances at San Carlos. Not one of them believed Sieber's death to have been accidental. The Apaches, they said, would not have killed him while acting as scouts but their dislike for him was so great that the temptation was great. Somebody undoubtedly knew that the huge rock could be dislodged and acted upon that knowledge."[46]

Fig. 12. Alberta Begay, daughter of Massai. (Courtesy Smithsonian Institution.)

ELEVEN

Massai

One of the more remarkable Apache stories is Massai's bold escape from the train of sorrow carrying vanquished Apaches to prison in Florida. Without benefit of compass or match, Massai and his friend made their way from Missouri to their old haunts. The account of Massai's feat in Indeh *is Eve's dramatized version, which originally appeared in* True West.[1]*

Here is Massai's story as told by his daughter, Alberta Begay, in 1955.[2] Eugene Chihuahua, who became Massai's son-in-law, corroborated the account. Others provided additional information.

"This happened at Mescal Mountain [near present-day Globe, Arizona]. . . . There is where my grandfather—his name was White Cloud—and my grandmother, Little Star [in Apache, Sos-tos-eh], lived. There is where my father Massai was born. He was a Chiricahua Apache. . . . Up 'til he was nine years old they lived there. And my grandfather started to teach him how to be tough. He would make him run about a hundred yards every day while he was growing up. As he got bigger he ran farther each day until he could run to the top of the mountain and back without stopping. That makes him rough.

"He taught him to make bows and arrows and how to hunt. Every time he goes out he brings in game—sometimes a deer or rabbits until the time he gets about fifteen years old . . .

"Then one day he saw another pal as his friend. A Tonkawa came up in the mountain. This little boy's name was Gray Lizard and they were about the same age and they went about together. They went hunting together and my grandfather told them to bring in a deer and they did. They went out after wild horses too. They made a log corral and put them in and tamed them. When he was grown up, a young man, he was strong and good looking. He could handle any horse.

"At Warm Springs Geronimo was living with his people [after the deaths of Cochise and Mangas Coloradas]. . . . The white people were treating Geronimo mean and he wanted to get help from the other Apaches. One day he came looking for Indians to help him in the war against the White Eyes. . . . Geronimo came in waving a white flag as he came down the canyon. He yelled to the Indians and they went to him and held a council. Geronimo made a speech and told all the Indians to help him make war against the white people. . . . He wanted to make preparations for two years ahead—to gather fruit, medicine, meat, etc. He made a long speech and told the Apaches that Ussen make this world and gave it to the Indians. 'He put us here to live before the white people came and He does not want the white people to take it away from us.'

"There were about a thousand Apaches on the hillside. They decided to go ahead and to take that plan and they did. He told all the Indians to gather their horses and to go out and hunt deer or whatever they could get and the men went on a big hunt.

"He told the ladies to gather the cactus fruit, Indian banana, piñons, mescal, and kinds of berries. They dried the berries and they stored them away. They prepare all they can for two years.

"My father and Gray Lizard went home and [Massai] asked his father if they could do as Geronimo said. His father said, 'You are a man and can decide for yourself.' So he went.

"They got four horses saddled and they went west clear down to southern California. They kept going for many days 'til they got there and they killed some game. They butchered it, tanned the hides, sliced and dried the meat on rocks, on flat places. They tanned the hides right there. That was wild country and they had to look out for themselves all the time. One would watch from the top of the mountain while the other worked. Then they changed to rest each other.

"After everything was dried they finally found there was too much to move. They had just four horses. They packed two horses with the dry meat and the hides. They had a big pile left. So they had an extra buffalo hide. They had found a cave and Massai told Gray Lizard, 'I think we better put this dry meat in that cave, for it is too heavy for the horses to carry.' So he took one buffalo hide, put the dry meat on it in the cave. There was a place . . . where they got a shelf way high in the cave. He told Gray Lizard, 'You remember this place. And if you get hungry and need food, you come back here. And I will do that too.'

"As they came out of the cave on the hillside they saw a big city on the ocean. The ocean was about two miles away. They had not seen it 'til they were ready to leave.

"They came home to Mescal Mountain. They stayed there for a while and in a few days they started to take the food to a safe place. They were the last to come in. The ladies and men all came back to Geronimo's camp near Warm Springs but nobody was there. The troops [San Carlos agent John Clum and his Indian police] surprised him [Geronimo] and take him away. [Massai and Gray Lizard] kept trailing them. Finally in the evening they saw the light of the camp and thought everything was alright. . . . So they got in there and the soldiers captured them [and forced them to go to San Carlos] . . .

"Massai married a Chiricahua girl [and had two children]. Gray Lizard had not married . . . but they were still very close friends and they stayed together much. The soldiers were not greatly interested in the Tonkawa but they watched the Apaches.

"Of this time at San Carlos, my father spoke little. Perhaps because he has a wife there my mother did not hear much of his life in captivity. But of his trip to the east he talked often."

Massai was one of Geronimo's warriors for a time. Eugene Chihuahua recalled, "He was in lots of places with Geronimo. Massai was one of Geronimo's band. He was a good fighter."[3] Jasper Kanseah said Massai was with Geronimo when he only had a few warriors.[4] After the group was moved to Turkey Creek, Geronimo broke out, but Massai didn't join them. Instead, he stayed with his family.

"For some reason he did not like to be with Geronimo's people," James Kaywaykla said. "He took his family and his wife and two children. They left the Indians, expecting to return to San Carlos. He wants to be alone, away from the rest. . . . Before the surrender of Geronimo he had left the band and returned to San Carlos. The agent there thought that he had been with the warriors but they found that he had been only with his family. The army officer seemed not to understand. I don't know of Massai's ever having made any trouble. I think he had been a scout. I think he went out after Geronimo."[5]

Massai enlisted as a scout during the 1880 campaigns against Victorio. Two years later he was on a train to Arizona with other scouts when he learned that Loco's band had been forced to leave San Carlos and was headed to Mexico. He jumped from the train and made his way to the Sierra Madre where he rejoined Geronimo's band. But he didn't stay long. He stole Betzinez's horse and, with his family, slipped back to San Carlos.

In 1885 Massai broke away from Fort Apache with Geronimo but grew weary of the warpath and again returned to Fort Apache. The authorities didn't arrest him but allowed him to rejoin his family.[6] Massai was one of the scouts in the battle when the scout company officer Captain Emmett Crawford was killed.[7] In this period, both Massai and the Apache Kid, who were about the same age, were scouts and could have gotten acquainted on one of the Geronimo campaigns.

"After while they decided that they were going to take them to Florida. [Jason Betzinez recalled that while the Apaches were held, Massai tried to provoke a rebellion but the others refused to join him and he grew silent.[8]] They saved everything up and took all their belongings, whatever they got, and they put them on the train. . . . Gray Lizard was not compelled to go but he stayed with my father. All the Chiricahuas and Warm Springs Apaches at Fort Apache were sent.

"There was a young guy who was always making jokes. He was talking to the two men. He told them—both had red handkerchiefs around their [heads], 'The captain say that the ones that have the red handkerchiefs are going to be hanged when they get to Florida.'

"Gray Lizard and Massai planned their escape. They had no weapons of any kind but they saved and hid a little of the food that was given them. . . . They planned to jump off as the train goes up a hill, for it has to go slowly. . . . Massai told his wife what he planned to do and she urged him to attempt to get away. . . . Massai told her he was going to do this and for her to go on to Florida and some time he would join her if nothing happened.

"When they were way over there in Missouri, the train was going up a hill slowly. . . . They watched for a moment when the guard should leave the coach. . . . They pulled up the window and both jumped out. They rolled over the bank and hid in the brush. . . . They saw [the train] disappear over the hill. Perhaps the guards thought that they were killed. But the escape was reported, for later soldiers hunted my father for years. Perhaps because Gray Lizard was a Tonkawa they did not mention him . . .

"Years later my father's friends told him that the guards talked with those in the coach:

"'Where is Massai?'

"Nobody knew. 'How did he look? What size man was he?'

"Now my father was a small but well-built man, not very tall.

"'High, like Naiche,' they told the guard."

This story was so effective that years later, even Apaches forgot Massai was small. "He was a big man; I don't see how he jumped off the train," said Kanseah. "I guess he got scared he get killed but he would have died anyhow."[9]

Alberta continued: "They lay hidden until it got dark and they started back toward their country. They saw many, many houses, and they had to avoid going near them. They had nothing but breechclouts and moccasins, so they suffered with cold as well as hunger, but it is hard to starve an Apache.

"They found food along the way—roots and birds. They killed quail and rabbits with rocks but they did not have enough. They were almost starving but it is not true that they ate dog—and especially raw dog. No Apache would do that. The small game they cooked. They hid in ditches and made a very small fire. One thing they had with them was their fire sticks. No Apache was without those in his belt. Always they traveled at night and hid in the daytime . . .

"After four or five days they got to the mountain, the first one they see. I think that maybe it was the Ozarks . . .

"One night they saw the light of a camp fire. It is easy to tell an outdoor fire. They crept quietly toward it. Between them and the camp was a little stream and they got water. They crept toward the fire. They got close enough to smell meat cooking and they were so hungry they could hardly live. They thought there might be Indians at that camp but when they could see plainly it was White Eyes. They hid in some thick brush and slept 'til dawn.

"Early next morning smoke again and good smells that almost kill them. . . . It was a mining camp. Those people got up and were making breakfast and there were several of them. When they had eaten [they] were going to work in the mine. So after they went down [Massai and Gray Lizard] came down from that place before [the miners] came out of the hole in the mountain.

"They went to the camp and they had some stuff that was left by the fire—meat, bread and coffee. They got hold of two [guns] and they got cartridges and belts and some knives. There were some sheep meat hanging in the tree. They cut a half of it and put it in the sack and they got whatever food they could carry. The miners were still in the mountain. And Massai and Gray Lizard left.

"They traveled and traveled until they got hungry. Then they stopped to eat. Sometimes they slept in the daytime and traveled 'til late at night. They would tell by the Dipper when it was almost morning and which way to go. Then they ate again. Now they could hunt deer. They stopped by a river where they could see another mountain. They saw a trail where the deer came to drink. Some came in and they killed the biggest. They butchered it and took all the meat they can carry with them. My father told Gray Lizard that they would take the stomach of the deer and clean it to carry water and they did that. They make a good water bag. They tied one end and filled it with water.

"After while they could see that they were going to cross a desert. Once Gray Lizard fell. He was carrying the bag. He fell against a prickly pear and tore a hole in the bag. Then they lose the water but they kept coming on anyway. The next day they were very thirsty—no water, no rain, no stream. My father was making medicine, was praying. And pretty soon it started to rain. Lots of water came down. They made a big hole to catch the water. It filled up and they had some to drink. They kept on going. Sometimes they travel by day but not much. They kept on 'til they can see the Capitans [in southeastern New Mexico]. They were very happy because it is not very far from there to the White Mountain [Sierra Blanca]. That's what Gray Lizard see. And not far from there to Mescal Mountain. [They reached home some time in the fall of 1887.[10]]

"They had carried the guns and ammunition and they took a day to rest, for they needed it badly. That was a safe place and they slept and rested. Afterwards they started on again. They crossed from there over the top to the White Mountain. They passed west on the other side of the White Mountain.

"Then my father said to Gray Lizard, 'This is the White Mountain and the Mescaleros live here. We will stay here. We will stay here a while.' They came on the west side near Three Rivers and back to the Rinconada. When they got to the top of the saddle Gray Lizard told him that he wanted to go back home to the Mescal Mountain where his father, mother and other relatives lived. So they agreed to separate. They bade each other goodbye. Massai pointed to the far end of the San Andreas [mountains]. 'Go right over there and straight through.' Gray Lizard left and my father stood a long time and watched him. . . . After he left here he never saw Gray Lizard again. The people there say they never saw Gray Lizard again. Something must have happened to him. . . . Then he went high up on the White Mountain. He sat on the side of it thinking what he was going to do. He thought that he would never see his family again and he stayed there two or three days.

"On the other side, my mother, Zanagoliche, a young Mescalero girl, lived. She was about seventeen years old and had been married to one man from Oklahoma named Chiwato. He was a [Lipan] and they had two little boys. The day he wanted to take himself back to Oklahoma she did not want to leave her father and mother, for her father told her it was too far."

Zanagoliche's sister describes what happened next: "I was about six years old when this happened. They were out picking piñons in the Rinconada . . . and Massai came and took her.[11] They tried to trail [Massai] but could not locate him. . . . My sister never said anything about his being bad and we don't think he was or she would have told her own family. She always said he took good care of her."[12]

While they traveled, Zanagoliche agreed to marry him, Apache way, and Massai took her to his people for a wedding feast. Then they traveled to California where Massai and Gray Lizard had years earlier hidden food and hides.

"The sun came up red and pretty soon they had an earthquake. The earth would open and go thick and the smoke would come up from the ground. He started to pray like his father had told him. He said, 'Don't run. Stay by the horse. The ground is not going to crack where you are.' And she was praying.

"Before noon everything settled down and the smoke kept coming up from the ground where there were ditches. He was looking way over here where he used to see those houses. . . . [T]here was nothing left. The place was just like everything is wrecked. He thought he should go over there. Maybe he would see something that would be of value to them. He told her to stay right there, to saddle up the horse, put the blankets on them and wait for him there.

"He took a hatchet and left afoot. He made a trail and came to the first place outside the town. He saw one Mexican fellow with a broken leg under a cottonwood tree. He had crawled into the shade.

"[In Spanish] he say, 'I am going to die. Please go and get me some water before I die. I know I cannot live.' And he put up his hands to him.

"My father can speak Spanish. My father felt sorry for him and took him a bag of water. And he went over to the place and was looking for things. Everybody was dead. Only one left is this old man. He got hold of some blankets, dresses, medicine, food and meat. And right there he saw something very shiny in a sack. It was not a big sack. It was gold. He don't want it at that time but he thought it must be good for it is sparkling. He took it to the old man and brought some more stuff and put it there. He told the old man to wait. Santos, he said he was called.

"He said he went back to my mother on the mountain, got a horse and took him to the Mexican. His leg was broken below the knee—the outer bone. He put him on the horse and took him and the food back to where my mother is.

"'He has a broken leg and I am going to set it. I could not leave him to die.'

"That same night—it was late—they camp there and the old man was very sick but he made it 'til morning. The next day they go on. There was another mountain over there and a medicine that is good for broken bones. He told Santos he try to make him live and he was sure happy that my father take care of him. My mother ride one horse and Santos the other and they start to Mescal Mountain where his father and mother were.

"In the evening about 7:30 they went to the place where he was talking about and there was a spring. My mother built a fire and cooked supper while my father look for this medicine. It is a kind that makes the bone grow together. He looked all over for it but could not find it. But when he went back to the camp to eat he look down and right in front of him is that medicine he is hunting.

"'This is what I want.'

"This root is round like a marble with about five of them sticking together. He started to make medicine for him that night and they have to stay four days to make the medicine so that it will heal him in five days. He cut a straight stick for each side of that leg and put the medicine over each side. That night he make a sing and pray for him. And Santos went to sleep. They do that for four [days until] the bone is sewed together by the medicine they use. And Santos is just happy for his leg is so much better. He made four steps and start to walk again. What he did was sure good medicine. He start to dig some more of that for he might need it for himself later. He took a lot of that medicine with him.

"They start again and they travel about six or seven days to get to Mescal Mountain. When they got over there he find that both his father and mother are dead and his relatives tell him that both are gone because they [were] told that he had been killed so they grieved to death.

"They started to live there with Santos. . . . During the day my father hunt but my mother is at home. He help my mother around the tipi when my father is hunting. He is a good man and help cut wood and water and help around the camp. That's the time my oldest brother, Herbert, was born. They live a long time there . . .

"[W]e stay there a long time on our home mountain; we don't go anywhere and my sister Cora was born there. When she was a small baby old Santos took care of her. Somehow he caught cold and died of pneumonia. He was old and could not stand much sickness and he died in the night. My parents felt sorry. They dug a grave and buried him and put a cross on it, for that was the custom of his people.

"Then another, Edith, was born. Then Mary. And I was the fifth child. Then Clifford, the youngest."

In this period of time local settlers believed Massai was raiding and depredating. His name appears in San Carlos agency reports from 1887 to 1890. Like the Apache Kid, he was blamed for crimes based on scant or no evidence and, like the Kid, he was accused of abducting women, keeping them a few months and then murdering them. According to one report, "A renegade Indian, supposed to be Ma-si, surprised a party of four women and shot one dead, slightly wounded two others and took with him a younger woman."[13] Given Massai's domestic obligations, it's unlikely he would waste effort stealing women.

In April 1889, Massai supposedly swept into the camp of two Mexican woodcutters and shot Sabino Quiroz as his partner Joe Guerena watched from cover. Then he took two saddles, loaded them with food and disappeared. Sheriff Glenn Reynolds, who would lose his life months later transporting the Apache Kid and other prisoners, searched for Massai for three days but failed to find a trace. The authorities in Globe were so sure of the killer's identity that a Gila County grand jury indicted him for murder.[14] There is no explanation of how his accusers knew it was Massai. During this time, Massai remained in hiding and it's unlikely they knew what he looked like.

In November of that year the Apache Kid escaped from Reynolds, who died in the incident, and was never apprehended. Scouts later reported seeing the Kid and Massai together.[15] Some Indian women claimed the two men had abducted them and headed for Mexico.[16]

Alberta recalled that around the turn of the century her father grew uneasy.

"My father was about 50 years old, I think. [He was probably closer to 40.] He was worried about his family. One night he had a bad dream he told my mother: 'Well, it has been a long time since I took you from Mescalero and now I know we have all these children. I want them to be safe. I want you to take them back to Mescalero. I don't want to have any more children because I am afraid that before I die something will happen.' He told my mother to get ready, fix everything that was of value — the food and blankets — just what is needed. 'Give what we have away to the people around us.' They were Tontos and Chiricahuas . . .

"My mother was getting ready. They have only two horses — bays. She got the children and herself ready to travel. My father was walking with his gun. From Mescal Mountain he went east toward the San Marcial Mountain. As they were going along about three days, they reached the foot of the San Marcial Mountain. Close to the mountain out in the flat they camped. The next morning very early we got back on the horses and started toward the mountain where it is safe. If somebody see you out on the plain they shot you. The white people are bad. We are trying to reach the mountain. There is a river coming down from the mountain. We water our horses. We have some bags of water. We put them on the horses. There is a little hill from which you can see the water. He told us to go on top of the hill and wait for him.

"'I want to stay right here and see that we are not followed.'

"Far in the west on the plain he could see some dust. When they got to the river my father told that two men were after him and his children to kill them. As they watered their horses my father hid behind a cedar. He thought that they were trailing us.

"He got his 30–30 and shot the small fellow on the horse. The other did not even know from which direction the shot came. This man was already dead. He fell from his horse. So this fellow got scared and put his brother on the horse. He took the dead man to San Marcial. When my mother heard the shot she was looking back.

"'Why did you kill that fellow? They will be after us now. You should not have shot him. Let's hurry. Let's go this way.'

"There was a canyon running to the east. They wanted to get up to the top before anybody came. They never saw anybody coming after us. When we got to the end of that flat they got over there and tied their horses — hobbled them. And right then we all went to sleep.

"Just as soon as this fellow reported that his brother was killed I don't know how many hunters or military police came after them that night. Well, they saw the two horses hobbled. All night they stayed and tried to ambush him. From where he was looking out there was a big bluff on this side.

"'I know something is going to happen. If we all scatter we will all get together on that bluff.'

"In the morning the military were laying for him in the bushes. Early my brother and he go after those horses. My brother heard a shot and my father fell. Herbert started to run. He jumped over that bluff, very high. I don't know how he escaped being killed. When my mother heard the shot she got hold of one blanket and some food. She told the children to follow her and they went way around. When she got to the place Herbert was there. We waited there a long time. We could see a long way down on the plain. Lots of soldiers."

In *Indeh*, Eve Ball wrote that a posse killed Massai, built a big fire and later boiled the head.[17] There are two other accounts.

On 10 September 1906, Charlie Anderson returned home to find that someone had raided his ranch, destroyed property, and stolen horses. He spread the word in nearby Chloride and asked for help catching the culprits and retrieving his horses. Anderson also got a John Doe warrant. He was joined at different times by John and Harry James, Bill Hiller, Walter Hearn, Bill Keene, Charlie Yaples, Cebe Sorrel, Mike Sullivan, and Bert Slinkard.

Some of the men found a trail left by four horses. That night they could see a campfire in the distance. The next morning they headed that direction and quickly found Anderson's missing horses. Keene, Sullivan, and Sorrel hunkered behind a log and waited. Two Indian men approached, one carrying a rope and the other with a rifle in a rawhide scabbard resting on his shoulder. The three cowboys opened fire, killing the first man. The other "jumped so high I could see daylight between the log and his feet. As he jumped and turned to run, he gave a war whoop that could be heard a long distance, a blood-curdling yell. He ran down over the San Mateos on the San Marcial side." He threw the gun down as he ran.

The cowboys collected the rifle and found the Indian camp. Meat cooked in a brass-lined, iron kettle, and coffee boiled alongside. Drying meat hung around the camp. In a sack Hearn found jewelry, pieces of china, a watch, a six-shooter, a saddle, and an ax—all taken from various ranches and camps in the area. The watch and gun had belonged to D. L. Saunders, who was murdered in Animas Creek in 1904. They also found two long spears with blades filed from carpenter's squares, butcher knives, arrows, arrow points, a three-gallon olla, and three rawhide panniers. The cowboys took what they wanted and then burned the camp. When they encountered Anderson, they announced triumphantly, "You are too late; the work is over. The Apache Kid was killed at sunup."[18]

The cowboys believed they'd killed Apache Kid, but the two were often confused.[19] Charlie Anderson said years later that they never claimed the reward on the Kid's head because they weren't entirely sure that's who they killed.[20]

According to a second account, the Apache Kid was raiding ranches near Hot Springs, New Mexico in the fall of 1907 and had vandalized brothers Ed and John James's South Fork Camp forty-five miles west of Hot Springs (now Truth or Consequences). The James brothers gathered a posse and after six days shot their prey in a thicket in San Juan Canyon. They removed the head and sent it to Yale University "where it became a prize possession of Skull and Bones, a secret fraternal society." Then because they were ashamed of mutilating the corpse, the men pledged to keep the killing a secret.[21]

Massai apparently didn't shoot anyone, although Anderson reported that someone shot at him and the others.

"Pretty soon they built a great big fire—too big for cooking. We watch. They throw him on top of that fire. We were afraid to go down. They might be hiding to kill us. We waited three days. Until then my mother could not cry. Then she did.

"'I know they kill him and put him on top of that fire.'

"We were all crying then. When we thought all were gone, we started to climb down that hill on the mountain. She told us to stay right there. I was only four years old but I remember it very plainly. We stood there for a long time.

"'I want to be sure what happened,' she said.

"She went over there but she saw nothing but bones. She was raking around in the ashes and she took a buckle from them. She knew that buckle—it was from his ammunition belt.

"'All the time you took care of me and the children. Now you nothing but ashes. I will keep this buckle. It is all I have to take back to the children.' And she took that buckle and came to us. She told us, 'Now we will go back to San Marcial.' [Alberta later gave the buckle to Eve Ball for safekeeping.]

"It was fifteen miles to the town right on the Rio Grande. We started there walking. We had food and water. All afternoon we walked. After while we stopped to rest. My oldest sister carried me on her back and my mother carried the baby. Close to evening when it is beginning to get dark we were dying of hunger and thirst. My sister was worn out and could not carry me any longer."

This part of central New Mexico is desert scrub, rocky, and sandy with a generous supply of creosote and cactus but little else. Imagine this woman, who just lost her husband, struggling to get her children to safety across miles of harsh landscape, cactus tearing at long skirts and moccasins.

"We got to a house. A Mexican lady lived there alone. My mother could speak her language. She took us in and fed us. She didn't even know what tribe of Indians we were. My mother had learned Spanish from Santos. Next day she fixed up our clothes and fed us. We stayed there two weeks. This Mexican lady was good to us and talked kindly to my mother. She told her, 'You must go back to the Mescalero Apache Reservation. I will take care of the children.'

"'I will go to my brother, Marion Simms. I will take Herbert and the baby. The others can stay here with you 'til we come for them. My brother will come for them.'"

One of the cowboys later wrote, "Two days after the killing of the Apache, his squaw and her kids were found eating from barrels behind the Harvey House in San Marcial. She said that white men had killed her husband in the San Mateos."[22]

"My mother said, 'I must leave for Mescalero.'

"The lady fixed her some food and she gave her a hatchet, a rope and a blanket. The three started. Mary, Cora, and I stayed. Mother told the Mexican lady not to give us away for she was going home for help. In the evening they left. Right below San Marcial Mountain there is a railroad that crosses the Rio Grande. They crossed on foot. On the other side there was . . . a horse.

"'Mother, that's an Indian horse. It is not afraid of us. I catch it and we ride.' He took the rope and caught the horse. He brought it to the fence and my mother cut the barbed wire with the hatchet. They put the blanket on and rode. All night they rode. In the morning they stopped and slept for a while. In the late afternoon, they started again. They could see the White

Mountain and they were very happy. For two whole days and one night they traveled across the San Andreas and got clear to the malpais [volcanic badlands near the Mescalero reservation].

"There were some cowboys camped there in the evening. They had been gathering cattle. There were lots of horses there. Their horse was worn out. My mother turned it loose and caught a black and white spotted one. They left toward Three Rivers. And right where the train station is that night they camped at Three Rivers . . .

"From there they tried to go over toward the mountain on the south side of Three Rivers where they came through when my father took her. She was going through that way again. Up toward the mountain Herbert say that he was sure hungry. He wanted something to eat. She told him to take care of the baby. She was a woman but her children were hungry. She saw some cows and a little calf sleeping in a shed. She hit it on the head with the hatchet and she killed it. And the Mexican lady had given her matches. She cooked her meat and she fed her children and herself. They took the meat that was left with them. Then they started back on the same trail on which she was kidnapped.

"It was late in the evening when they got to the river. She heard somebody hollering over there. . . . She was afraid and she passed by the fire and went on toward Mescalero. It was a moonlight night and she kept going 'til about one in the morning. She got on top of the mountain on the north side of the mountain. She felt glad that she was nearly home. She told Herbert that she could see her old home and that they were nearly there.

"But she was still on the mountain. 'That's how we were going.' And she told him all about it. After they got a rest they got on the horse again and went down. The first tipi to which they went was her relatives'.

"'Who is that?'

"'It is me.'

"'Is that you? Is it really you?'

"'Yes. I am the one who was kidnapped many years ago.'

"And they were happy and cried."

Zanagoliche asked her family to bring her brother back and when he entered the tipi, he was surprised by their appearance. "Marion Simms thought that my mother looked strange. Nobody was ever [dressed] like that. We had buckskin clothes—nothing else. And they looked strange, for they were wearing white man's clothing at Mescalero."

The Mescalero agent gave Simms permission to leave and some money. They took a wagon to Tularosa and then caught the train to El Paso and, the following day, back to San Marcial. They found Cora with the woman who had helped them but two families had taken the other girls and planned to adopt them. Alberta was with a white couple on the train; she grabbed her mother's skirt and when the white man tried to interfere, her uncle said he had come for the children. They found Mary at another house in town. Then they returned to Mescalero.

It would be nice to say they lived happily ever after, but real life, especially in those days, was never that simple. Irving McNeil, a doctor at Mescalero, recalls Zanagoliche returning to the reservation with her children. He examined the children and found them to be in good health. He described the twelve-year-old boy (Herbert) as "a very handsome lad. Seldom had I ever seen a finer physical specimen."

The reservation by then boasted modern buildings with steam heat, bathing facilities, and a cook who prepared nourishing food. "But our newest pupils did not thrive. Exposed to multitudinous infections inexperienced by them in their wild retreat, though common to any people who gather in groups, they soon sickened. At first there were minor ailments as colds and digestive disturbances and then more serious illnesses. Briefly, before the school term had ended, these three children had all died. The younger children who stayed in camp through the winter, in a half-wild state, remained healthy. . . . The inference is that they could not stand civilization so suddenly thrust upon them."[23]

"Mrs. A. E. Thomas, a former teacher at the Mescalero Indian School, said that the older children, accustomed to a free, animal-like existence, pined away and died."[24]

Simms adopted Alberta and she attended school at Mescalero, Las Cruces, and Bernalillo. In 1936, a WPA writer said Massai's wife (he assumed it was the Apache Kid's wife) was still living on the Mescalero Reservation, along with two of their daughters. "His widow asserts that the Kid never killed unless he was driven into a corner. . . . She declares her captor was always kind to her and her children."[25]

The infant Zanagoliche carried in her arms, Clifford, was murdered in his teens by an unknown assailant. When Zanagoliche died, only Alberta remained. On her deathbed, the courageous mother told her daughter, "Some of these days you must remember all the story. Your father was not a murderer. He killed only to protect us. He did not do it for meanness—only to protect his family. I want you to clear his name if you can. . . . Be sure and keep this buckle that belonged to your father."[26]

TWELVE

Gordo and Juh

One travesty among many shameful stories in the Apache wars was the Army's treatment of its Apache scouts, who had served faithfully only to be interned with the very people they'd helped the Army bring in. Here's the story of one scout, Gordo. While the journey of scouts Martine and Kayitah to bring in Geronimo is much told, the similar story of Gordo's effort to bring in Juh, legendary Nednhi chief and strategist, is little known.

As trackers Apaches had few peers, and among the Apaches a few had extraordinary gifts, or Power.

"Maybe a stone be moved and turned over," Asa Daklugie said. "Maybe the grass or weeds be stepped on and broken off near the ground. But one doing it could almost tell how long ago it was done. Just a few were experienced trailers. Maybe three or four of the band. They go ahead and study the trail. Maybe a wild country and they try to find the trail. They find it in a few hours. We up there on top of the mountain and still traveling. That what they do."[1]

James Kaywaykla said, "Their sense of smell was much keener than the white man's. If the Mormons brought fruit—peaches, apples—we could smell that for a long distance, maybe several miles.

"A man left Fort Apache and Asa told me that he and Mangus [son of Mangas Coloradas] and party are out with him and this man came to him.

This man told the Indians that when he went to their camp he could smell them, that he followed the scent like a wild animal does. . . . He was a Warm Springs."[2]

"Trailing was an art," said Eustace Fatty. "In soft places he could trail but in the rocks I could not but some Indians could see it. I don't know how they do it. It was some kind of a Power. But they did follow it on a run."[3]

When General George Crook arrived in Arizona to put an end to Apache depredations, he learned that only an Apache could even find an Apache, much less engage him in battle. Crook was soon sending large numbers of Apaches into the field, and he boasted of their effectiveness and loyalty.[4] But Eve had her doubts:

"Once pointed out to me, it seemed logical that the scouts were not so loyal as officers portrayed them. Obviously, Gatewood questioned it. The old Apaches didn't, for they knew that what he said was true: that the scouts provided others with ammunition and at times protected their friends and relatives when the officers believed them absolutely reliable."[5]

Becoming a scout was initially an honorable thing to do; Apaches aided the Army against their traditional enemies. And in the humiliating confinement of a reservation, it allowed a warrior to have a horse and gun. After Crook began using Apache scouts against their own people, scouts were alternately branded as traitors or respected for their effort to bring a futile war to an end. Sometimes, weary of running and fighting, the most loyal Apaches became scouts.

"It better to be a scout now because you be all right if you are a scout," said Percy Big Mouth, a Mescalero whose father was a scout. "And we can't do nothing like in old days. We can't fight any more against this long-range rifle. They tried out a rifle from Blazer's mill—a tree a long ways over. Our little 44s won't range that far. It better to be at peace now."[6]

Gordo,[7] a Bedonkohe chief who was often with the Chiricahuas, was first a peacemaker and later a scout at Fort Apache. He was also known among Apaches to be the first man who buried whiskey in bottles to keep it cool, which became his Indian name, Tooteen-chi-hlejh-yea-cee-ah-een. He was a half-brother of Daklugie and Charles Martine.[8]

"When my [grand]father was back in Arizona with Cochise he ... and his two brothers used to go round by themselves," said Gordo's grandson, Eustace Fatty. "Came to Mescalero and stay by that big mountain. That's where was his real station. Used to hang around there and cross to Mexico. Would visit Indians down there and would come by to the mountain and Deming. Go all over, looking for something to eat."

Gordo married Nat-ah-yah, a Chiricahua, and had five sons.[9] He and his son Fatty were among the chiefs hauled in chains to San Carlos in 1877.

Despite Gordo's close ties to Juh, he agreed two years later to help the Army bring in Juh, who had bolted to avoid being sent to San Carlos. Gordo was chosen, along with Adis, because they had many relatives in Juh's band.[10]

"Asa's father [Juh] just like Geronimo. He was down in Mexico somewhere and must be close relation to my [grand]father," said Eustace Fatty. "He was pretty mean. They had a meeting and they got my father and two fellows, told him he was some relation to you and you can go up to him and bring him back, he is your relation. That's what they told this old man. Took the two men and travel many days. [Juh] was all there and they talk to him. He say, 'I am not going in . . . for anybody. . . . He get his gun out. 'If they get me they kill me.'

"But my [grand]father talked to him a long time: 'You got lots of children, girl children, and I don't see why you run like a wild man—no sleep and food, no water. Why you stay when you go back to white man's village? Nobody kill you. They give you food and you not going to starve. Little children—you carry them around and get them killed and like the coyote, crow eat you. Now you got a good finish. Nobody going to hang you.'

"Kept talking to him and toward morning he gave up and say they going back with my father. 'You take me back over there.' And he gave up.

"They brought him back and he was all right and the white people were coming to him. This old man got a big medal for that and a little book and some kind of protection. That officer say, 'Take care of that book and the badge and they protect you.' He was drinking tiswin somewhere and had it in his vest and he lost both."[11]

Juh and Geronimo, then camped in the Guadalupe Mountains along the border between Mexico, Arizona and New Mexico, agreed to surrender in December 1879, persuaded by poor grass, thin ponies, and Army officers "assisted by friendlies."[12]

"When my [step]father was on his scouting trips I was at Fort Apache with my mother," said Sam Kenoi, Gordo's stepson. "All the scouting the Indians did against Juh they did it afoot, and most at night with carbines—Springfields."[13]

Eustace Fatty recalled one outbreak, probably in 1881, when Gordo's group joined the Chiricahuas.

"Finally [Geronimo's band] took out . . . at night even with the soldiers there; everybody was moving out and my father said, 'Let's go. They are taking out. Not stay here by ourselves.'

"'We not fight nobody. Why should we go off at night? We not bothering nobody.'

"Go a long way after Geronimo's group and finally in the mountains somewhere the oldest man stop and said . . . he want to say a few words and want you to get it. Little kids on horses with a sack like a basket on each side of horse stop and this old man talk to them. This old man say, 'Why should we go any farther? We have not done anything. Geronimo's going out for trouble and we can't keep up with him. Let's go back there and let's stay there. If we go we won't sleep like we used to. We just be like a coyote or a deer. Let's go back. Now we got plenty food. Why we travel around?'"

Gordo agreed. "'Okay, let's pull back. It is like you say.' And they turned back. The people behind asked why they were turning back and they said, 'We want to go back.' The next morning, they met soldiers who told them to go to the fort."

Soldiers trailed Geronimo but couldn't catch him. At Fort Apache soldiers asked Apaches to become scouts and help them bring in Geronimo. Fatty, then about twenty-five, enlisted. (The Army apparently called him David Fatty and his own people later called him Old Fatty.) He served five years as a scout. "And they trail him and could not catch him. And they all went after him and circle around in different directions." They managed to capture Perico's wife. "After that we could not catch Geronimo. Trail him around and could not catch him."[14]

Gordo apparently died between 1881 and 1883. Fatty and his family were interned with the other prisoners of war, and he served in the Army again in 1891 at Mount Vernon Barracks in Alabama.[15] He survived to live his remaining days with his family at Mescalero[16] and died when he was about seventy-six.[17]

Gordo's people apparently didn't think ill of him for scouting, and in fact, he was respected.[18] Martine and Kayitah, the scouts who persuaded Geronimo to come in, were likewise well regarded. Martine, a Nednhi, was Juh's orderly "and he was respected." Kayitah was brother-in-law to Daklugie's mother. "They became scouts, but the Chiricahuas did not hate them. They were relatives to us and they stayed together. If there are things they don't like, they say so."[19]

Despite their service to the Army, the scouts were rounded up and imprisoned along with the hostiles they'd helped capture, a travesty the Apaches recall with bitterness even today.

"After that we came to Florida and they [took] the guns back. They turned everything in," Eustace Fatty said. "They shipped them off like cattle, without asking anything, and after that they treated the scouts just like Geronimo's band. They called the scouts and took the guns and cartridges, butcher knives and everything. Then they lined them up and hauled them to Holbrook and put them on a train to Florida. . . . We did not kill anyone and my father had been a scout and helped the white people and they treat us like criminals or wild animals."[20]

Juh

Juh was chief of the Nednhi band of Apaches, closely related to the Chiricahua band. Known as a strategist, he assumed leadership of the Chiricahuas after Cochise died. His wife was Ishton, sister of Geronimo, and their sons were Daklegon, Delsezhenne, and Daklugie, who was Eve Ball's primary informant for *Indeh*.

"I had a brother [Delsezhenne]. We were at Casas Grandes and he and another brother [were] in the soldier camp there. He came in dressed like a Mexican soldier. The Mexicans did that to him and kept him there. . . . He was taken to Chihuahua City and from there to Mexico City. The president of Mexico wanted to see him. We never knew what became of him. Maybe they executed him. He was much older than I and he was a good warrior."[21]

Jacali, daughter by another mother, was wounded in a Mexican attack, and Ishton was killed.[22]

"Juh stuttered badly when he talked but he could sing well and he had good songs and many of them," Kanseah said. "When he talked he kept moving his foot because he stuttered so badly. That seemed to help him say the words."[23]

One little-known fact is that one of Juh's warriors was blind. "Blind Tom been pretty blind all his life. He was with Juh most of the time. Could not see well enough to be a warrior but he traveled with them and stay in the camp with them."[24]

Daklugie said of his father, "Juh tried to keep his people out of trouble. . . . Fighting was not the main thing a chief had to do. Sometimes he had to fight but he had to be the manager for his people. He always cared for the women and children and had an appointed [place] for the men to come after they stopped the soldiers."[25]

Juh died about 1883 and Geronimo took over.

Sam Kenoi

When anthropologist Morris Opler was researching the Chiricahuas in the early 1930s, Sam Kenoi was one of his leading informants,[26] but among his own people he was controversial. Kenoi was born in 1875 at Balas, Arizona.[27] His father was a member of Juh's Nednhi but he didn't stay with them long. He went to the Fort Apache (White Mountain) Reservation and was never with Geronimo on the warpath.[28] After his father died, his mother, Tsaltey-koo, married Gordo, a Warm Springs chief. Kenoi's uncle was Fun, one of Geronimo's bravest warriors.[29]

In notes and one article, Eve wrote that Kenoi was born in 1881, called Coso as a child, raised by Mangus (son of Mangas Coloradas), and was with Mangus when he surrendered in 1886.[30] She apparently confused him with another child. Kenoi says he was with his stepfather, Gordo, among reservation Apaches rounded up during a social dance; his mother joined them in Holbrook before they were entrained for Florida. He believes he was ten or eleven at the time.[31] In 1892 his mother died in Alabama at the Mount Vernon Barracks and his sister Daisy took care of him.[32] Kenoi learned English there when soldiers began teaching him words, beginning with profanity. "I learned the bad words first. Didn't know the meaning. When I say the bad words they laugh."

When the tribe was moved to Fort Sill, he lived in a shack with his aunt until she died. Kenoi attended boarding school for four years.[33] "I began to learn things. It was too late to have any hard feelings. My relatives were dead . . . and I was an orphan. My father was not living; my stepfather did not like me. So I cook for myself. I pull out and go to Chiloco in 1895." Then he went to Carlisle. An intelligent youth, he learned quickly. He spent five years and advanced to the tenth grade, returning home with Spencerian penmanship. He also lived with a Pennsylvania Dutch family, worked hard, and learned a lot about cattle and farming. "I studied the way they lived."[34] Probably because of his life at Fort Sill and in the East, Kenoi was one of few Apaches to enjoy fishing and eat fish.

When the Chiricahuas moved to the Mescalero Reservation in 1913, Kenoi, like the others, moved to White Tail. There he industriously cut brush, planted trees, built fences, and installed electricity, which a lot of people didn't do, he said. "I love my home, my family and my neighbors. I try to make my family happy and comfortable."

Kenoi had married Anise Simmons at Fort Sill and they had two daughters, Catherine and Constance, who apparently didn't survive. Anise died of pneumonia after they moved to Mescalero. He was then working for the store for sixty-two dollars a month and caring for his surviving daughter, Catherine. At thirty-three, Kenoi married Sarah, a Mescalero girl, over the objections of her father, Nyuka, who felt that she was too young and didn't care for her marrying one of the Oklahoma newcomers. But Sarah's mother (the daughter of Uncas Noche, sergeant major of scouts) approved and the wedding went forward. "And I was a lucky man and she is lucky too."[35] (At the time of the interview, in 1954, the lucky couple had been married forty years.)

They had three children—Opal, Ulysses, and Sam Jr.[36] "In 1918 a flu epidemic took our children. Soldiers die too—sixty or seventy a day. We have just the one son now."

Kenoi was in the Fifth Cavalry at Fort Bliss, along with his half-brother David Fatty, having joined when Pancho Villa was fighting. He was highly involved in tribal politics and policy. At one time, he headed the business committee, the equivalent then of tribal chairman. His fine handwriting gained him a position as secretary of the tribal council.[37] One of the first things he did was have letterhead printed that said "Chiricahua Apache Tribe," which offended the Mescaleros and embarrassed the Chiricahuas.[38]

"We are just like visitors to the Mescaleros. It is the way we feel about it," Kenoi said. It always disturbed him that Apaches who stayed in Oklahoma got land of their own, while those who moved to Mescalero didn't.[39]

He and Daklugie never liked each other. Even as old men they maintained what Eve described as "a deep and implacable hatred."[40] Said tribal member Dan Nicholas, "Each would call the other an outlaw."[41]

In his life and official duties, Kenoi was outspoken in his criticism of the government's approach to Indian affairs. In 1931 when the Senate investigated conditions at Mescalero, Kenoi testified about mismanagement on the reservation and demanded the agent's removal.[42] With Eve's help in 1951 he wrote, "No broad, constructive policy has been inaugurated to make the Indians self-sustaining, to teach them manual pursuits, and to give them such educational advantages as would qualify them to discharge the duties of citizenship." He complained of the Apaches being driven from their lands and herded into reservations to starve and demanded a change in policies.[43]

"I live a long time. Have a little education. Always sorry I don't have more education. What I know is from experience, not out of anybody's history book. I live long time, seen some smart Indians just get smart enough to do harm against their own tribe but not smart enough to get away with something from the white man. . . . Some smart ministers I know—Indians . . . [Eve noted on the transcript, "Chino."]

"If we quit and say nothing, somebody going to make us take bitter medicine all the time. We not blame the government, Congressmen and lawmakers. . . . We have the right to make complaint to Congress in Washington . . . and all this time I have never seen it done yet. Nobody has used that privilege. They don't have enough understanding of their constitutional rights to profit themselves as Congress intends."[44]

Fig. 13.   Perico, one of Geronimo's warriors, later had a treasure-hunting mis-adventure. (A. J. McDonald, courtesy National Archives.)

THIRTEEN

Gold and Treasure

It's not surprising that people who lived from the earth would notice mineral deposits, but gold was the symbol of Ussen. While Apaches could possess silver and barter gold nuggets they found on the surface, mining was deeply offensive to them. Typical of their attitude is this comment by Charlie Smith: "I got this gold on the reservation. . . . I know where that gold is but I don't touch it."[1] That didn't keep them from repeating treasure stories.

"I learned that if one discovered gold nuggets or smelted ore that it was his obligation to impart his information to his chief but to withhold it from everyone else," Eve wrote. "If one died, the other must give the location to another and do it immediately.

"Did the Mescaleros know of the cave in Soledad Peak?

"Ace [Asa] Daklugie shook his head. The chief, he said, or perhaps two of the chiefs may have known. He recalled that soon after the Chiricahua came to Mescalero in 1913 that Peso, the last Mescalero chief, and Magoosh, of the Lipans, had each taken his oldest son and left the reservation for several days. Not even their families knew their destination or objective. Consequently, it was assumed that they went to give their sons exact instructions as to the location of hidden treasure."[2]

In time the gold taboo became a little less forbidding to impoverished reservation dwellers, at least for a few. One of the stories told in *Indeh* was about Perico's journey to Mexico.[3] The original accounts differ in significant details.

In 1928, Perico, one of Geronimo's most faithful warriors, decided to look for a cache of treasure he remembered near Casas Grandes, and he set out with Marion Simms, Yanosha, and Kanseah.[4]

"Perico went to Mexico with Yanosha and Marion Simms to find that gold hidden in that cave not too far from Casas Grandes," said Darlene Enjady, Perico's daughter. "They saw it when they were living down there. Way deep in a narrow canyon the Indians camped and they saw stepladders [notched poles] leading up from one ledge to another clear up to the rim.

"They climbed them and found that near the rim there was the opening to a cave. You could not get to it from the top of the mesa. And in there were bars of gold stacked like cordwood. Who put them there? The Spaniards maybe, or the Mexicans, but you know no Apache would mine gold. It is the forbidden metal. You can pick it up off the ground but you mustn't dig for it because the Mountain Spirits would get mad and make an earthquake.

"Well, many years after they got back from Florida and Mount Vernon Barracks, Alabama, and had come down here to the Mescalero Apache Reservation, five of them decided to go down and get some of that gold.

"When Perico was a boy he had known some Mexicans near Casas Grandes and they had been good to him. He went and they found the canyon and the smoke-blackened stones used for cooking when they were young men. But there was no ladder at the bottom of the canyon. They found a pole and notched it. On the first ledge, they found an old one but it was so old they were afraid it would break. They knew that at the top was this cave and maybe the gold [was] still in it.

"That night my grandfather—something talked to him and warned him that if they got that gold the Mexicans would kill them. He lay awake 'til he was sure that all the rest were asleep and he stole silently away and walked to the home of the friendly people he had known so many years ago and they knew him. He didn't have any money, for Marion Simms had all they had and he had the tickets to El Paso. So these Mexicans, they wrote a letter to my mother. They addressed it, 'Isabel, Mescalero.' And she got it."[5]

George Martine said, "Yanosha and Perico went to look for that silver in that cave in Mexico. It was down near Casas Grandes. But they discovered sign that they were being watched. They found that cave all right but they didn't go up the cliff to it. They separated and Perico made his way to the home of a family at Casas Grandes that he'd known when he was a boy. They gave him money to go home on the train and he repaid them."[6]

Other Gold and Treasure Stories

An old Nednhi man told of following a deer up a canyon and seeing it enter a hole in the cliff. He followed but the cave was too dark to see. He stumbled over something partially buried in the dust. He bent down to examine it and then went outside and created a torch from a branch. When he went back inside he couldn't find the deer and returned to the buried object. It was too heavy to lift. Maybe it was iron. But he found that the mineral was soft enough that he could cut strips from it. It was white inside—silver. It was too soft for bullets and he didn't know it could be traded for things. Later on there was a silver mine in the canyon. Mexican miners sent mule trains of ore to Chihuahua City. He warned Apache boys to never go there.[7]

"The Indians were camping in a canyon. They were playing hoop and pole. One Indian said, 'Way over there in the wall of that bluff there is hidden treasure—gold bricks.' It was a long bluff—no telling how long. Old Man Peso . . . went down to try to trace it but did not do it."

A man who lived with the Indians on Pajarito Mountain used to take gold to Ancho and sell it to buy whiskey. "The side [of the mountain] is like the fingers of my hand. I don't know which gully you follow," said Sam Chino.[8]

"Geronimo hated the miners," said Asa Daklugie. "They did not want the land, just to mine. They catch the Indians and make slaves of them. Mangas Coloradas could have shown them plenty of gold. All the chiefs know where it is. He was not lying to them. Once they have the best gold in the main ridge of the mountains. They not care anything about the gold. Just don't want the white man there."[9]

Said Eustace Fatty, "[Between] El Paso and Alamogordo are two big mountains. . . . There was a battle in this dry canyon. The soldiers were coming to Fort Stanton with a payment and they [surrounded and] killed all of them; only one fellow from Tularosa got away. The Indians took all the harnesses off and pulled out toward Rinconada. [The survivor] came back that night and got some bags with silver in them; he took a lot of it and covered it up and took a wagon wheel and left it sticking out to mark the place and went back to Tularosa. He told his old man and the old man [couldn't find it]. It is supposed to be there yet."[10]

Woodrow Wilson (Choneska's nephew) said, "There is a place in Deming where a house was built on top of the gold—it was buried there. Old Man Choneska was in a raid and got these gold bars . . . from White Eyes and he placed it in one hole. About 1914 they went back over there and found that there was a house built over that gold . . . but he did not tell the people."[11]

Money

"And talk about money! My goodness! Man got a belt that start from the button and put it around and button it up under his clothes. Indians get that belt and get that money and throw it away. They think it nothing but paper. They don't know nothing about money. They had some red money in Mexico, give it to the children to play with—copper, I guess. They don't care anything about it," said Daklugie.[12]

Jack Tortilla, a Mescalero woman who lived to be 104, remembered when the people robbed a stagecoach. "They got a big lot of cartridges, a big leather bag full. They got bundles of paper tied up with strings. They just cut the strings and threw the money into the mesquite. The long pieces blew all over the desert. All that money! They just threw it away. They kept the silver."[13]

Perico

Perico (Spanish for "white horse") was Geronimo's second cousin[14] and his chief lieutenant. (Perico and Fun had the same father.[15]) When the Chiricahuas were camping with Britton Davis, Perico became a scout and served as second sergeant but bolted when Geronimo broke out.[16]

He married a Chiricahua woman named Hah-dun-key, considered one of the three outstanding young women of the band, along with Geronimo's daughter and Betzinez's sister.[17] After the Davis outbreak, Hah-dun-key was captured, along with their children. Geronimo, Perico, and three other men attempted to rescue their families from the reservation but Perico was unsuccessful. The group had stolen a White Mountain woman, Bi-ya-neta, and she became Perico's wife. They stayed together permanently, even through captivity.[18] She was also known as Bonita.[19]

During final negotiations with Gatewood, it was Perico who tilted toward surrender, saying that his wife and children had been captured and that he wanted to be with them. On the way in, Perico invited Gatewood and two officers to join them for dinner and Bi-ya-neta made a well-cooked dinner. Geronimo sent Perico with interpreter George Wratten to tell General Nelson Miles the group wanted to surrender.[20] Perico told his daughter, Isabel Enjady, that Geronimo sent him as a hostage to the white man to ensure that Geronimo would come in.[21] Army records list him as about thirty-seven at surrender, and his wife Bi-ya-neta, about twenty-eight.[22]

Perico became a scout again at Fort Sill, where he headed his own village. Presumably, both of his wives lived there. When a portion of Oklahoma was opened to white settlers, Perico was with Daklugie guarding the reservation line when Perico was shot in the stomach.[23] Hah-dun-key died at Fort Sill, but Bi-ya-neta and their surviving children accompanied Perico to Mescalero in 1913.[24]

Part II.

The Mescaleros and Lipans

FOURTEEN

Cadette

Cadette, a diplomat given to poetic speech, was one of the most important Mescalero chiefs during the 1860s and 1870s. His Apache name was Zhee-es-not-son, and he is said to have had seven wives.[1,2] His father, Chief Barranquito, was hostile to the whites filtering into Mescalero lands, but when he died in 1857, the more conciliatory Cadette succeeded him, becoming one of the principal Mescalero leaders, along with Santana and Roman Grande. Santana was probably the most powerful, but the more sociable Cadette, with his flair for negotiation, came to be regarded by whites as the main leader.[3]

"Cadette was a great Apache who actually succeeded in keeping most of his people out of trouble, but even the greatest chief could not prevent them from being hungry in those lean times, or keep them from occasional thefts and pilferings," Sonnichsen wrote. "He did his best, however."[4]

It was Cadette's bad fortune to confront the ruthless General James H. Carleton and his California Column. In 1862, Fort Stanton, which Confederates had taken and partially burned, was reactivated under Colonel Kit Carson. Carleton had ordered Carson to kill all Mescalero men and take women and children prisoners. Cadette fought valiantly but ultimately was no match for the Army's superior firepower and numbers.[5] Worn down by Carleton's relentless campaign, the Mescaleros surrendered to Kit Carson, who in November 1862 sent them to Santa Fe. There Cadette made his now-famous speech:

"You are stronger than we. We have fought you as long as we had rifles and powder but your weapons are better than ours. Give us like weapons and turn us loose; we will fight you again. But we are worn out; we have no more heart; we have no provisions, no means to live. Your troops are everywhere. Our springs and waterholes are either occupied or overlooked by your men. You have driven us from our last and best stronghold and we have no more heart. Do with us as may seem good to you but do not forget that we are men and braves."

Carleton ordered them to a new post, Fort Sumner, at the Bosque Redondo along the Pecos River,[6] and Cadette reluctantly took his band to live there.[7] Urged to send his children to school, he told the commanding officer that he didn't want his children to become slaves to their possessions as the White Eyes were.

"You desire our children to learn from books, and say, that because you have done so, you are able to build all those big houses, and sail over the sea, and talk with each other at any distance, and do many wonderful things; now, let me tell you what we think. You begin when you are little to work hard, and work until you are men in order to begin fresh work. You say that you work hard in order to learn how to work well. After you get to be men, then you say, the labor of life commences; then too, you build big houses, big ships, big towns, and everything else in proportion. Then, after you have got them all, you die and leave them behind. Now, we call that slavery. You are slaves from the time you begin to talk until you die; but we are free as air. We never work, but the Mexicans and others work for us. Our wants are few and easily supplied. The river, the wood, and plain yield all that we require, and we will not be slaves; nor will we send our children to your schools, where they learn only to become like yourselves."[8]

On the night of 3 November 1865, Cadette and all but nine Mescaleros ran away from the despised reserve.[9] Cadette had warned officers that his people would leave, saying they would return when the Army set up a more humane reservation.[10]

They spent the next five years wandering and hiding. Game was scarce.[11] By 1870, the Army was trying to persuade the Mescaleros to come in, this time killing them with kindness. Santana's group worked with military details to raise crops, José La Paz had returned with his people, and Cadette sent word that he wanted peace. His band arrived in July and during a council at Fort Stanton, Cadette, with his usual eloquence, promised peace and even asked for a school. Agent A. J. Curtis promised protection and provisions.[12] But while Cadette lived up to his end of the contract, settling with his three wives in La Luz Canyon and attempting to farm, the government, as usual, did not.

The Mescaleros were living quietly at the fort until a few scattered at the rumor, probably started by a local liquor dealer, that the Cavalry would attack their camp. Cadette stayed and later testified against the liquor dealers before a grand jury in Las Cruces.[13]

On 7 November 1872, Cadette and interpreter Juan Cojo left Mesilla and were last seen on the road leading from Whitewater to La Luz.[14] When they failed to return, Chief Santana began a search and followed a trail eight miles up La Luz Canyon. There he found Cadette's horses, still saddled and tethered, grazing beside the trail. Nearby was Cadette's body. Shot through the chest, he had ridden until he fell.[15]

According to the newspaper account, Cadette was shot near the settlement and traveled for eight miles until he dropped from his horse. "There is great sorrow manifested by all the citizens whom Cadette had been thrown in contact with, for he had won the confidence and esteem of all by his prompt and decisive manner in ever seconding the views of the agent. . . . The tribe are apparently feeling very bad and are quite excited, the braves cutting their hair and evincing such other signs of Indian grief."[16] Cojo's sons had ridden in search of him and returned a week later carrying Cojo's head, bits of his clothing and his blanket, all of which they found five miles from Whitewater on the road to San Augustine. His horse too was dead.

Eve Ball wrote of two explanations for Cadette's murder. In one she said the Mescaleros at first believed Cojo had murdered the chief, but apparently both were murdered. A second account appears in Eve's handwritten manuscript: "Cadette was shot during a drunken brawl, allegedly by Juan Cojo. The wounded chief lived long enough to cut off Cojo's head and set it up on a pole in the road near La Luz. After stumbling a short distance, Cadette dropped dead."

The newspaper reported, "A portion of the body of Juan Cojo, interpreter for the Mescalero Apache Agency, [was] found a few days ago about twenty miles from La Luz Canyon under circumstances which show that he must have shot Cadette with his [Cadette's] pistol, and was then killed by Cadette with a knife, who afterwards shot the interpreter's horse which accounts for the two balls lacking in Cadette's pistol at the time he was found."[17]

In 1873 Superintendent L. Edwin Dudley blamed Cadette's death on the Mexican bootleggers against whom he had testified in Las Cruces.[18]

Cadette and the Comanche Fight

Mescaleros regarded Cadette as one of their greatest chiefs. This is one story told of him. The source is probably Bernard Second.

"Always we thought of defense. We had our main camp behind a hill, away from the river. But between the ridge and the Rio Grande we put a few tipis and some horses. Cadette was a wise and brave chief. He knew that if an enemy saw those few tipis they might not think of the main camp's being hidden. Those tipis would keep us from being surprised. At our back was a small mountain where the people could hide if we were attacked. Cadette and the medicine man had chosen our camping place well.

"A band of Comanches had been raiding in Mexico. They crossed the Rio Grande with many horses, stolen from the Mexicans. They had other things too—blankets and food and they had bracelets made of silver. They had never been good friends to us. Sometimes we had made peace with them and they had made promises but Comanches are much like White Eyes—nobody could trust their promises.

"They saw the few tipis and the horses. As we had planned, they did not expect to find more. There were a great many of them—two chiefs and their bands. That night they held a council to decide what to do. One of our warriors could speak their tongue. Cadette sent him to go close to the council and hear what they said. One chief wanted to attack us. He said he would kill all the Apaches and take their horses.

"The other said, 'No. When I have enough horses, why do that? Let's go camp with them and have a good time. We can dance and have a feast. Then we can go to our own country. There will be plenty of buffalo for all.'"

The two argued back and forth, the pacifist saying, "This will not be like fighting Mexicans. This will be a real fight. Let's give them presents and have a dance."

In the end, the belligerent chief held sway. "So they got up early, before daylight. They put on their paint. And they gathered the horses between the hill and the river.

"Cadette got his men ready for the battle but the medicine man [probably Choneska] was away in the hills gathering herbs. Cadette sent a runner for him. He was a great medicine man and my grandfather. He was Solon Sombrero's grandfather too. They find him and tell him a big fight is coming.

"'I know,' he said. He could tell before what is going to happen. 'I am ready to go with you. I fix!'

"He knew and he had taken his war horse, bows, arrows, spear and shield with him. He rode back with the young men. . . . Cadette had sent the women and children to hide in the high hills. He had saddled up. The warriors had kept only their best war and buffalo horses. The rest the women took. Cadette told them to guard their horses well.

"A Mescalero rode up on the hill. He could see the big Comanche camp and all their horses. He could see the enemy driving off the little bunch of horses that belonged to us. They were getting ready to charge the tipis. The chief said, 'Every man who wants to fight, come on!' They started up the hill.

"Then Cadette signaled our men to ride. They are just out of sight, just below the top of the hill. They charge the Comanches. They shoot their arrows and then they fall back. Many Comanches fall to the ground but the rest charge us. We drive each other back and forth, back and forth, using arrows. When they are all gone we use slingshots. Can throw a stone far. And then we charge them with spears. One of their chiefs was killed.

"The medicine man say, 'Now they will start to cry. It will be easy.'"[19]

Choneska

Choneska was a Chiricahua medicine man who married the Mescalero sisters Amelia and Florence, which made him Mescalero. The women's father was Yellow Flowering Weed.[20]

Choneska "was a brave warrior. He lived to be an old man. . . . Choneska had known Geronimo before he left the Chiricahua. . . . Choneska did not like Mexicans. The Apache would grab their lower lips and push it up. That was very painful—many nerves in that area."[21]

Choneska may also be the warrior referred to by the agent as Ho-nes-co, one of Victorio's warriors who on 12 August 1882, came to the reservation and tried to persuade some of the young Mescalero men to go on the warpath. He was arrested and disarmed.[22]

He died in fall of 1931, in his seventies.

FIFTEEN

Bosque Redondo

❖

From inhumanity can come heroism, as the Mescaleros proved. In 1863, the Army began one of its most ill-conceived and cruel initiatives—the settlement of Mescalero Apaches and their enemies, the Navajos, at Bosque Redondo. Much has been written about the Navajo Long Walk. Less known is the Mescalero experience.

❖

Kit Carson arrived at Fort Stanton in the fall of 1862 with orders from General James H. Carleton to kill all the Mescalero men "whenever and wherever you can find them." If they asked for peace, the chiefs and twenty principal men were to come to Santa Fe for a talk. Major William McCleave, with two companies of the California Volunteers, pursued 500 Mescaleros into Dog Canyon and fought 100 warriors on 11 October 1862. The survivors asked Kit Carson for protection and he sent the leaders to Santa Fe.[1] Captain Thomas Roberts, with two companies, went south by Hueco Tanks and engaged another group, which may have been Magoosh's Lipan Apaches.[2] In early 1863 Carleton sent the Mescaleros to a reservation just established at Fort Sumner.[3]

"I was a boy when they moved the Mescaleros from their homeland on the Bonito to the bosque near Fort Sumner," said Big Mouth. "I was big enough to ride a horse in 1863. My people had been hunting with bows and arrows. The soldiers spied their camp and there was a big fight. They whipped the soldiers for a while. But how could they fight long against long-range guns with only rocks, bows, and arrows?[4]

"For a long time we fight and hide and starve. Then our chief Cadette and some of his men make a council with the White Eyes. Many warriors been killed, many peoples hungry and cold and Cadette think we better do what Kit Carson say. He tell us if we go to the Bosque Redondo on the Pecos, they feed us. What can we do? The men say, yes, maybe that is good. Not so good as on the White Mountain but they won't let us stay there. So they agree to do that. And dig hole and Cadette and Kit Carson and all the council, they spit in hole and cover it to show that the trouble is buried. And Kit Carson tell us to bring everything we got to Fort Stanton and be ready to go to Fort Sumner . . .

"In 1863 I must have been eight or nine years old. I had been riding a long time. My mother and I had horses and we rode and led a packhorse with our tipi on it. Most of our tribe had horses. Only a few walk. We start and go north. Go through Capitán Gap and on to the bosque. It was a sad, sad trip. We did not look at each other."[5]

In a report to Washington dated 19 March 1863, Carleton said his troops had brought in 400 Mescalero prisoners to the Bosque Redondo; about 100 fled and joined Apaches in Mexico. However, Bernard Second maintained, "Not more than a fourth of the Apaches were there. The rest scattered in every direction." His grandfather, Choneska, said there were more than 2,000 at the time.[6]

Carleton intended to feed the Apaches at the Bosque Redondo, keep an eye on them, and encourage them to farm. For a time, Carleton's plan seemed to be working. Mescaleros didn't like the alkali water and weren't happy about their internment, but they were making the best of it. By summer the camp had fields with crops planted. In 1863 and 1864 the army brought in 9,000 Navajos. Food and provisions were scant, crops failed, and disease was rampant.[7]

"At Fort Sumner the Mescaleros fixed up the place to raise corn," said Big Mouth. "They dug the ditch for irrigation. Lots of people, especially the older ones, died at the Bosque. They had good little farms started when the smallpox broke out among the Navajos."[8]

Solon Sombrero said, "Fort Sumner was used like a concentration camp. Our parents went there and made ditches for farming. They taught them how to cultivate. . . . We got the land all improved. . . . We didn't want to farm— we are a hunting people. What the Apaches always do, they are wanderers. They don't stay in one place. If one chief want to go this way, they go."[9]

"They did not like the Fort Sumner country," said Big Mouth. "They did not like to farm. They were a hunting people. They loved the mountains of their own country. They did not like the water. It had worms in it. They did not like to be prisoners; they were a free people. It was just like what they call a concentration camp, only they did not say that word then. They were very unhappy."[10]

"The Bosque Redondo was a bad place . . . but we stay. Sometimes they give us some food, sometimes not.[11]

"Then the Navajos were brought there and camped above us on the Rio Pecos. They had got the sickness from the soldiers—what you call the small-pox. And they died, lots of them. The bodies were thrown into the river, and the Mescaleros saw them and knew that if they drank the water it would make the disease. So they just left. And they went back to their home. They camped up the Bonito from Fort Stanton. And they were hungry and almost naked."[12]

On 3 November 1865 every Mescalero who could travel slipped into the night and scattered. The nine left vanished a few days later. Soldiers didn't pursue them. Some headed to Mexico; some joined their cousins, the Warm Springs or the Lipan Apaches; and some joined Comanche bands.[13]

Two Girls

Eve Ball wrote a dramatized version of this story about one family's flight from the Bosque Redondo in the July–August 1971 issue of *True West*. This is the story as May Peso Second told it:

"So that some might live, they scattered and don't stay together. Families were separated so that some might live. Two girls, sisters, very young, maybe thirteen and fifteen, were to go together, but not with their parents, alone. They were warned not to travel by day but to hide so that they won't be found and carried off as slaves. [The older girl's name was Ooh-nah-kah, which means "grass and flowers," and the younger Too-neh.]

"But they are more afraid of ghosts than of Navajos. And crossing an open place, they saw a hill. They think they can see far from there, maybe see some of their people and they go. And a Navajo saw them and race his horse toward them. When he got close they know he is a chief because he is so well dressed—buckskin and beads, many beads. He don't carry a gun, just bow and arrows, but arrows are bad, very bad. And fast. A good fighter can keep maybe five or six in the air at one time, and he can hit something far off. No use running from that man.

"He caught up with them and talk. They can understand some of his words. He tell them to get on horse, the bigger girl first, behind his saddle. Then he throw the younger one up behind her and mount. He start off fast and the larger girl hang on to him. Her little sister put her arms around her waist. And the big girl think if she just have a knife, or even a rock, maybe she kill that man. But she don't have a thing to fight with.

"Then the little girl take her hand loose and put it on the older one's arm and pull it gently. The big girl let her arm slip slowly down and hold on tight with her left hand. The younger one slide her sister's hand down to her high moccasin. And that girl feel a knife in it, a butcher knife. And she stoop sidewise, enough to get that knife. And she rear back and hit that Navajo chief in the back. . . . She hit that Navajo right between the shoulders where he can't reach to pull it out.

"The horse jump and the little girls slide off. The man lean down on the horse's neck, then slowly slide to the ground. The girl jump into the saddle and get the reins. Then she ride off far enough to be out of bow shot.

"The small sister cry to her to come back, not leave her to be killed. The man sit up and fit an arrow to the bow. And the girl's heart stand still, for she think her sister going to be killed. But the Navajo shoot at her—a tired arrow that don't come very far. But he getting another ready. And she tell the little sister to grab the horse's tail when she ride by fast. And she did. But the little one so close to the Navajo that she can't get to her. More arrows flying but don't hit. . . . If he'd had any strength he could have easily killed both of them. . . . But the fourth time she try, the sister catch the tail and the horse bring her out of range of arrows. The little girl climb up behind her sister. And the Navajo slump down. They don't know if he is dead or just fooling them, but they don't go back to see. They need that knife awful bad but with a horse they feel much safer than if they are walking.

"So they turn it toward the White Mountain and they go back to their old home. They get there before their mother does but the next day, she come. Their father and the other men, they stay back to protect the women and children who ran away from the bosque and they all get together every one.

"Their Apache names are not said, but [Ooh-nah-kah] was the grandmother of Fred Pelman, and I have often heard her tell that story."[14]

SIXTEEN

The Mescalero Reservation

After fleeing the Bosque Redondo, the Mescaleros wandered for the next five years, largely invisible except for an occasional raid.[1] Their often-told tales of hardship and suffering in this time have an almost biblical ring to them.

In February 1870, José La Paz led the first group to return to Fort Stanton.

"José was out east of Fort Stanton," Percy Big Mouth said. "All the time they tell him to move in so he went to the Guadalupe country. His folks, his wife, and children were gathering fruit out in the hills and valleys and the old men say they were gathering the lamb's quarter seed. The Fort Stanton soldiers ran onto the camp of women and children. The men were out hunting and when they got back his wife and children were gone. They tracked them to . . . Fort Stanton."[2]

In July Cadette led in a bigger group. Amid councils and speeches, they promised to live in peace, and agent A. J. Curtis offered them land and protection. The Mescalero Reservation was established on 29 May 1873, but peace proved as elusive as the agency's rations. White predators, including Billy the Kid, attacked their camps. "White mens steal Indian horses," said one woman.[3] Corrupt agents and traders cheated them out of their provisions. The army pushed them from place to place. Deprived of guns and horses and unable to hunt, they were frequently starving. To save themselves, they fled again and again.[4]

Fig. 14.   This Mescalero Apache boy was photographed at the Bosque Redondo in 1866. (Courtesy Museum of New Mexico, #38195.)

On one occasion some women, on their way to Mescalero to receive rations, were camped in the Sacramento Mountains when soldiers spotted them. The soldiers, from Fort Defiance, were returning from a scouting expedition in search of a group that had made trouble on the Plains, possibly Comanches or Kiowas. The soldiers had Navajo and Chiricahua scouts with them, as well as Alabama Charlie, a Mescalero who was responsible for finding water holes.

Percy Big Mouth told the story this way: "'Are you going to go over there and kill them?'

"A Navajo said, 'No, my friend, no good. They not doing anything. They just going back to Mescalero and they make talk. And a child cry. It not fair.'

"'We are paid to kill them.'

"'No, that just women. They do no harm.'

"And they killed that woman right there and shot the little girl in the ankle. Her name Mary Armstrong. . . . That was Peso's first wife before Peso was chief. They took the children back to Fort Stanton and the soldiers up there got the children back."[5]

"After while they make an agency at Fort Stanton and give us some cattle. At first we kill the cattle ourselves. Then they have a white man [Heiskell Jones] kill the cattle, cut up the meat and we go to the issue house and get beef. . . . Every Saturday we get beef, 'bout 'nough to last us 'til Monday. We don't get any more beef 'til Saturday. And they take our weapons away from us."[6]

"We got no horses so we will pick up what we can carry on our backs and move it to Nogal or White Oaks, about four days' journey on foot. We got almost to Nogal, very tired. We found some who had a few horses.

"Then the poor Indians were out in the timber. They rounded [us] up in the timber and shot at us. Old Dad could hear the bullets whistle around us. He was about fifteen. They go to the Guadalupe Mountains. The white people over there treated them good. They move that night and the soldiers made a raid and burn all their camp. Starvation is bad, pretty bad. One of those old-timers say, 'We just are never going to have anything to eat.' So we go down there and get some cattle to save our children. They just cry for something to eat. Pretty bad to hear them cry for food. A few camped there and got plenty of deer meat and make jerky. And gave them some meat and mescal and then they found a settlement and got eight head of cattle, for they had to eat. They drove the cattle over there and butchered them.

"A few days later the officers sent another fellow out . . . to talk to these Indians. Finally they found them way over here in the Oscuros. . . . 'They sent me out here to get you Indians all back to Fort Stanton.'

"And the leaders said, 'They already sent us away so why should we go back? We are going to Fort Marfa. They offered us an agency there. Better country.'

"'No, let's all go back to Fort Stanton. Let them finish us up right there. They made a raid on us and clean us out; now let them take us back and chop our necks off.'"

After more discussion they decided to return to Fort Stanton. They started out on foot in the cold. It was March. They traveled sixty miles and the only water they found was from a salt lake. Finally, they arrived at the mouth of Three Rivers where a wagon was waiting with food for the group.

During the raid Big Mouth's aunt had gotten the small children under a blanket and told them to be still so they wouldn't be found. But one child in a cradleboard was left behind. A boy returned for it but when soldiers shot at him, he jumped over a high bluff and let the cradle slide down a rock. The baby was injured and died a few days later.[7]

"Some say, 'Let's go back. That save our children. Stay here we starve to death. Some already dead.' I think it in March but cold, snowing. They start back, all afoot, sixty miles and very little water; that bad water. But have to drink that or nothing. One woman way behind the rest. She feel very bad. She not have but a few rags, not want them to see her. At wagon the cook tear up flour sack and she make a dress the best she can. Cook tell her to ride in wagon but she walk with her people. It rain and turn to snow. Very little clothes, very few blankets but they got hot breakfast. And come back that time."[8]

The group continued on to Fort Stanton. "It rained and turned to snow and was very cold. Very little clothes, very few blankets. Had to keep up a fire all night to keep from freezing." When they got back they found that the Kiowas and Comanches had raided Mescalero for their horses.[9]

"Then an officer say, 'You got to get out. You make the water polluted. Go away, just anywhere.'

"It all our country, from the Rio Bravo [Grande] to the Rio Pecos and across it and over in Texas. But we don't go over there, only when the buffalo run. And our country way down in Mexico and up the Pecos to the mountains. It always been our country.

"But white people coming in along the rivers, along the Ruidoso and the Bonito and on the Pecos. And our people talk about where to go. They can go anywhere they want. It all their country. . . . Our people don't know what to do. They can go anywhere they want but maybe no food there.

"Soldiers not want us to live near Fort Stanton—they need land for horses, maybe cattle too. They not want us live there. Not want us live anywhere. Want us all dead . . .

"We 'fraid if we go they follow and make us come back. We pack everything—we not got much—and carry on our backs. Take old peoples, babies, everything, and go in night, afoot, very quiet. Children, they cry for food and not any food. Starvation is bad, pretty bad. We don't got any horse to kill. And can't build fire. It cold, very cold. One old woman take her blanket and cover little children and give them what food she have, just a little mouthful apiece. And keep them still so soldiers won't find. And next morning they still alive but she dead.

"Soldiers follow. They shoot at us and kill womens. Old Lady Peso, she little girl then. She remember . . .

"'We talk with soldiers. They want us come back to Fort Stanton.'

"'No, they push us out and tell us to leave.'

"'That's right. Now they tell us come back.'

"We can't go Old Mexico, got no horses. Pretty far for womens and old peoples to walk. We talk again to soldiers.

"'The best thing for you Indians to do is come back. You will get beef.'

"We go back but same kind of troubles. The officers say we must go somewhere. Say it all our country and we pick a place and they move agency so we get food. They say it don't matter whether they white peoples there or not. They tell it to the three chiefs who go to Fort Stanton—Natzili, Gregorio, and Roman Grande.[10] They come back and call their mens together and tell them. [According to medicine man Woodrow Wilson, there was a fourth participant, a medicine woman who was his uncle's sister.[11]]

"Gregorio say, 'There's the Hondo and the Bonito. Plenty water. Can raise gardens.' That part was going to the Pecos, all Mescalero country.

"Natzili say, 'The Guadalupes and the Pecos, that a good country. And the Peñasco, that good river. And up where Weed is, that good place.'

"The peoples listen.

"'You pick place for your peoples, you other two chiefs.' It all our country. We can go anywhere we want—the officers say it. The Tularosa, that a good country. On west slope of the White Mountain plenty water, wood, game.

"Roman Grande say, 'That is the place I pick for my peoples. White man on Tularosa good man—Dr. Blazer. Let him stay. White peoples at Tularosa our friends, trade hides for things they got. Plenty food on the Tularosa—deer, elk. That good. Bear too and mountain lion and turkeys . . . not good.[12] Plenty water, plenty wood. All belong to us. That's where we go. What you do, Natzili and Gregorio, when you run out of wood on the Pecos? You two will be already dead but your childrens will have to build little fire and reach out for little twigs to burn. You make big mistake to go to the Pecos.'

"'That's right. We never thought about timber and food—just water. We all go to Tularosa with you, Roman Grande.' [In 1875 the agent's office was moved from Fort Stanton to Blazer's Mill.]

"Agent go too but then get paper to show if government don't need that land 'round Fort Stanton no more it belongs to the Mescaleros. 'If we don't want it no more, it your land,' that's what they promise. 'You keep this little book to keep this land on. Don't let that book run wild. Take care of [it] and get land when we don't need it no more. Government will keep you good, feed you, you be their childrens. As long as you keep little book nobody can take this land away from you.'

"Gregorio—he medicine man too[13]—keep book in buckskin bag and carry it with him all time. He not got no other place to keep it. When new agent come he show it to him. Godfroy agent that move them to Tularosa. This next man, he see book.

"One day Gregorio ride up on mountain where lots of brush. When he get back book gone. String broke and buckskin bag lost. Indians scout everywhere he go—can trail horse easy—but not find. It lost . . ."[14]

Roman Grande enjoyed his chosen site until 1885.

"Then there was some kind of disease among the people at Tularosa—smallpox, I think." Roman Grande's group was camping in the Rinconada "and the agent told them not to go down there . . . but they don't listen and a bunch went down and they got some drink and some other stuff too and the whole camp got sick and began to die. Roman Grande died and the most of them died."

The agent told them to leave the area, so they went toward present-day Weed. "They camped there and it was beginning to snow and it was four feet high—up to the horses' bellies, way high—and looked like a log had been dragged through it when horse move. And some of the people froze to death. They saved a few horses. Then we had to go on again. Starvation was bad again. . . . Some women joined them but they were afraid and they could not keep up. They left food for them but they all died except Juan's wife. She got near the camp but stayed way off. They gave her food but she stayed away."[15]

"Old Dad old now and blind but he remembers good and he tell us this long ago, when I just a child."[16]

SEVENTEEN

The Apaches and Comanches

Apaches had little fear of other people until the 1700s, when Comanches began to appear on their Plains hunting grounds. The eastern Apaches—Mescaleros and Lipans—suddenly faced an intruder more ruthless than themselves. Sometimes enemies, sometimes friends, the two groups began a complicated relationship that endured into the nineteenth century and fuels some of their best stories.

History tends to remember the Mescaleros as mountain people, but the tribe's easternmost bands ranged from the Texas Panhandle south toward Big Bend and into Mexico. They once numbered more than 2,000.

"The Mescaleros were [once] more numerous than the Chiricahuas and we fought many times until only one member of the family or very few of the band was left, for we had enemies on every side—numerous enemies all ready to attack us," said Bernard Second. "Our history is both romantic and tragic."[1]

Their close allies were the Lipan Apaches,[2] who lived in the San Saba River valley of Texas and lands to the north; they were a menace to the Spanish colony of San Antonio.[3] The Lipans probably numbered five hundred to one thousand for most of the nineteenth century;[4] by 1910, just twenty-eight remained.[5]

"Lipan means 'no water.' They just had rainwater in the holes," said Percy Big Mouth.[6]

Fig. 15.   Chief Natzili led a band of Plains-dwelling Mescaleros. He was so strong that, like Ulysses, nobody else could string his bow. (J. R. Riddle, courtesy Museum of New Mexico, #57614.)

"They fought with the Comanches long before they're settlers in the Southwest—also with the Kiowas, Cheyennes, and Arapahos and sometimes with the Navajos but seldom with other Apaches," said Woodrow Wilson, a medicine man. "The Navajos were our enemies. The Mescaleros went by themselves. They roam from the panhandle of Texas to far south in Mexico but always they return to these mountains and there is one time that they all got together in Mexico close to Chihuahua in the San Perras [Blue Mountains]. They all got together, all those tribes of Indians got together and they dig a hole for all those tribes to spit in. And from then, everything old trouble gone and they did not fight. The Spanish came. And the English. And they did the same thing with them. We were at Fort Sumner. They dug a hole and spat in it—White Eyes, Mexicans, Indians, everybody. And they never would have any more trouble if the White Eyes keep their word. But they don't."[7]

Apache conflict with Comanches began with the horse. Apaches had stolen Spanish livestock since 1598 but in 1621 the Spaniards made horsemen of Pueblo people so they could serve as herders. Some deserted with their mounts and took refuge with the Apaches. The rest is history. With a horse the Apache could raid over far greater distances, and a new source of wealth was created. Apaches likely traded horses to Comanches and other Plains tribes[8] but were less dependent on them. The lithe and hardy Apaches always said they were faster on foot in mountain country; the heavyset and ungainly Comanches were only graceful on a horse.[9] While Apaches simply pilfered horses as they needed them,[10] Comanches became expert breeders.[11]

Bernard Second said, "[T]he Cheyennes have a song about us. They honor the Apaches for giving them the horse, and that is great recognition and honor. We mounted a lot of other tribes too. . . . Nobody should say that the Apaches were influenced by the Plains Indians—just the contrary was the case. Our old people say that the Plains Indians were originally just river tribes [before they got horses]. . . . The Mescaleros used horses much more than did the Western Apaches, who lived in the mountains. The Mescaleros lived on the flat plains and horses were [more] essential than in the mountains."[12]

During this interview, Second showed Eve some old beaded moccasins. They were ankle high and without the turned-up toe Chiricahuas used to protect themselves from thorns, but with fringe about a foot long attached to the heel. "The fringes streamed in the wind when the Mescalero was riding, and he usually was," Eve wrote in her notes. "When on foot they trailed behind his feet."

Percy Big Mouth said, "These Lipans and Comanches could never get along together. All the time they fought each other for the horses. Lots of wild horses that probably got away from the Spanish, many of them around San Antonio. That's where the old Lipans' country and the old ones tell me about it. My mother told me much about that—they were her folks."[13]

By 1700, horses were widely dispersed and within fifty years, the Comanches had used horses and guns supplied by the French to drive the eastern Apache bands west and south,[14] some across the river into Mexico. The Comanches also allied with the Spanish in making war on Apaches. By 1750, a map of Comanche territory nearly replicated a map of former Plains Apache lands.[15] However, they were no match for mountain Apaches. By 1821, Comanchería was well defined but it stopped short of the western New Mexico and Arizona Apache strongholds.[16]

The Plains Apaches didn't yield without a terrific struggle. In one nine-day battle in 1725 at the Rio del Fierro, probably the Wichita River, the Comanches prevailed over the Lipans.[17] In another big fight in 1790, the Spanish, Comanches, and their allies attacked a group of Mescaleros, Lipans, and other Apaches west of Bexar in Texas, killed two Apache chiefs, twenty-eight warriors, twenty-eight women, and one child, and captured thirty women and children.[18]

The Apaches hand down stories of their own victories.

"They used to go on the warpath with the Comanches sometimes but not very much," said Alton Peso. "This battle, the way I heard it, only one Comanche got away and he was wounded. His people called him a woman because he ran away and was saved."[19]

Around 1822, after yet another outbreak of hostilities, the Lipans slit the throats of all Comanche men who had married into the tribe during more peaceful times.[20] Spaniards tried for a time to convince these groups that they should listen to the missionaries and become farmers, but with bigger troubles in Florida and Mexico, the Spaniards lost interest. Similarly, the Mexican Republic also had more vexing concerns than the Plains Apaches and largely let them be.[21]

Not so the Texans. President Sam Houston worked hard to establish peace with the tribes of his republic and signed a treaty in 1838 with the Lipans, but whether the Texas lawmakers ever ratified the treaty is unknown. His successor, M. B. Lamar, took the opposite tack—extermination. The Lipans chose to help the Texans against their old enemies the Comanches, who, pressed by Texans, increasingly occupied Lipan lands.[22]

"My grandfather [Magoosh] saw the fall of the Alamo when he was a boy," said Richard Magoosh. "The Apaches were sympathetic with the Americans. They hated the Mexicans."[23]

The Texas tribes were at peace when Texas was annexed to the United States. The U.S. military promptly began pushing the Lipans from here to there, at the same time wiping out the game on which the Apaches lived until they were starving and had to steal to survive. The Texans at one point established reservations for some of its tribes but not the Apaches and soon abandoned any reservation policy at all. The U.S. Army continued to hunt them down and destroy their belongings wherever they were found or failed to defend them against rampaging settlers and Texas Rangers.[24] Ultimately, they were driven from Texas and took refuge in Mexico and with the mountain Mescaleros in New Mexico.

Except for a brief period, around 1776 when the Spanish succeeded in driving a wedge between them, Lipans and Mescaleros raided together, later attacking gold hunters on their way to California. They harried anyone who traveled the El Paso-San Antonio Road.[25]

Some Apaches retreated, becoming a greater menace to the Spanish settlements in the Rio Grande valley,[26] while others allied themselves with the fierce Comanches, raiding together and intermarrying. (Given the Apaches' prudish attitudes toward male-female relations and the Comanches' lack of the same, their camps must have been interesting.)

Comanches took advantage of the Mescaleros' internment at the Bosque Redondo to raid the Mescalero homeland and burn Blazer's Mill in December 1869.[27] In 1871 agent A. J. Curtis reported that the Mescalero chief Cadette had come in with 300 people but said more of his band were with the Comanches.[28] The following year Curtis counted 350 Lipans at Mescalero, along with a group he referred to as Aguas Nuevas, a Mexican band that had come in from Comanche country in the past year.[29] The Lipans were probably the band led by Magoosh.[30]

"Magoosh roamed mostly from Roswell to the Guadalupes all the time," said his grandson Richard Magoosh. "He was born in Mexico. . . . When they were free they would go south for the winter and up here for the summer. What the government did was to pen them up here and keep them here."[31]

In 1873 Curtis observed, "For some years they [Mescaleros] lived with the Comanches and participated in their depredations; but they have been gradually collected about the agency although the communication between them and the Comanche seems to be only partially interrupted."[32] Writing in 1874, agent W. C. Crothers indicates that the Plains-dwelling Mescalero came in from what he calls Comanche country that summer. In 1876, the Plains Mescaleros led by Natzili,[33] which means "buffalo," took refuge with their mountain cousins.[34]

Natzili's band had inhabited the High Plains from the Texas panhandle to the Pecos Valley.[35] "Natzili was a large and powerfully built man, much taller than the average Apache, most of whom do not exceed five-feet-six-inches in height," Eve wrote. "He was so strong that, like Ulysses, nobody else could string his bow." They lived on bison, eating the meat and using hides for clothing and tipi coverings. They traded hides with the Western Apaches and the Nednhi, who also used them for tipis.[36]

"Nogal Canyon to Las Vegas was ours," said Solon Sombrero, a grandson of Natzili. "And to Santa Fe from the White Mountain, follow the ridge to Sandia Mountains and Tijeras Mountains and to the Organs and to El Paso, San Juans. . . . That Natzili's, who were originally Plains Apaches—clear up close to Lubbock and Rabbit's Peak, near Tucumcari and Amarillo too, and the Panhandle of Texas. They had a trail up to Oklahoma. . . . When they went visiting to Oklahoma it took them thirty-two days to make the trip and back. Sometimes the Apaches went there for a visit to their people who married Comanches."[37]

In 1877 a smallpox outbreak forced the Mescaleros and the newcomers led by Natzili to break into small groups to prevent its spread.[38] It is likely that this was the same period the Lipans split up for the same reason. The bands scattered, one heading to Mexico where it remained for years.[39]

"An epidemic hit that country and they drifted into Mexico and made it their home," said Eric Tortilla. "There was some kind of Apaches down there."[40]

Even after moving to Mescalero, the ties with Comanches persisted. Following their flight from Bosque Redondo, some Mescaleros joined Comanche camps,[41] and returned to their Comanche friends at other times when conditions at Mescalero became unbearable. Both Comanches and Mescaleros were in Victorio's party when the great guerrilla leader was raiding in 1879 and 1880.[42] And a small band of Mescalero and Comanche renegades was still committing depredations in the Rio Pecos and Rio Peñasco as late as 1883.[43] Apparently, even the Chiricahuas rode with Comanches on occasion.

"One of the Chiricahuas went as far as the Wichita Hills looking for some lost Indians. We heard that they were killed down by Fort Davis. I think some of them took part in that big fight for about fourteen or fifteen miles—just slaughter one after another—but fighting with white soldiers long, long time ago. Red Bird was the chief, a Comanche. They were helping the Comanches. I was not there but that's what I heard. Two or three fellows, good men, went to talk; they guide and talk. . . . Red Bird was killed. Whenever they [were] fighting, he was in the middle of it all the time."[44]

When the Army swept through Mescalero after Victorio's departure, rounding up the peaceful Mescaleros and Lipans, the Lipans fled.

"My grandfather, Chief Magoosh, went to Mexico about the time Victorio did," said Richard Magoosh. "My father, Willie Magoosh, was born down there on that trip."[45]

"When the army [came] to the [agency] they started to round all of them [up] there and they had done nothing. . . . Some of them got away. They went on Jacinto Peak. My daddy was a small boy then. They were going up the side of the hill and trying to get over that into Nogal Canyon.

"They opened fire on them just like wild game. They were not fighting, just trying to get away. They killed some of them—I don't know how many. When they got over that hill they went toward Bent. Just this side of Bent there is a crossing of the Tularosa [road]. From there they went toward the Rinconada and then over into the Three Rivers country and into the Capitans. They didn't camp 'til they got to the east side of the Capitans. And they hid and went from there to Roswell, the Guadalupes, and then to Mexico. They went with this bunch that ran away. Magoosh went to his friends in Mexico. He stayed there a long time. . . . When they got back [to Mescalero] they got rations. They did not bother them any more. They were all friendly again."[46]

When Magoosh returned, he asked his old friend Peso for permission to stay.

"Magoosh had two wives and children with him," said May Peso Second. "He left them at the south end of the Sacramentos toward El Paso. [He asked for Peso and said they wanted to return to Mescalero.] Peso let them return. Took them to the superintendent and told him. And he sent some of the scouts over there to get them . . ."[47]

Magoosh would be the last chief of the Lipans and also served with Peso as a scout during the Geronimo campaigns.[48] The Lipans remained at Mescalero in relative peace except for one incident. In 1887 the agent reported that as the Mescalero chief San Juan lay dying, the medicine man blamed the witchcraft of two Lipans who had feuded with San Juan. The Mescaleros were enraged. Hiding their women and children in the mountains, they prepared to fight. The agent found San Juan's people saddled and ready to attack the Lipans' camp. The Lipans, well armed, were also ready to fight.

The agent told the Mescaleros that he would investigate and then chastised the medicine man and threatened to imprison him if he continued to practice. The agent also reported, "Fifty Indians, chiefly Lipans, wish to return to the Comanche reservation in Indian Territory. Quannah Parker, Comanche chief, is here and says he and his people would be glad to have them too. Because of the trouble with San Juan's people it might be best to let them go."[49]

In 1905 the Lipans were reunited with their missing cousins in Mexico after a member of the Mexican band had made his way to Mescalero and asked Magoosh to rejoin the other Lipans. Agent James A. Carroll had Father Migeon, parish priest at Tularosa, arrange to bring the group of thirty-seven to the reservation.[50]

"Several hundreds of Lipans were in Mexico and the Mexicans killed them," said Sam Chino. "Those who were left were brought back."[51]

Solon Sombrero said, "Mr. Carroll had a priest go down in Mexico. Some Indians were down there without land—just on public land. . . . Father Migeon went after them and brought them back. One used to live right here—my neighbor Philemon Venego."[52]

Washington

At one time the government's Indian relations included bringing leaders to Washington, and several Mescalero chiefs were so honored. These visits were the occasion for some humorous culture clashes.

"Natzili went to Washington as a delegate several times," said Solon Sombrero. "President Garfield, I think. They went in and introduced themselves. The President came out to meet them. My grandfather . . . hugged him. The President got scared. That's the way Indians shake hands—no harm about it."[53]

May Peso Second told of another visit.

"When they went to Washington, there was a long table and both white people and Indians at it. Old Man Shanta used to stick his fingers in the dishes and taste everything before taking any on his plate. He tried to cut his meat and [the knife] was not good. He took a big butcher knife out. He would put a strip of meat in his mouth and cut it off like the old Indians used to do.

"Maria Boy, he was looking through a window watching a lady half-dressed. A man chased him with a broom. Peso said, 'Don't look into houses. White people don't like it.'

"'Then why do they have windows?'

"Magoosh got a long-tailed coat and a derby hat and the Indians called him Grasshopper, he looked so funny."[54]

EIGHTEEN

Comanche Stories

The Lipans and Mescaleros often told stories around the campfire of their scrapes with the Comanches. They were all buffalo hunters and fought when they encountered each other.

Once a few Mescaleros were out hunting buffalo. "They were close to a cliff, way up on the mountain," said May Peso Second. "There was a very narrow path up that cliff, dangerous [even] in daytime. And there was a big rock split off where many could hide. It was way high on the side of the mountain, and the path went to it. Some Mescaleros were hiding behind it, and they thought nobody could climb that path. They had caught many rats and were cleaning them at night. They were hidden behind the rock. They were going to throw the refuse down the cliff. And the Comanches were sneaking up on them and they didn't know it. They didn't fight at night. One that was sneaking around got the offal in his eyes and mouth and the other Comanches started laughing at him. He must have had his mouth open from climbing. When this Mescalero started [laughing] . . . so did the Comanches. And they didn't fight, not that time.

"But on that hunt they had a bad time, for some other Comanches chased them clear back to their own place. They chased them clear there for several days. They did not bother them any more that year. And next time they were afraid . . .

"They killed several Comanches there. Then they moved to another place. But after that they went back there, they could hear the Comanches talking. It was the ones they had killed that night. A man went to see if he could find where they heard the Comanches talking and he heard them himself—those they had killed in that fight, and their bones were still there and not buried. This man stayed all night there all alone. In the morning he burned the bones in a fire and so they don't hear them any more."[1]

In another story about Comanches, a Lipan woman was the hero. Eve Ball relates a dramatized version of the story in *Indeh*.[2] Here is the original told by May Peso Second, daughter of Chief Peso:

"Big Mouth stayed with my father but my father was older than he. Big Mouth was about fourteen when he stayed with Peso, who took him into Texas and Mexico on hunts first and later on raids.

"On one trip to Mexico [around 1870] they went down the Pecos and raided Sonora. It was the month of the Comanche moon and Peso realized that they might encounter roving bands who went to Mexico to steal horses.

"Big Mouth and another boy were riding about fifty yards or so back of the main group of Apaches. They turned and saw the dust of a big band behind them. They laughed and instead of reporting it to my father, just kept on laughing. Then they turned back. Instead of riding toward the approaching dust, they turned their horses up a mountain side so that nobody would know they had seen the approaching party.

"A man with the chief called to them to come on, to join the rest, for there were Comanches coming. They knew by the cloud of dust that they were being followed by a big band and that it was coming fast.

"My father got after them because they did not report seeing the dust. The main party had not known of it until they missed the boys and turned back to find them. They were going to go up on the hill until the Comanches stopped fighting the Apaches.

"'You were trying to get out of fighting!'

"The boys laughed.

"'That is nothing to laugh about. You were acting like cowards.' [There is no worse insult one can give an Apache than to call him a coward.]

"The Comanches caught up with them just before dawn the next day and they attacked the Apaches but they got away. Their medicine man was with them. I cannot say his name but he was the father of Bessie Big Rope. He always went with them on the warpath and whatever he told them, they did. And always everything he told them came true . . .

"A few days later the Apaches and Comanches met. They did not fight the first day. Just a few Comanches and they waited for others to come. And they did fight. The first time out the Comanches kill some Lipans [who had joined the Mescaleros from Mexico]. Among this band was a young married couple, and the Comanches killed the boy.

"After that battle, the girl got her buckskin suit. They did not wear it except for ceremonials and special things. The Comanches went back to their own country. And this girl, she knew that a good Indian wife must be the servant of her husband's people after his death. And she could never marry again unless they gave their consent.[3]

"So she slipped away from them but she took her buckskin suit. And she followed those Comanches. It was very easy to do because they left a big trail. She took a little food, but most of what she ate she found along the way. She knew she could not go back to her parents but must stay with her in-laws and she didn't want to do that, not always.

"She walked from the place of the battle far, far to the north, many days. And when she found the Comanche village, she did not let herself be seen until they had the dance. They had scalped Apaches, and they had scalped some Lipans.

"And when the dance began she put on her beautiful beaded buckskin dress, and she joined them. She waited until late, late at night to go to them. It was the chief who had killed and scalped her husband and she looked until she found him. She had something on her head, and she went to him. As is well known, it is the woman's privilege to ask a man to dance with her, and she chose the chief. She was beautiful and her dress was beautiful, and the chief was drunk. And at his belt her husband's scalp dangled beside his knife.

"They began dancing and soon he began trying to put his arm around her. That is not good. Indians do not touch each other when they dance. And the girl knew what the chief had in his mind. That man kept trying to make love to her and pretty soon she could not talk to him. He walked her off a long way and she started running. And she ran into some tall weeds and there was some brush too and she could not run fast. She knew that they were so far away from the others that nobody could see them and if she screamed nobody could hear her."[4]

This account doesn't describe what happened next but in the *Indeh* story, lacking a knife, she used her teeth to slash his throat as she held the drunken chief in a death grip. She then scalped him with his own knife, took his clothes, and stole away on his horse.

"They had been searching for her and thought she might have returned to her parents. And she went to the door crying and singing the Apache war song. For Lipans, they too are Apaches. And when her in-laws came to the door she had that scalp on a stick and she had his clothes. And they ran to her. And they cried. And they put up a big dance. And they told her, 'You may marry anybody you want.' The in-laws used to do that—keep the daughter-in-law to do the work. But they tell her, 'You are free and can marry again because you are brave and you are true.' And she was brave and the Lipans respected her.

"I have often heard my father tell this story, and Elmer Wilson's father also, and Magoosh too. He was the chief of the Lipans who came to our reservation and brought his people to live."[5]

The Mescaleros from then on called the girl Gouyen.[6] "*Gouyen* means more than just 'woman'—it means woman but it means a very special one, like 'wise woman' or 'faithful woman,'" said May Peso Second. The commonly used word for woman is *ishton*.[7]

Big Mouth

In May Peso Second's story the teenaged Big Mouth behaved badly, but he would go on to distinguish himself as a scout. His son Percy was a storehouse of knowledge about his people's history and culture.

Big Mouth was born about the time Fort Stanton was built, around 1856.[8] The names of his father and mother are unknown. His father, uncle, and maternal grandfather were killed in Mexico before he was born.

"My father's grandfather was Juanito. They grab him—he was the chief—way down in old Mexico. They capture him and took him, chained him, and hauled him to Santa Fe. They never knew what became of him, thought probably he was hanged. A bunch of Chiricahuas were down here near Santa Rita when he came from Old Mexico with *carretas* [carts]. They stopped right here . . .

"'Have you Indians ever come up among the Mescaleros and know about my children? I am Juanito. I want to know if my children doing good. . . . If you happen to go to Mescalero country tell them you saw me.'"[9]

Big Mouth never mentioned having brothers or sisters and describes being moved to the Bosque Redondo with just his mother.[10] Peso, his uncle, assumed parenting duties when Big Mouth became a teenager.

"Peso name Big Mouth. When Big Mouth was very young Peso took him and trained him. . . . Big Mouth stayed with my father but my father was older than he. Big Mouth was about fourteen when he stayed with Peso, who took him into Texas and Mexico on hunts first and later on raids."[11]

Big Mouth married at about age twenty to Eliza, who had a Mescalero mother and Lipan father.[12] When the Army asked for Mescalero scouts, Big

Mouth was one of the first four scouts enlisted at Fort Stanton. He was about twenty-five. Government records show he enlisted as a scout twice, on 11 July 1885 and 5 August 1886.[13] Mescaleros remember that Shanta Boy, Crook Neck (brother of Sans Peur), and Big Mouth went after Geronimo as scouts in 1886.[14]

Big Mouth was one of the last people to see Colonel Albert Fountain alive. The Mescaleros were friendly with Fountain, who had done some legal work for them. On that fateful day in 1896 Fountain passed through and stopped to talk.

"Sans Peur, son of San Juan, my dad, and some others talk to him and [he] say, 'I have been to Lincoln and I am going back on to Las Cruces.' He got a little boy with him.

"Then Sans Peur . . . speak and say he go along with them.

"'No, it is not necessary. Why, I got little boy and nobody bother me.'

"They went on. They went in a buggy and way up in the White Sands along somewhere he was killed. They never could find his body—his son's neither. Soon as they heard, a bunch of Indians went out and tried to trail them but [it was] pretty hard. Somebody had driven a herd of cattle over his tracks. Way out toward the Sacramentos they find horse tracks, just two, going toward Dog Canyon. After they went out of Alamogordo [there were] too many horse tracks and they couldn't find much."[15]

Big Mouth had four sons, of whom Percy Big Mouth became one of Eve's best sources of information.

"When he was a small child his spine was injured by a fall from a horse, and Percy never married. After the death of his mother he lived with and cared for his aged father, who died at the age of 108. Percy was well informed as to the history and traditions of his tribe, and he was also expert in making bows and arrows, lances and shields. His knowledge and skill brought many men interested in Boy Scout work to Mescalero to learn authentic accounts and learn the authentic methods of preparing not only weapons but foods as the Apaches did those things in their primitive state.

"In addition to the excellent care he gave his father, Percy did much for the youth of the tribe. He attempted to help preserve their traditions and make them aware of their heritage. . . . It is not an exaggeration to say that he was one of the best known and most beloved individuals on the reservation."[16]

Percy Big Mouth died of a heart attack in December 1958, five weeks after his father's death.[17]

Fig. 16.   Big Mouth, a Mescalero, was an army scout during
the Victorio campaign. (Courtesy Smithsonian Institution.)

NINETEEN

Victorio and the Mescaleros

For years the Mescaleros told stories of the great Warm Springs Chief Victorio's visits to their reservation and of the Mescaleros who rode with him. Everybody had a different view of Victorio. The Army considered him a menace; the agent suffered him with anxiety. The Mescaleros welcomed him as a brother, but to some he was a troublemaker. Either way, Victorio gave the Mescaleros their last opportunity to live the old way and die as warriors.

In August 1878, the government ordered Victorio's people from their beloved Warm Springs a second time. They fled rather than return to the despised reservation at San Carlos. In December Nana came to Mescalero with a group of Warm Springs people, but not until June 1879 did Victorio arrive with thirteen men.[1] They told agent S. A. Russell they were willing to settle at Mescalero and wanted to receive rations,[2] but Russell said he needed permission from Washington. They waited at the reservation, growing more suspicious as the days passed. Chief San Juan brought Victorio and his men to Dr. Blazer, who gave them from his own supplies a steer, flour, sugar, and coffee in hopes of placating the restless warriors.

Still, Victorio was suspicious, and in August 1879 when soldiers arrived from Fort Stanton at the request of the timid Russell, who expected an uprising, their bugle was enough to send Victorio scurrying. Victorio went to Blazer, shook hands, and said goodbye.[3]

"Victorio and his band were here and he brought some of those people with him. . . . One was Kaytennae, and he was just like Victorio," said Sam Chino. "He loved to go out and hunt trouble. . . . Kaytennae was very well known then. And Broken Ankle [Nana] . . . Victorio went into the Rinconada and there were many Mescaleros camped out there. He sent word for all the people to come to the Rinconada so that he can talk to them.

"San Juan was chief and he went over there and talked to the Indians and [Victorio] told them, 'Join me and we are going out and fight together. That the best thing you can do. Join me and we will fight all who come.'

"San Juan: 'No! I think we don't do that. I have already shaken hands with the agent and I don't want to fight any more; I think what it mean to lose my people. The government is giving us food and I don't expect to do anything of that kind any more. It is useless.'"[4]

"Victorio was here and was given a place over on the Rinconada," said Percy Big Mouth. "Victorio didn't like San Carlos and all the time he come back. He told his men, 'Well, this pretty bad. This our country and the miners, store men, and farmers all time cheat us.

"'Then we go to our cousins and brothers, the Mescaleros.' They came over here to speak with our chief, Natzili, and with Gregorio and Roman Grande. They came over here and talk with them and the three agree: We are relations. They give them the rights . . .

"They give them the Rinconada and over on the west side. They getting along good and . . . they don't disturb the store men and soldiers nor the miners. [Men from Silver City] say some of Victorio's men steal back in the mountains and kill sheep and herders and they want to come back and get this man . . .

"Saturday was ration day and then Victorio came up there with his people. They were in line at the commissary—you get rations there. On the west side there is a window where they get their rations. Mescaleros come first. When Victorio come they tell him, 'You wait.' They give Mescaleros food first. Every time he come in, 'Not yet.' And finally get mad and think, 'Maybe they going to do something to us.' Think they saw soldiers coming down the hill where the hospital is now. Looks like trouble. And they still don't want to give them rations. . . . And Victorio think they after him because he is the leader.

"'They don't want to issue rations, well, here goes my ration card.' And he tore it up. 'I got something in the hills to eat. . . . This is my last day. I am going to leave.' And he took his men and left. They stopped at Dr. Blazer's and he got little store. Victorio shook his hand. 'My friend, this is my last day,' he say. 'Going back to my country.'"[5]

"Victorio and five Warm Springs Indians came in and the agent refused to issue rations to them," said Paul Blazer, the mill operator's grandson. "They had camped in the little canyon back of the Blazer Mill. They were there several days and in course of time went on a tiswin drunk. They went again to the agency. José Carillo interpreted for them. Again Russell refused to issue rations without authorization from Washington. Since three weeks was the minimum time required to get a reply, that meant little.

"Agent Russell was a very sanctimonious man who believed in going by the literal statement of his office. He had a waist-long white beard of which he was very proud. Victorio grabbed him by it and began dragging him about the room and stopping occasionally to kick him. Russell cried to José, 'Habla bonito to them.' José had realized that it was useless to try to reason with Victorio but had tried to make Russell understand that hunger is a pressing affair.

"Victorio finally released Russell and administered a parting kick, much to the enjoyment of his warriors. They went down to the mill and Dr. Blazer gave them food—beef, flour, sugar, and coffee. They returned to their camp and settled down for the night. The Mescaleros were coming in occasionally to visit them. They were out of sight of the road but close enough to be heard . . .

"Russell telegraphed Fort Stanton that there was an Indian uprising. . . . The post sent a company of cavalry. Dr. Blazer had a trading post and quartermaster place. The detachment took their horses and went down there to feed them. A bugle was blown and the Indians heard it."[6]

"The soldiers were coming on account of Victorio—scouts from San Carlos. . . . The chiefs said, 'Don't leave. Don't join Victorio's band,'" Percy Big Mouth said. "Two of the chiefs went to the White Mountain and they wanted to send somebody from the agency, two men to go hunt all these other bands. But the main thing was to get Natzili and Gregorio—they were up there somewhere. Finally my dad went. They had taken all the horses. After they went out of Mescalero they saw a train of wagons from Fort Stanton. If they found any of Victorio's band they would take them. They stopped and did not move, the Mescaleros. Then old Dad started over to Rinconada and met a man on this side and he told them where these two chiefs and their wives and children were at the Mescalero Agency. 'Then we hunt 'til we find them.' Some came back to the agency and two chiefs were on the south slope of the White Mountain at a spring. One is ready to go to the Capitans. He has some folks over there. Dad got there just about time they were ready to go and got his horse ready to go look for his wife and children."[7]

Despite Blazer's entreaties, Victorio rode out. The only dealings he would have with the whites from that day on was at gunpoint. And despite the efforts of their chiefs, many Mescaleros rode with him. "They . . . say they are going to die fighting."[8]

With Victorio were the Mescaleros Running Water, Manchito,[9] Caje, and Muchacho Negro. Caje was a Warm Springs Apache who had married a Mescalero woman and lived with his wife's tribe.[10] "Many Apaches from Mescalero went with Victorio," said Muchacho Negro's grandson, Ralph Shanta.[11]

Almer Blazer, the trader's son, had a close call about then. The boy had gone hunting in the Rinconada with two men. They camped out several days. One man suggested leaving the trail and moving cautiously. Soon after, they saw five Indians camped near a spring they had been heading toward. From their dress, the three knew they were Warm Springs people, and they crept away toward Tularosa. There they learned of Victorio's flight the previous evening.[12]

Many restless, bored Mescaleros, up to 300, joined later, including Mescaleros from the Davis Mountains, as well as Lipan Apaches and Comanches.[13] On 3 March 1880, the Mescalero chief Caballero got a five-day pass to contact Victorio and bring him in. On the tenth, he sent the pass back with his wife and promised to return later. He didn't. San Juan asked permission to go look for Caballero and he too apparently stayed out. Army and civilian reports of 1880 also describe Mescaleros and Comanches fighting alongside Victorio and the capture of ponies with Comanche brands.[14]

As Victorio and his growing band raked the border, news of his feats drew more Mescaleros to the warpath,[15] all the while chased by the Army, which was aided by Mescalero scouts.

"Big Mouth, my father, was a scout for the cavalry at Fort Stanton during Victorio's wars. They asked for a local scout and one-fifth of the Mescaleros joined . . ."[16]

Solon Sombrero said, "Most of the young men volunteered for scout duty. There were scouts in every Indian village or band."[17]

Returning from Mexico and El Paso during one sweep, Victorio's group reached the Guadalupe Mountains. By then some Mescaleros were having second thoughts and held a council.

"'We better not go. You fight for [your] country but we got a peaceful place to live.'" Two scouts decided they didn't want to go and turned back, said Percy Big Mouth. "And a bunch of Mescalero join in with them."[18]

After five months, Caballero also wanted to go home. In August 1880, he saddled his horse to return to Mescalero and ordered his people to follow. Victorio confronted the Mescalero chief and in the argument that followed, Caballero died and the Mescaleros stayed.[19]

One woman's experience illustrates the hardship of riding with Victorio: "An old lady who died here told of coming back from Mexico on horseback with nobody but her baby with her. . . . She said they come down that year running all summer and she was on horseback," said Isabel Enjady. "She stopped for her baby to be born. Then they got on their horses again and traveled all night. And the baby lived. . . . She was worn out from riding. She didn't have time to be sick. They just had to keep on traveling. . . . Nowadays you young women have to stay in bed. . . . In those days we could not even stay in one place. And sometimes we have to leave them and go on."

She stopped to get help from a Mexican family. "My father said early in the morning while it was still dark she left that baby and came on alone. She was far away from [home] . . . and she came to a river and just as she crossed the river, it rained so hard that the river overflowed. It was evening time. She stopped on the top of a big mountain and spent the night there. Then she traveled again all day and got back to her people in Arizona. She never got her baby. The Mexican family got it. I think she was with Victorio, for it was about that time. She died here."[20]

Willingly or not, Mescaleros followed Victorio into the trap laid by Mexican soldiers. Some sixty Mescalero men, women, and children were killed or captured in the Tres Castillos Massacre on 25 October 1880.[21] A few managed to escape; San Juan returned to the reservation. Muchacho Negro, Maria Boy, and Ishpia survived because they were away hunting or raiding.[22] Another survivor was Nai-yoki, a Warm Springs who married a Mescalero.

"So he was a Mescalero then," said Percy Big Mouth. "He is the one who, when they surrounded Victorio, he slipped out at dusk and he crawl and go to the hills. Victorio said, 'No, don't go. Let's die together right here.' He came back by Fort Van Horn. He and some others got back here. They live here 'til they die. I know them well.

"Caje was a Warm Springs who went with Victorio but he did not see the fight where Victorio was killed. He was up in the hills with his family when Victorio lose his life. He used to come over to our house and talk with Big Mouth."[23]

With some Mescaleros, Caje returned from Mexico by way of the Peñasco. Soldiers shot into their camp while they slept, and several women and children were wounded; Caje's wife took a bullet in the lower leg. Afoot, the men carried their wounded for miles up the Peñasco until they could catch horses. Caje was thereafter called Packs On His Back. (Eve Ball wrote that this happened in 1871 when Cushing attacked the camp.[24])

One small group of Mescaleros who stole away from Tres Castillos holed up in the Davis Mountains and made life dangerous for hapless travelers until Texas Rangers ambushed them in 1881. Nana became chief of the Warm Springs remnant, reinforced again by Mescaleros. At one point, they were believed to be camped near Mescalero, and Peso and Choneska, then scouts, tried unsuccessfully to find them.[25]

Mescaleros would drift back to the reservation and surrender until 1882.[26] Those who arrived first found their people held captive by U.S. soldiers. Although Natzili and other chiefs had tried to keep their young men at home, their reward in the spring of 1880 was to be brutally rounded up, disarmed, dismounted, and confined in a corral by soldiers who believed they were aiding Victorio.[27]

"Then they surround all the Mescaleros here," said Percy Big Mouth. "Some of the men go to the hills. They very nearly had a big fight up here where the road goes to the cemetery. The Mescaleros camped. Some stay way over. There were many Mescaleros down around Camp Horn in Texas, some at the Pecos and up around Amarillo. Then fighting was going on. They surrounded us and all the old men left. Right there the soldiers were coming—some of the cavalry at the hill by Blazer's and some on the hill where the Catholic Church is now and right here near the hospital and there was a bunch of cavalry. Then Indian scouts from Arizona, San Carlos, and Yumas, and even Maricopa scouts. And way up to Head Spring and Mescaleros up on the high point of the mountain. And the Indian scouts come and see the camp and shoot at them . . .

"One of the leaders say, 'Don't shoot!'

"'No, let's fight! We have a battle and they finish us right here. That what they want.'

"'No, here's the children and the women. We got no ammunition, just bow and arrow. What good we do? Let's give up.'

"And they march them to the agency ground. Some stay on the hill and never came back. Some over in the Rinconada and some over south don't know about it. They put them in prison here at Mescalero and keep them about a year. They don't want us to join them [Victorio]. Our chiefs told us not to join them: 'We must remain on our own reservation.' A few slip away from here and go with them. Some of the men and women follow Victorio. And they catch them way over by San Carlos."[28]

"Soldiers camped here above [what is now] the feast grounds, right across the canyon on that point they rounded up the Indians," said Sam Chino.

"There was no battle. Some tried to run away and were shot at to stop them and make them come back. But there was no battle. But they were corralled. It was there they were deprived of horses, guns, and ammunition they had. Their personal belongings were not taken."[29]

More than thirty warriors escaped. Some joined Victorio, others formed independent raiding parties, and still others headed for Texas.[30] The Lipans escaped into Mexico. Said Percy Big Mouth, "A long time 'til everything peaceful."[31]

Muchacho Negro (Black Boy)
Mezcalero Apache Chief.

Fig. 17. Muchacho Negro, a Mescalero warrior, rode with Victorio. (Courtesy Western History Collections, University of Oklahoma, Rose Collection, #883.)

TWENTY

The Battle of Round Mountain

In the lore of southern New Mexico, the battle of Round Mountain is always considered the turning point for Tularosa. To Mexican farmers, who settled here in 1861 for the good soil and available water, the battle saved their village. To the Mescalero Apaches, not only was the whole episode a misunderstanding, it wasn't even a good fight. "There was not much fighting—just a few Mexican volunteers from Tularosa," Percy Big Mouth said.[1]

On 27 April 1868, soldiers accompanying a wagonload of supplies from Fort Stanton to Fort Selden turned back five miles from Tularosa, believing that the wagon was out of danger. Ten miles from town near Round Mountain, a cone-shaped hill also called Dead Man's Hill, they met up with Mescaleros and a fight broke out. Five men took cover in an old fortification near the mountain while the sixth rode for help in Tularosa and returned with twenty-six men.

In the heat of the battle, one Apache jumped up on the wall, where he was promptly dispatched. During a lull, a teenaged boy stole down to the Tularosa River to get some badly needed water for the party. The Apaches saw him hurrying back to rejoin the Tularosans and thought he was the advance guard of reinforcements and retreated. The settlers believed they had saved their town and in gratitude built a church.[2]

Mescaleros remember the skirmish differently.

"Mescaleros were camped out in the Guadalupes," said Percy Big Mouth. "A young woman—this girl was the age of the ceremonial—talk her dream. It was going to be peace with our friends at Tularosa. Now the dream told her to go over there and make a big dinner and friendship and then everything will be peaceful for all. That was during the ceremonials. She told her father."[3]

A girl during her puberty rites was believed to have great power and vision. If a girl made a pronouncement in this time, the Apaches took it to heart.

"Next day they held a council: 'Make a big council with your friends who used to live at Doña Ana. They are building a town on the Tularosa. Make a peace treaty and it will last a long time. . . . You dance for them. We have a big feast and everything be all right.' That's what the medicine told them. They decide to go. They started, a bunch of them—women and children too—and they leave part of the women and children. . . . Then they fix up for the dance with headdresses . . .

"The Indians were going there walking and one fire a shot. . . . Two more guns go off and women [scream]. Three! They got scared. Four! They came running back. They did not have any arms. It was in September. Corn and pumpkins ripe. Harvest time. Then they come to Round Mountain. They met some more going down with a load of lumber, four or five wagonloads. I saw this bunch coming down and chasing them. They ran down in the creek. They just took some horses. They went down to Tularosa, got people and follow up. Then the people from Tularosa caught up with them and fight them.[4]

"There are trenches one-half mile from Round Mountain. . . . [The people from Tularosa fought from a protected position inside a trench.] They throw rocks and shoot arrows but can't tell if they hit anybody. One Indian got shot in the leg. He fell and they not see him. . . . They track him into the trench and kill him.[5]

"Henry Treas's father was Dah-eh-wol[6] [He Went Forward] and he got that name at the battle at Round Mountain," said Byron Treas. "This man took all the bullets—they didn't have many—and went out there and shot them at the Mexicans. Sixteen Mexicans were killed but no Apaches."[7]

Eric Tortilla said, "The Round Mountain fight, only two Indians were killed. Most of the fighting occurred because they did not understand each other. . . . Old Man Peso, I heard him tell a white man that only one Indian was killed; one Indian somehow was crawling right up that thing, very close range. . . . Peso was there in that fighting."[8]

Peso's son Alton also remembered his father's stories: "Of Round Mountain, he told us there was a deep, square trench. He was a boy then. That

Fig. 18. Mescalero Chief San Juan left the reservation to bring renegade warriors back from Victorio's campaign but instead stayed. (Ben Wittick, courtesy Museum of New Mexico, #15893.)

square was pretty deep. . . . I read a story about it, that ten Indians were killed, but my father told me that only one boy was killed and he was crazy. He ran right into that trench and he was the only one killed. The people in the wagon train were held in there and starved out. That was not much of a fight. They called it a skirmish. It did not amount to very much. He told them he did not call it a big fight."[9]

In fact, just one Indian was killed and one Tularosan wounded by an arrow through the wrist. One account says Cadette led some 200 Mescaleros in the conflict, but Cadette was probably far away. Another story credits San Juan.[10]

Fig. 19. Peso, shown here with his daughter, was one of Mescalero's last chiefs and an army scout. (Dana B. Chase, courtesy Museum of New Mexico, #14216.)

Peso would go on to become the last Mescalero chief. Son of chief San Juan and Nagoo-nah-go,[11] he was born in the Guadalupe Mountains, near present-day Carlsbad, and was a child when his people were sent to Fort Sumner.[12,13] As a boy Peso had ridden the Plains with Chief Natzili, who led an eastern band of Mescaleros. Their home country was in the area where the Army built Fort Stanton.

"He said he roamed around Fort Stanton when he was a boy. They used to stay there. On the flat they used to have horse races. They had target practice with the soldiers, too."[14]

Peso also joined Magoosh and his Lipan Apaches from time to time. "They used to roam around San Antonio," said Alton Peso. "It was just a little town with white buildings. They used to roam to the Gulf of Mexico and down into Mexico. The Lipans and Mescaleros are mixed but most of the time the Lipans were down toward Mexico City. My father and Magoosh used to be together a lot."[15]

Daughter May Peso Second explained his name: "Peso got his name because he took a lot of money away, much silver. And he dug in a ditch and put it there. And they gave him that name—Peso."[16]

Peso was an expert tracker and served as a scout for the Army during the Geronimo campaigns.[17] In the 1880s he was a respected tribal police captain.[18]

His daughter says he became chief at twenty-eight;[19] an agent's report for 1878 mentions Peso's band leaving the agency because of the Lincoln County War.[20] In the early 1900s he was one of a trio of primary leaders on the reservation—Magoosh, Peso, and Sans Peur (Without Fear).

"Magoosh was at Elk Springs; Sans Peur at Tule Canyon; Peso lived in Tule Canyon part time but represented Rinconada and the Three Rivers part of the country," said Paul Blazer.[21]

Peso had four children: May Peso Second, Katherine Sombrero (Mrs. Solon), Alton, and Bill. Peso also raised his nephew Big Mouth, who would become the last surviving scout.

Peso was probably about eighty when he died in 1929.[22]

TWENTY ONE

Billy the Kid

One clash between the acquisitive white interlopers taking over the Mescalero homeland was a chapter of the notorious Lincoln County War. That was the struggle for power between two rival merchants, John Tunstall and Lawrence Murphy and their respective partners, that flared in 1878. The feud should have ended with the murders and financial collapse that finished both mercantile houses, but their partisans carried on.

One of Tunstall's cowboys would gain notoriety at the pens of dozens of hack Western writers: Billy the Kid. Anglos regarded Billy as an outlaw, and Hispanics, as a friend. To the Apaches, however, he was another horse thief in the company of the Texas trash who menaced the reservation in that period, taking anything of value the Apaches had. "Everybody was afraid of him," recalled Carisso Gallerito, brother of chief Sans Peur.[1]

"At Fort Stanton Billy the Kid was making a raid on the Indians all the time for their horses," said Percy Big Mouth. "We made a big brush corral at Fort Stanton right near the fort. We got a brush corral and to protect us against Billy the Kid. One night they came over, tore all the brush down and got all our horses. The soldiers would go after Billy."[2]

Two incidents and three murders of the much-chronicled war took place on the Mescalero reservation. One was the battle at Blazer's Mill, on 4 April 1878. The second occurred on 5 August. Billy, with a party of some twenty

Regulators (Tunstall men), rode onto the reservation. While part of the group stopped at a spring, the rest continued toward the agency and, when they encountered Apaches, began firing. Agent Godfroy and his clerk, Morris J. Bernstein, were doling out rations but at the sound of gunfire, sprang to their mounts and rode out. Bernstein, in the lead, was shot down and Godfroy turned around and hurried back to the safety of the agency. The Regulators made off with all the horses and mules in the agency corral.[3]

Again, the recollection of eyewitnesses is different from existing accounts. Mescaleros say there were just three rustlers—Frank and George Coe and Billy.

Leroy and Darlene Enjady said during an interview, "My grandmother saw Billy the Kid and his gang ride down the road from the east and turn off there at the old trail near the spring. She went on to the trading post, which was about where the old post office stands now. There was a hill between them and the spring. A man came into the agency to report that the White Eyes were stealing the Apaches' cattle. Bernstein took a saddled horse at the hitch rack and rode over the hill. In a few minutes they heard the shots that killed him but it was a half hour or so before anybody went to investigate."[4]

"Dad was here when Billy the Kid's bunch killed Bernstein," Percy Big Mouth said. "This happened on Saturday when Billy's bunch came over from the North Fork and [some Mescaleros] were getting their rations and they saw a cloud of dust above the agency and knew somebody must be doing something. They told it to the office and the chief clerk said, 'I will tell them not to come. I will send them back.' He got his rifle.

"'Wait 'til we get our rations and let them alone.'

"'No, they will mind me.'

"'No, they outlaws. They will not listen.'

"Peso told the clerk to wait until they got their rations. Then they would send their women away and the men would go with him but Bernstein said he could handle them. So he rode up there and put himself just north of the present office just about 200 yards. The outlaws came up on the hill.

"'You go back.'

"'Who said so?'

"'I am saying so.'

"And they shot him right then. Some Indians got on their horses and rode around where the Catholic Church is now and got some horses away from the outlaws.

"The Indians said that when they killed that clerk two men jump off and search that fellow and took his gun and they got two of those horses."[5]

Another comment suggests that if Bernstein had been less impulsive, he might not have died. Bessie Big Rope recalled, "When Bernstein was killed the Indians were prepared to ambush the horse thieves."[6]

"In the minds of many people the killing of Bernstein was a sequel to the Roberts-Brewer fight," Eve Ball wrote in a note attached to a letter from Paul Blazer. While history remembers Bernstein as one more shooting among many of the Lincoln County War, the Apaches remember their own people who paid with their lives when Billy the Kid and his gang wanted their horses.

Percy Big Mouth said, "One hundred yards from the office these two went over a little hill. . . . Just over this side Eclode's mother was gathering her horses and hobbling them. Next morning she went after her horses again and the outlaws came down here gathering up horses, all they could find. This woman hobbled her horses and saw them up on a hill. Probably they wanted to take the horses but the woman got mad and tried to fight. And one of those outlaws shoot and killed her and take her horses.

"Same thing happen down Round Mountain right near Nogal Canyon. Billy's gang came and shoot the camp up. One woman still in the tipi. They see her shadow and shoot and kill the woman. They took her horses and left. And Crook Neck know about it too. One Saturday the horses [were] by the cemetery. This gang came and saw the horses. They cut the hobbles and drive them off. 'The broad hat people steal our horses and drive them away.' They mean Billy the Kid's gang."[7]

On 7 November, agent Godfroy asked his superiors if he could organize an Indian police force. Between the lingering Lincoln County War and other crime on the reservation, the Mescaleros were too frightened to stay near the agency and camped instead in small groups at a distance. They were particularly upset about the murder of Bernstein. "In the last council the Indians demanded that if they organized as police that they should be armed with Winchester rifles, which, of course I would not permit," he wrote.[8] The Mescaleros did ultimately get a police force but the fear of Billy lingered, even after he was gunned down by Pat Garrett.

Said Eric Tortilla, "I worked with Mexicans over here in a logging camp in 1920 who told me that Billy the Kid was still living."[9]

Part III.

The Apache Way

TWENTY TWO

The Apache General Store

Apaches were as resourceful as they were wily. Pursued by troops who couldn't function without wagonloads of provisions, Apaches—men, women, and children—could disappear like sprites and sustain themselves on desert or mountain. Exhausted, frustrated soldiers scanned a landscape they considered God-forsaken while the Apaches' God provided more than a hundred plants and a dozen animals they could use for food, drink, medicine, weapons, clothing, and tools. When pressed, they could endure days without food or water.

Apaches followed wild foods from place to place through the seasons. "These people knew nature's calendar by heart, and no matter whether a grass seed ripened or a certain animal's fur or flesh was at its best at the particular time, the Apache was present to share in the harvest."[1]

The best-documented food source was the cherished mescal, also known as agave or century plant (*Agave parryi*), collected in May and early June.

"They dried it and kept it. It was their staple food. It is a century plant," said Paul Blazer. "It is like a cabbage—a big globe above the ground. The body of the plant, they chop off the leaves. They cut the head off. The root is three or four inches and the head six to eighteen. A pit is [dug] three and one-half or four feet deep with lots of wood, rock, fire coals. They put green stuff on rocks and pile mescal in, cover with green and then cover it with soil. They would have a few of the long leaves stuck down where the heads were. They pulled these out to test the cooking. They would work the pulp out of the leaf and dry it. There would be a large center mass. It was cut into thin slices and dried. It would keep indefinitely."[2]

The green stuff was wet grass, probably bunchgrass (*Sporobolus airoides*), side-oats grama (*Bouteloua curtipendula*), Texan crabgrass (*Schedonardus paniculatus*), big blue stem (*Andropogon furcatus*), mesquite grass (*Muhlenbergia neomexicana*), or bear grass (*Nolina microcarpa*). They preferred bear grass because it doesn't burn easily.[3]

"There are three kinds of century plants that ripen one after another. A small one grows close here — they are not so good as the others. A middle-sized one is very good. Also the large kind," said James Kaywaykla.

"These things have much sugar; when baked they candy. They cut the leaves off and bake the cabbage underground, covered with wet grass. They heat the rocks red-hot and when that is burned down they dampen the grass and put it against the heads and cover it with dirt. They cook it two or three days. That was a great food for the Indians."[4]

The other two plants Kaywaykla referred to were probably sotol (*Dasylirion wheeleri*) and the narrow-leafed soapweed, or *palmilla* (*Yucca elata*). Both were prepared in the same fashion as mescal but weren't as tasty.[5] Chiricahuas also ate the fruit of the saguaro (*Carnegiea gigantea*)[6] and the prickly pear (*Opuntia*), both of which taste like figs when dried.[7]

The saguaro, said Asa Daklugie, "had fruit which we use. It has many thistles. Lots of them. You have to hunt it and take a long stick and hook a little piece away from the end of the stick. . . . It could be made dry like mescal and it could be carried as long as you have any left."[8]

They ate fruit of the barrel cactus. To remove the spines off the barrel cactus and prickly pear, they gathered "red-tasseled grass," probably sacaton grass (*Sporobolus wrightii*)[9] and bound it with sinew like a broom, put the fruit down and brushed the spines off.

"Got to be very careful to clean them thoroughly before eating them or get thorns in your mouth. Cholla has no fruit and we never bother it," Daklugie said.[10]

Tunas, or prickly pear fruit, were prepared by splitting the fruit lengthwise, seeding it and placing it on grass to dry, or mashing the fruit into pulp and storing it as cakes.[11]

"They knew that country [Mexico], where to get food and water," said Jasper Kanseah. "They been there before. They can locate every water hole. Had plenty deer and eat fruit — cactus fruit is good, *pitahaya* [organ-pipe cactus, or pitahaya dulce (*Lemaireocereus thurberi*)] is good to eat. They can live on that and wild bananas, mesquite beans, lots of walnuts too and the red fruit on the prickly pears. Wild honey. Acorn."[12]

Mesquite, which Apaches called "that which lies about," is one of the most ubiquitous plants in the Southwest. Apaches ground its sweet, nutritious bean into flour and made bread. They also cooked the beans with meat or boiled and then pounded them.

Apaches used all species of oak in the area. Typically acorns were eaten raw or roasted slightly, pounded, and mixed with dried meat or fat and stored in hide containers.[13]

"We lived mostly on meat but ate piñons and acorns ground on *metate* for dessert," said Dahteste.[14]

"Cracked the shells and got the acorns out, grind them into flour and make good food of it," said Daklugie. "Make like a dumpling and throw it into a kettle of hot water. Chop the meat and make a stew."[15]

Kaywaykla recalled that they used to find acorns at Ash Creek and in the mountains of Sonora. "And honey grows on trees and near the top of cliffs. They would shoot it loose and catch it." They also ate wild onions and cattail roots.[16]

Wild onions (*Allium cernuum* and *A. geyeri*) were eaten raw or used to flavor soups and gravy. Similarly, cattail roots (*Typha latifolia*), gathered in the spring, were cooked with meat.

Piñons (*Pinus scopulorum*) were a favorite food of the Apaches, as they were with other tribes. They ate the nuts raw or roasted and stored them. Sometimes they were combined with yucca fruit pulp in a pudding or were ground and rolled into balls.[17]

Eustace Fatty recalled, "They ate roots, berries, and piñon nuts, wild sweet potatoes grown out on the flats—they smell like sweet potatoes but taste different."[18]

The sweet potatoes were probably the Indian potato (*Hoffmanseggia densiflora*), a sweet but tough tuber eaten raw or cooked.[19]

Apaches depended more on acorns and mesquite than grass seed as a source of flour for bread. They gathered seed of wild grasses by holding a basket under the heads and striking the grass sharply.[20] Types of seed they used included drop seed (*Sporobolus cryptandrus*) and grapevine mesquite grass (*Panicum obtusum*).[21]

Apaches weren't farmers, but they did plant a little corn. Eve said, "They didn't cultivate it; they'd just plant it down in a damp place, right close to the bed of a stream. And they tried to get back there at roasting ear time. If the bears hadn't beat them to it, they'd have roasting ears. But not many of the ears would mature."[22]

Tiswin

Tiswin was an intoxicating brew the Apaches probably brought north from Mexico.

Dahteste described how it was made: "To make tiswin you grind corn fine on metate. Build a big fire, boil meal twenty minutes. Take it out, squeeze mash out good. Throw grounds away. Put in jar and let ferment with yeast twenty-four hours. It took much longer when we had no yeast."[23]

Eustace Fatty said, "My mother used to make tiswin. Shell the corn, put it in a can of water and let it soak well. Then get a gunnysack, pour the corn in and spread it out and put it under grass or heavy cover. Cover good and the warm water on it and it would sprout. Then get it out and grind it on the metate. Then boil water, put it in 'til the foam comes up and go back down. Take it out and squeeze it out with the hands and just use the juice. After that they put [it in] some kind of jugs. Then put some that in it, grind it first, then put it in and put some yeast in it. Then it black. Set it away. Next day it is all right. It tastes very much like beer. After a while it gets stronger."[24]

"It was not much stronger than water—took a lot to make you drunk. No use drinking it to get drunk," said Charlie Smith.[25]

Eve said once in an interview, "Anything you've read about these tiswin drunks, that's all hooey. That's what Father Albert told me, and nobody knew them any better than Father Albert did . . .

"They brought me tiswin two or three times. I wanted to know what it was like. I found that it's about like beer. Well, people can get drunk on beer. But it took an awful lot of tiswin to get drunk, and they didn't have it. That is what Father Albert told me. He said, 'I've gone out to dances out in the forest, when they'd have tiswin drunks, as they call it. Usually when they got drunk, it was because some white man was bootlegging bad liquor to 'em, and it wasn't a tiswin drunk. They just didn't have enough tiswin to get drunk on."[26]

Hunting

Apaches were choosy about their meat; there were as many animals they didn't consume as those they did. They would eat deer, antelope, elk, mountain sheep, opossum, and wood rats. The Mescaleros hunted buffalo. Cottontail rabbits were hunted but not jackrabbits. Creatures never or rarely eaten included bear, coyote, turkey, quail, dove, and fish.[27] They wouldn't eat a snake or hunt animals that ate snakes.

Enjady[28] was a Mescalero scout who hunted game for the cavalry. "They [the soldiers] were awful. They would eat bear and fish," said Leroy and Darlene Enjady. "You know the old Apaches wouldn't even eat turkey. They liked venison and mule meat. Well, my grandfather killed plenty of deer for the soldiers but he wouldn't kill a bear. If one tries to kill you, it is right to kill it in self-defense but not other way. I don't know what my grandfather's name was in Indian but the soldiers called him Great Hunter and so we say it in Apache. . . . My grandfather learned to eat bacon. You know we didn't eat pork either. I guess that was because the wild *javelinas* [boars] were so dangerous. They'd tree a man and keep him there 'til he starved or fell from the place and then they'd eat him."[29]

Deer were a staple and Apaches took males and females year round; they avoided shooting pregnant or nursing females unless in dire need.[30]

"When a man killed a deer he must divide with everybody, not just his family. After the meat is cut he takes a piece and takes it to his home but if it is cooked he eats it there. But nobody went hungry if anyone had food. There were lots of deer and antelope," said Daklugie.[31]

Deer hunting required more skill than any other kind of hunting. Hunters had to approach from downwind, sometimes crawling for hours while pushing a weed ahead for cover.[32] Frequently hunters wore masks and hides for more effective stalking and they avoided smoking tobacco or eating onions before a hunt. Some rubbed themselves with deer tallow or antelope musk. They hunted on an empty stomach and avoided thoughts of hunting or feelings of optimism because both alerted the game and offended the spirits.[33]

"In the old days they used a mask to stalk deer—put the head and skin over them and fed among the deer," said Percy Big Mouth. "That is too dangerous now. One time in the Sacramentos—out beyond, really in the Guadalupes—the Indians were camped and had only bows and arrows for hunting. One man killed a deer and was playing a joke. He held the deer horns in the bushes and moved them as though the animals were feeding. Another man shot him—just creased him across the stomach.

"'Hey, You shoot me!'

"'Well, it is your own fault. Anybody would shoot you.'"[34]

After their father's death, Daklugie and his brother got a pass and went hunting near the headwaters of the Black River.

"Each day we killed deer and almost every day we jerked it. Pounded it if we had time, put it in flour sacks. We would put the fat in another sack. When we wanted it cooked we put some fat in with it. But when we are in a hurry we eat it raw [as jerky]."[35]

Women normally didn't hunt with the men but when the opportunity presented itself, they were quick to act.

"My grandmother said the men were hunting and nobody there but the women and children and a deer wandered into the camp and everybody chased it," said Evelyn Gaines. "She outran the rest of the women, grabbed the deer by the neck, threw it to the ground and killed it. With a knife. She was very much like the sister of Victorio. She was Victorio's daughter."[36]

To harvest antelope on the plains, the Apaches rode horses in relays; one chased the antelope until his horse wore out and then another took over.

"They get those antelope so tired that they can be roped and butchered. They take the intestines out and then at the camp the women skin them and cut them into pieces to cook and to dry. They broiled or roasted meat—just brush out the coals and lay it in the middle. When it is done they turn the other side. Can cook a big piece of meat in a half hour or forty-five minutes."[37]

After contact with whites, Apaches ate horses and beef and were particularly fond of mule meat.

"Sometimes have the beef already cooked and tied to the saddle. Eat as we ride. That's the way we travel."[38]

Always on the move, preservation of meat was important.

"The meat was pounded enough to smooth it down so it would pack well but it was not pulverized," said Kaywaykla. "When they got ready to eat, it was pounded to bits and made it something like meal. They mixed it with fat and if they dared build a fire, cooked it. If not, it was eaten raw."[39]

"They like horse and mule meat. [Gordo] and Old Man Peso used to go back in the Rinconada and kill wild horses and dry the meat and pound it up, put grease in it, and it was good. It is not good when it is fresh but after it is dry it is good and very strengthening," said Eustace Fatty.[40]

Mescaleros and their Lipan cousins hunted buffalo, but so too did other Apache bands, including the Warm Springs and Nednhi. To kill a buffalo with a bow and arrow, they aimed near the kidneys.[41]

Said George Martine, "From San Carlos and Ojo Caliente they went to the Pecos sometimes, even as far as Roswell. They camped and laid in a supply of meat and hides."[42]

In the late 1870s the Apaches, like other Plains groups returned in horror to their once abundant hunting grounds.

"When they were camping in the Guadalupes they used to go on the buffalo hunts across the Pecos and they could not find any buffalo," said Percy Big Mouth. "Further up a whole herd and hunters kill them . . . and did not use buffalo meat either, just cut tongue or hump and take skin. It make the Indian pretty sad. Soon they all gone. Then next time they went on a hunt they found very few alive. Then the wagons way over there and a pile of white bones and they haul it away. 'What those people do?' They sneak around in the mesquite and gather all the bones. The last time they went over there even the bones most all gone.

"They are loco. [Indians] just kill what they need for food. When they wanted a tipi they kill enough to make tipi, maybe twelve or fourteen hides. The Indians wanted to save the game for next year. And they used the meat—jerked what they could not eat.

"When the big herds came from the north—thousands, like water flowing down the hills—we camped when it was time for the buffalo to go to the south. They just beautiful—look like dark flood. They came as far west as Carrizozo, to the malpais [volcanic badlands near the Mescalero reservation] but not every year, just once in a while. They crossed the Pecos near Artesia [New Mexico]. That was a good hunting place. We would make a robe. Buffalo skins tan easily. They had a tender skin, not like beef. We would tan it like buckskin with the hair on."[43]

Game disappeared in a similar fashion.

"One time they were going up the Pecos to hunt buffalo—my dad, his uncles, Ishpiye and Eclode. They see a band of Tonkawas—scouts—come over here and tell Mescaleros not to go down toward San Antonio. 'Soldiers kill all the game and they kill [you] if you go. They think you are raiding and they sure get you.' And they never did. A Lipan scout, Dah-nos-ti, was with the Tonkawas so they never went there any more."[44]

As game became scarce, raiding increased by necessity.

"When game all killed, how we going to live? We have to have meat. The Mexicans got many cattle—not so good as deer, but still, it is meat," said Jasper Kanseah.[45]

"We are at war because our land taken from us by forces and compelled to be shift to places against our will," said James Kaywaykla in a letter. "So what can we do but making raid on whom we can, Mexicans, Americans, Indians, they are all our enemy."[46]

Cooking Tools

The mobile Apache kitchen was nothing if not efficient. Because their way of life didn't encourage pottery making or transport, Apaches had only crude clay cooking pots, but they ingeniously fashioned a heavy rounded base that would right itself if tilted. These were usually cached in caves with supplies of food, skins, and fabric.[47]

"It was just when they were in a permanent camp that they have the cooking pots," said Daklugie. "When moving they used the baskets coated with gum."[48]

"Water jugs holding from six quarts to two gallons were tightly woven of willow," Eve wrote in a manuscript. They had openings about three inches in diameter with a flaring rim. To prevent leakage they were plastered inside and out with piñon gum. If it scaled off, it could be replaced with another coating."[49]

"I think water never tasted so good as from those jugs," said Kaywaykla.[50]

"My people did not use pottery, for it broke too easily. They had hot stones in one of those [basket] jars and shake it back and forth and melt the piñon so it stick to the inside," said Daklugie. "It lay for a few days and then they fill it full of water and leave it. In a few days it take the taste of the gum from the inside so that water can be carried in it. It can be hung on the back of the saddle; tie it on. And they plugged the middle with grass or weed. I never saw them use the intestines of an animal for carrying water—always the jar."[51]

"They used to carry water in the intestines of cattle. They washed them and they did not taste bad," said Eustace Fatty.[52]

For food harvest and storage, they used large baskets. Eve wrote in an unpublished manuscript: "Because they were trading baskets, Apache women decorated their baskets beautifully. Split yucca strands usually formed the background. Designs were created from long leaves of other plants, usually shading in color from cream to dark brown.

"Very important was the medicine basket. It was shaped like a shallow bowl and was tightly woven with designs in the sloping sides. Without the medicine basket the opening rite of the annual Puberty Ceremonials cannot be performed. So scarce were these baskets that for several years Lizzie Comanche, wife of one medicine man and mother of another, borrowed mine . . .

"The medicine basket was used also in the primitive wedding ceremony. It was filled with a dish of very thick mush, the surface of which was divided into four parts. Each person took a small pinch from each of the four sections. This rite had not been observed on the reservation for sixty-five years until Bernard Second and Eileen Gaines were married several years ago. They shortened the rites from four days to four hours. Again my medicine basket was used."

The most important tool was the fire stick, which every Apache carried.

"There is plenty fire and the Indians used to make a split half stick and cut notches and have one in their hands and roll stick in their hands and put

Fig. 20. Tanning was women's work. (Courtesy Arizona Historical Society, Tucson, #26250.)

bark in that hole and the wearing away of the stick make fire. . . . I can make a fire with a drill," said an unidentified speaker. "My people did it when I was a boy. It take maybe ten or fifteen minutes but it make a fire. It was much quicker with flint. They strike it on a knife. They have wild dry grass. You keep that dead grass down in hole so when everything wet you can still make a fire . . .

"Sotol is the plant for a fire. You split that and get a piece of it and cut your notches. And take the stake and whirl it fast and it will begin to smoke and then keep on. Then get it on the dead grass and you get a fire. I learn it from the old people. And you can bring the fire back and you keep your stick and carry it with you and you got something that will help you."[53]

Tanning and Decoration

Like other tribes, Apaches used everything.

"They used to make rattles of deer hoofs. They boil them and dry them and make a hole in them," said Darlene Enjady. "Leroy can make those rattles. He'll make you some."[54]

Tanning was one the most important camp chores for women and was practiced well into this century.

"To tan hides you soak the hide two or three days, scrape hair off with the rib of a cow or horse, put it on pole and scrape down," said Dahteste. "Stretch and dry on ground. Protect from insects. Soak again and stretch. Maude Geronimo tans buckskin."[55]

"To tan a hide, don't lay it away too long," said Daklugie. "I can peel a deer hide in about forty-five minutes. If you want buckskin you first remove the hair. Then you stretch it and peg it out on the ground. You put the brains on both sides. . . . And then you soak it about two days and then use a stick for small pieces and rinse the hide. Put it around a post or tree and twist to get it dry as you can. Then you work and stretch it back and forth and get all the water out of it. Then step on it and pull it with your hands. Without the brains it will dry just like a piece of tin. But the brains make it soft. You draw it through your clenched hand. Pick it up and shoot the water out and if you tend to it, it won't beat you to being dry. You always working to tan hides. If you let the air come and dry it you have to put it back twice. You have to watch it very carefully. Lots of work to tanning buckskin. Ramona was very skillful in tanning buckskin. Always I helped her do the work and we always had buckskin whenever she wanted it."[56]

Bone beads were once commonly used by Mescaleros for decoration.[57]

"Before they obtained commercially made ones, the Apaches, as did other tribes, made beads from shell and bone," wrote Eve. "Hand-drilled strands of beads are rarely seen today. I have one I bought from Maude Geronimo, daughter-in-law of Old Geronimo. In the center front there is a large chunk of turquoise and at about inch intervals on either side, smaller ones graduated in smaller sizes toward the clasp.

"Paul Blazer, whose grandfather owned the famous mill of his name, told me that fifty years ago one seldom saw an Apache woman or child who was not chewing. . . . They were softening sinew for sewing beads or buckskin."[58]

Saddles

Sometimes Apaches could appropriate saddles from the Cavalry, but mostly they did without or crafted their own.

"Much of the time they had no saddle. . . . They had nothing but a piece of rope tied around the lower jaw," said Kanseah.[59]

"Not everybody had a saddle," said Daklugie. "Most of them were made of rawhide. They made a frame of wood tied together with buckskin cut like a belt to hold it together. And we [made] a saddle horn of flat wood. They cut a piece of oak that they find [from] a tree easier to cut—sycamore or cottonwood. It is softer to cut and much faster than oak. When the frame is finished, they take rawhide, which has been soaked in water, and they cover the frame. Some have a hook in front—a little hard limb cut off. On this they can hang water jug, gun, or bundles . . .

"We had nothing but an ax and a . . . knife to work with and our knives were just straight knives, much like butcher knives. And they could do nice work with them."[60]

Tobacco

Kanseah and Kaywaykla said, "A long time ago the Indians had no tobacco. They used very dry oak leaves for cigarette papers. They also used corn-husks. For the tobacco they used a plant called *nato insay* [big tobacco]. . . . The Apaches did not smoke the peace pipe nor use the sign language. They smoked when they made medicine. They would say a few words of prayer and blow the smoke upward."[61]

"I never see any Apache smoke a pipe. They use a stick out of cactus. They shave that off and use it for cigarette paper. And they use oak leaves too," said Eugene Chihuahua.[62]

"They use it for a peace council," said Percy Big Mouth. "Not like the Comanches who used big pipes. They use corn shucks and made cigarettes of sotol leaves—it made a good cigarette paper. They used oak leaves too."[63]

TWENTY THREE

The Apache Pharmacy

Army doctors were always surprised at what a healthy, vigorous group Apaches were.

"My people lived out of doors and wore little clothing, got fresh air. They had no bad colds, no pneumonia, no disease bug viruelas *[smallpox]," said Christian Naiche. "They didn't use sugar and flour at that time—mostly wild fruit, mescal and mesquite beans, venison, of course. Beef too."*[1]

But they did get occasional ailments, and obviously warlike people had wounds to treat. In the Apache pharmacy were a variety of cacti, herbs, and even clays with healing properties, almost always used in combination with prayer.

"Our medicine men had healing herbs, but without the prayers and the faith in Ussen they were not effective," said James Kaywaykla.[2]

One handy ingredient was the prickly pear (Opuntia), which was used for wounds and even for therapeutic bloodletting.[3]

"My father used prickly pears—burn the stickers off, bite it in two and bind it over the wound," said Christian Naiche. "It will take the soreness out of a wound."[4]

"Enjady had a wound in his neck and breathed through it," said Solon Sombrero. "They used prickly pear poultices on it to heal so that he breathed through his nose."[5]

Said Asa Daklugie, "Prickly pear—cook the leaves and use for poultice. Athletes foot can be cured by it. Mr. Peña cooked and made a poultice and cured me of it."[6]

This raises one question about Eve's references to Apache medicine. In *Victorio* and *Indeh*, she has her subjects applying a raw, split prickly pear so often that I began to think of it as the Apache Band-Aid. I found only one observation of this use of prickly pears among her sources, but located a number of references to herbs and poultices for the treatment of wounds. Herbalists describe Indian use both ways—peeled raw and bound on wounds or pulp scraped from the roasted plant and used as a poultice. They would also chew the pulp to make a poultice.[7]

"There is another Indian medicine too, a root—the *o-chin-ah*, not a cactus, different," said Christian Naiche. "It is smooth and clean. You chew the root or grind it and use it but you put it on a sore and it will heal it. It grow right here on the reservation [Mescalero]. . . . And it is good. They used it for any sore."[8]

This plant was likely one the Mescaleros called *i-ze ho-chi-ne*, or "black medicine." San Carlos Apaches pounded and dried the root; Mescaleros ground the root, mixed it with water and applied it to the injury. They were also known to eat small quantities. This could either be arrow-leafed balsam root (*Balsamorhiza sagittata*) or deltoid balsam root (*Balsamorhiza deltoidea*).[9]

"I got shot in 1938," said Eustace Fatty. "Bunch of boys drunk. I had a gun. They jerked it from my scabbard . . . and shot me through the hand and another shot through the leg. . . . My father came over and gave me an herb. He got it in a buckskin bag. He broke it in four pieces and put them in my mouth and he was praying. I was suffering. Pretty soon it got cool. In an hour I could feel that burn going down slowly. . . . [The medicine is called *i-za-ho-ge*.] He put that in my mouth and he was singing a little song. My father used to know it pretty good. It cured lots of people."[10]

Besides black medicine, the Mescaleros had a number of plants they used to treat wounds. One was *i-zebi-ne*, or night-blooming cereus (*Cereus greggii*). The dried and powdered root was applied to wounds and sores. The Mescaleros and Lipans used sagebrush (*Artemisia dracunculoides*), or *i-ia-ai*, by pounding fresh or dried roots, mixing with cold water and applying to bruises, contusions, and fractures. This remedy kept the injured part cool and prevented swelling.[11] For sores and small wounds, San Carlos Apaches applied the cottony part of the brownfoot root (*Perezia wrightii*), called *me-tci-da-il-tco*. Chiricahuas also held the latter, which they called "narrow medicine," in high regard for use in a ceremony against tuberculosis.[12]

Apaches did not use peyote for its hallucinogenic properties (they were exposed to the peyote cult in Oklahoma but disapproved), but rather for pain relief. Daklugie said, "They used peyote. This cactus would kill the pain. We used this cactus for medicine."[13] Tribes of Arizona and northern Mexico were all known to use peyote to treat pain by chewing the root and applying the poultice to fractures, wounds, and snakebites.[14]

Medicines were also taken by inhalation.

"My grandmother was a good medicine woman," said Eustace Fatty. During the winter one time people sickened and died quickly. "And finally they brought up some kind of strong weed like sage. They stand in the smoke and got over it. Put blanket over smoke and they got alright."[15]

One plant that was used in this way was silver sage, also called wormwood (*Artemisia frigida*). Mescaleros called it *chin-de i-ze*, or "devil's medicine," and put some of the root on a fire and inhaled it.[16] Chiricahuas often used the smoke of burning juniper and piñon boughs to ward off disease.[17]

Apaches, like other Indian people, had a number of cures for arthritis.

"And our people went to the Sacramentos to get medicine," said Woodrow Wilson, a Mescalero medicine man. "A little herb there is good medicine: *saw zha*. It cures arthritis or injuries but you don't boil it, just chew it. . . . I have herbs that bring sleep when people suffer and need rest. You saw what they did. They cause the patient to sweat and he wakes up feeling much better. This medicine grows along the river and it is better fresh and green but is also good dried. That's what we call panther foot. It is strong but it will help you every way, for when you get sleep and rest, you improve."[18]

Wilson's arthritis cure might have been a plant Mescaleros called *ce-xa-ne sa-iu*, or "grows through the rocks" (Latin name unknown). It was used in the form of a decoction or rubbed into sore joints. The San Carlos Apaches used a plant they called *chil-check*, or chaparral (*Covillea tridentata*), which was common along the Gila River. They heated the tops over fire and applied a dry poultice directly to the affected part. In fact, Southwestern tribes commonly used members of the same family (greasewood, creosote bush, and chaparral) for everything from arthritis to bruises.[19]

In high elevations they collected osha root (*Ligusticum porteri*). Apaches called it *ha-chi-de* or *hai-chi-di*. Its odor was so strong men couldn't chew it before hunting. They mixed it with water and rubbed it on the forehead for headaches.[20] The Mescaleros drank a tea for colds and cough. They also ground it, mixed it with water, and rubbed it on sore parts. Sometimes they chewed the root for cough, or inhaled, chewed, or smoked it for headaches.[21]

Apaches were also known to put mud on wounds to draw out poisons and use cobwebs as gauze to soak up blood.[22]

"When I was a little boy I was out in the wilderness with my father and mother and the chief [Mangus]," said Eugene Chihuahua. "I had sores on my body from a vine. And they carried me on a stretcher—they carried me across a canyon. They went along a ditch and I say, 'Throw me in that ditch.' Mangus scolded me and said, 'Don't talk that way, my nephew.' Someone applied white clay from a spring. 'They paint you all over with that white clay. When it dries, the sore and itch come away with it.'"[23]

Fig. 21.   Geronimo was a medicine man whose powers were legendary among his people. Wearing a medicine hat, he's shown here in 1897. (Courtesy Western Collections, University of Oklahoma, Rose Collection, #860.)

TWENTY FOUR

Medicine Men and Women

Medicine men and women could treat wounds and heal the sick, but they were more than just healers—they had Power. Apaches were reluctant to define Power, but anthropologists have described it as a force that pervades the universe. In their youth, men and women could gain access to Power through some medium, such as an animal or plant during a four-day fast on the sacred mountain.

"Four days and nights the seeker goes without food or water and prays to Ussen for a sign that shall thereafter be to him a symbol of God's acceptance of him," Eve wrote. "And it may be in the form of an animal, a bird, a tree, a bit of quartz, the cone of a tree, etc. If it appears to him during his lonely fast, it becomes his medicine. He places a bit of it in a small buckskin bag and wears it beneath his shirt.

"If it is an animal, he has a bit of its fur, or a claw, tooth, etc. And he attains a Power over that particular animal. . . . Other medicine men had the Power over a certain illness, usually over only one . . ."[1]

Eugene Chihuahua said his father had Power over horses: "When anybody get hurt by a horse my father do things, work on him," said Eugene Chihuahua. "I never saw anybody can handle horses as well as my father did. And when horse get sick or snake bit or hurt they bring it to him to cure. And he does cure lots of them but not all. When one gets bitten by a rattlesnake, no medicine seems strong enough."[2]

Besides the expected treatments and prayers, many medicine men were credited with miraculous deeds. Eustace Fatty describes one: "There was a big medicine man. Nothing could see him. Even [when] he is right in front of the army, they could not see him. He just like light. This medicine man cook the meat off the striped cat . . . and he could kill the white man with the sword quick as lightning. This meat made him strong and fast. They could lie on the ground and nobody know they were here until they jump up right in their faces. . . . They never turn back, not this kind of people."[3]

Among his people, Geronimo's feats became larger than life.

"Tissnolthos was a very reliable man," said Dan Nicholas. "He told me that they were in a [unreadable] and could not move without being seen by the cavalry. Tissnolthos said that Geronimo went through some kind of ceremony and ritual and the soldiers were gone. When they went by the Indians saw a drove of cattle passing.

"Geronimo: 'Alright, you look the other way, not at the soldiers. Look the opposite direction.'

"When Geronimo talked . . . they turned around and could see nothing but a bunch of cattle passing."[4]

"When they were after him they could not find him," said Daklugie. "Maybe he is there but they don't see him. That's the way he goes. And he sings for his people who were sick and made them well too. . . . Geronimo's medicine tells him what is going to happen before it does. It tells him to move out—troops coming. If somebody say that to you, you got to roll up your bed and hit for a high hill or somewhere that you can't be seen. He could foretell things and it happened just like he said. And my father [Juh] too could do that. That's why he was hard to get."[5]

"He could make a white man get out of the way by his medicine," said Eustace Fatty. "Sometimes people coming after him and a big rain would start. That's the way Geronimo did it. When he took his people out, his power would start a rain or send a storm or something like that. The soldiers thought they could not hit him with a bullet."[6]

"He said as long as the sun shone nobody going to kill him. . . . I heard this, . . . he can talk to the moon. He can make them stand still and we can find our way where we want to. And he won't be killed. And he was not."[7]

Apaches also believed that Power could be abused, and they believed in witches.

"I know these fellows gone crazy," said Daklugie. "I met one in Mexico who was living in the willows. He cut some and made a wigwam on top of the mountain where he stayed [at night and left during the day]. I saw him. He came to us right in our midst and cried and said, 'I am glad to see you.' [He said] he used to have a good time and talk when he wanted but he can't do it now. 'Somebody have the charge of me and tells me to come over here a little while and I can't help myself. I got to stay. I don't want to go but they put me there and tell me to go on.' He thought somebody had the Power over him."[8]

An old medicine woman who stayed with Kaywaykla's family in Oklahoma told a story about the Guadalupe Mountains.

"There was a party went down there with a woman and [she] told them she wanted to go into a cave and the rest were to wait a while," said James Kaywaykla. "She went in. The rest were to stay about a half-mile away. They waited a long time for her to come back and when she came back she brought a little lamb. When she went she had nothing. She told the Indians that it was given to her in the mountains. She became a medicine woman. . . . It is always strange, things that are told about that mountain."[9]

Sam Kenoi tells of another medicine man:

"There is a story of a medicine man by the name Ha-tan-e-ged-eh way back many years ago, got some real Power that he talk with One from above. All Apaches know of him—Chiricahuas. I have heard their stories ever since I can remember. It has been told for generations . . .

"[He] was one of the greatest medicine men that ever lived. . . . He had about twelve [grown] sons and one wife. . . . And he had a little bag handed down to him. This bag was from Above but nobody see who give it to him. And in that little bag he carried with him was an Army sword and with it . . . the book, and he told the stories just like that from the old people. . . . He told his wife, 'When I die don't throw this book away. Don't burn it. Keep this saber and keep this book and you shall be increased in population and nobody going to hurt you. . . . Give my book to my oldest son and when he die to the next one . . . '

"The medicine man was allowed to ride a paint horse. . . . And the Apaches were so plentiful—keep increasing everywhere—and the Indians all look upon him and mind him.

"One time he went out hunting. . . . He happened to be close to the border. Lots of Indians mixed up with Mexicans." The Mexicans went to their camp and captured the medicine man's family and took them to a Mexican jail. When he returned his gun and horses were also missing. He trailed the group.

"He rode right in and inquire for his family. They say, 'Big office over there—that's the place to find her.'

"He went over there . . . and say, 'Where's my family?'

"Officers not there. They call and say, 'They in jail over here.'

"In a nice way he say, 'Give those folks to me.'

"Now, course, in those days the Mexicans began asking who he was. He had fought against Mexicans and he tell them who he is—a man who never run away. It don't make any difference how many coming, he not run. "'Oh yes, we hear about him. He pretty bad man. What going to do if we don't give your family back?'" There was a big chair in the room. Soon all the chairs were spinning around.

"'All right. We see. Make the chairs stop.'

"'Get my family and big horse and lots of food.'" The Mexicans complied.

In another version of the story the Mexicans had him in jail with many guards. He was lying down and saying little. The Mexicans told him he could never get out. "In the morning all the doors were open and all the guards sleeping and he was sitting outside. He don't run away. And those doors all open, [the guards] all asleep, and how he do it I don't know. The Mexican officers took him to his family and supplied them with several days' food."[10]

And what are we to make of this recollection from Eugene Chihuahua? I found nothing similar in other accounts or in references, but have included it for readers' interest.

"It was up on that high flat mountain where Juh lived that I first saw one of the little people. I thought at first that he was another child about two or three years old and that he might be lost from his mother but when I got close I saw that he was a grown man, not a child. I told nobody but Daklugie and he explained. There are little people living in the forest and they sometimes come around the outskirts of a ranchería [village] but never inside. They are not ghosts nor witches but just small people who never die. And they mean good to the Apaches."[11]

Christianity

Some Apaches, like Naiche, became converts to Christianity; others, like Daklugie and Geronimo never abandoned their traditions. Many covered their bases by attending church and still maintaining Apache tradition, a source of conflict at times.

"Jasper [Kanseah] never accepted Christianity—believed implicitly in the old Indian religion," Eve wrote. "He said Ussen [God] spoke to him—that he heard his voice clearly, just as he did that of people about him."[12]

"Eugene is a member of the Dutch Reformed Church; and when Daklugie's wife [Eugene's sister] died, he was so torn between his belief in the old tribal remedies and the teachings of the church that he wept in agony, fearing to use the rites of his people in his sister's behalf. Of late he is off with the church, and using the old Power."[13]

Sam Kenoi described his religious inclinations as "fifty–fifty." He was a member of the Dutch Reformed Church. "I go [to] my mountains, pray to God direct. And I also believe in the Indian religion. The younger generation—you can't tell them anything. They don't care anything about their own religion and will go the white man's way foolishly."[14]

"Chihuahua became a member of the Reformed Church, but Daklugie never accepted the concepts of any church," Eve wrote. "He once said, 'I never could understand what White Eyes believe about your queer three-headed God. Father and son, yes. We have them too, but what is this Holy Ghost? . . . '

"Of those I knew well enough to get an honest expression of religious ideas, those who never accepted Christianity were the best sources. Those who had, seemed ashamed to admit that they had ever believed in their primitive religion. However, in times of crises, death and other tragedies, they reverted to it."[15]

Missionaries

"Why were the missionaries disliked? Some of them were kind to us, some were not, and we thought they tried to force us to stop having our religious dances," said Amelia Naiche. "We knew they did. They told us not to attend them. Some of them still do. They thought that the Puberty Ceremonial for the maidens is a pagan rite and that it should not be observed. One minister ordered the members of the Reformed Church not to attend nor to permit their daughters to participate. Did we obey? Certainly not."[16]

Daklugie said, "The missionaries may not have openly opposed observance of the Puberty Ceremonial and rites for healing. They protested against their being observed by attributing sickness and pneumonia to exposure and cold during the night."[17]

Frank Love, minister of the Reformed Church said, "I had orders to erect a huge tent and conduct a revival service during the four-day Ceremonials. The tent was very expensive. The church sent an evangelist, and a soloist led the singing. Only one night did anybody attend. That was one very feeble old lady. What am I going to do this summer during the Ceremonials? Take my vacation."[18] Love, a member of the Omaha tribe, later came to question his service in the ministry and resigned to work in a social center for Indians.

Generations

Woodrow Wilson was a Mescalero medicine man. He was the son of a famed medicine man, Elmer Wilson, whose Apache name was Bal-i-go.

Elmer married Say-a-no-tish (Nina Treas) and their daughter was Eloise Shield. Elmer Wilson was the first medicine man Eve met, introduced by Eloise, and she called him "a dedicated and conscientious man."

"This is what my grandmother told me: [Elmer Wilson] was the greatest medicine man. . . . Elmer Wilson was very religious. His father gave Elmer all of his Power. That was before he married my mother," said Eloise Shield. Wilson was interested in wind Power and the Power to save people from winds. "He knew all the songs and would help everybody. But after he got blind he had to give up Power . . .

"Elmer went to Florida with them [Chiricahuas] and went back to Fort Sill too. Elmer was an interpreter. . . . [At Fort Sill he was also a guard.] He was gone with his mother's folks. When he came back his father was very old and his mother was blind . . .

"His father was a Lipan and they had a little Spanish blood too. Elmer could read, write, and speak Spanish."[19]

Elmer's sister Amelia married Choneska, a Chiricahua medicine man, and their son was José Second, whose son was medicine man Bernard Second. "Elmer and Amelia raised Bernard. . . . Bernard learned his medicine from my father. He used to live with him after he [Elmer] got blind."[20]

The position of medicine man isn't hereditary but "often occurs in families. It depends largely upon the boy's experiences when he undergoes the four days spent on the sacred mountain fasting and praying.

"The young medicine man, Bernard Second, made his own tribal costume. The headdress is of tanned beaver skin with fur left on, rimless and shaped similarly to our pillbox hat. His moccasins are ankle length and completely covered with beads. The background is turquoise blue and a sort of insignia for the Mescaleros. His breech clout is eight feet long and eight inches wide and completely covered with beads. Bernard's is, however, not made of buckskin but of felt."[21]

When Bernard married his wife Eileen it was the first traditional Apache wedding in seventy-five years, held in a remote canyon with just three white people present, one of them Eve Ball. It was four hours instead of four days, followed by Anglo rites performed by a justice of the peace, a dinner, and a dance.[22]

Weapons and Warfare

"The Indians say the Lord gave the Indians bows and arrows but to the White Eyes he gave a shovel."[1]

Consummate warriors, Apaches were deadly with their traditional weapons— the bow and arrow, knife, slingshot, and lance. (Apaches never used a hatchet.) When the opportunity presented itself, they lost no time adopting new materials and later, new weapons.

The wooden bow was both weapon and work of art, strengthened with layers of carefully layered sinew.

"Our local wood is used for bows," said Percy Big Mouth. "Oak is good at first but does not last long. It does not hold up in shooting. The best wood is the wild mulberry that grows east of the Pajarito and in the malpais [volcanic badlands near the Mescalero reservation]. It makes a good bow that lasts. Locust is strong, so is bow d'arc but we do not have it here. They use the sinew of a beef or deer. . . . The sinew comes from the tenderloin or sirloin, parallel the backbone. The arrow also is wrapped with sinew.

"The long bow is spliced—lapped and pinned together and the splice covered with leather. . . . The bow string would surely sting the wrist so they made bow guards of leather, used rawhide. Really old-timers made a small groove to give it a straight go."[2]

"My father made arrows. . . . He used mountain ash for the bow," said Eustace Fatty. "It is not easily broken. The arrow, a brush that grows on the plain, small like cedar but is bigger. Must be straight stick."[3]

"Magoosh [a Lipan Apache chief] always chewed sinew for bows and arrows," said Paul Blazer. "After chewing, it can be soaked and made soft. Saliva seems to condition it. They would put feathers on the arrows and never tie it. It would then stick and never come loose. The Indian children went around with a mouth full of sinew. I have a bow forty years old that is still good. It was a glue as well as a binder; if put on smoothly and evenly it dries almost transparent. The grain of the wood could be seen through the sinew."[4]

Arrows were made of wild chokecherry and sometimes Apache prune.[5] More than a yard long, their points could be stone, bone, or iron. Charlie Smith said his people made points from barrel hoops and would ambush a wagon train for weapons and hoops.[6]

"They used some kind of hard rock. It breaks out like a knife-flint." said Eustace Fatty. "They used it for arrows and spears, but they got tin cans and still finally, they got the knife."[7]

Eugene Chihuahua said, "Echos[8] was one of my father's warriors and a brave man. . . . He taught me many songs for the Dance of the Mountain Spirits. . . . He would come to our camp to work on arrows. He had a name for me and would call for me to come and hold a feather while he scraped it with a knife to make it fine."[9]

The lance was fifteen feet long. A warrior charged his enemy holding his lance above his head with both hands and directing his horse with his knees.[10] And the slingshot could do considerable damage. Kaywaykla recalls early training when the Warm Springs band was corralled on the San Carlos Reservation.

"In the mornings the boys went out for the horses and either the San Carlos or the White Mountain boys would attack our boys. Each side would have a group and they would have battles. The boys always carried their slingshots no matter where they were. If only one or two went and were attacked, somebody went for reinforcements. Sometimes even the men took part. And they meant to hurt one another. It was no play but our training for battle, but very seldom was anybody seriously hurt. We learned to throw straight and we also learned to dodge stones thrown at us. It was a very necessary part of our education. It trained us for defense in case of attack. You would be surprised how good a weapon a slingshot can be."[11]

"When I was a little boy my cousin told me to get out of the way," said Eugene Chihuahua. "He threw a rock at a squirrel in a tree. This was at Fort Apache. . . . He threw the rock with an Indian sling[shot] and the rock busted. A piece hit me above my eye and knocked me [out?] and almost killed me.

"An Indian named Motzos, Owl's Feather, he made medicine for me. He was a big medicine man. He knew what herbs to use and what songs to sing and what prayers to say. I don't see how I lived but I did. We just told big lies to my folks, for my father [Chief Chihuahua] would whip me if he knew it. He tried to get me to tell him how I got hurt and I told him I fell and bumped my head on a rock. So we all got out of it. I don't know if he believed it or not."[12]

Jasper Kanseah, Geronimo's nephew and his youngest warrior, rode with the Chiricahuas from the time he was thirteen. He describes how Apaches entered the Iron Age:

"At first we don't have anything but bow and arrow and slingshots. And a long pole with a knife on end. No gun at all. Steal a horse. Ride one horse down and then get another. . . . When the Indians go to Fort Thomas they make a knife out of a stone. After they kill some Mexicans they get knives and guns." In a Mexican house "you can find metal of some kind to make a knife. Pretty hard to make a knife. . . . We don't like to steal. That's the only way to get anything then."[13]

In hunting and in combat with the Americans, Apaches soon learned the limits of their weapons. "If the bow was strong enough you can kill an animal at one hundred yards, maybe one hundred and fifty if the bow is good," Daklugie said.[14]

"For a short distance they could fight well but not over a hundred yards," said Percy Big Mouth. "They could shoot three hundred yards but not accurately much over a hundred. I make bows and arrows and know how they can be used."[15]

And yet, under certain conditions, the bow and arrow had its place. John Cremony observed that even though Apaches might have guns, they were never without bows and arrows, which were silent, light, and reliable.[16]

Although Betzinez said Apaches didn't use bows and lances much after 1882,[17] personal observations indicate they never lost their fondness for the bow and arrow—or their touch. Many Apaches remember a relative making them well into this century.

Once at Fort Sill there was a contest between a soldier with a gun and an Apache with a bow and arrow.

"This soldier doesn't believe in this arrow shooting," said Eustace Fatty. "And they went out there to see who was going to win. So they went to fight it out with Indian with arrows to see if he could win over gun. Soldier on horseback and Indian dodge so far and the Indian shoot him with arrow clear through neck. The soldier can't hit with the pistol."[18]

Guns

In terms of firepower, Apaches soon had everything their white adversaries had, plus field glasses, Sheffield knives, and McClellan saddles.[19] The first guns were no doubt the crude and sometimes antique muskets the Spanish and Mexican governments supplied to their colonists.

"Lead? Most of them used a Mexican rifle. They used six-shooters but not too much," said Sam Chino. "That's where they got their lead and bullets. Hard to load cap and powder. They used the same for the six-shooters. They fight every day."[20]

During the Civil War, repeating rifles were introduced. Although troops didn't have Sharps or Spencer rifles and carbines in great numbers, some made their way into Apache hands. Ironically, these same weapons would evolve into the buffalo guns used to destroy the big animals on which the easternmost Apache bands depended.

The breech-loading system was developed to keep panic-stricken soldiers from blowing themselves up on the battlefield by overloading their muskets. The user released a breech cover, which ejected the spent casing, slipped in a cartridge, and snapped the cover shut. Apaches were also known to use breech-loading Winchesters. When entrepreneurs discovered they could make a buck selling cheap shotguns to settlers, Apaches obtained these too but didn't like them.

In 1873, Colt brought out its Single Action Army Revolver, the so-called "Peacemaker" or "Frontier Six-Shooter." The Army's order of 8,000 in 1873 put many in Apache hands, helping equalize the lopsided contest between the Apaches and the Army. Also in 1873 came another weapon dear to the Apaches, the Winchester repeating rifle, which became the most popular shoulder arm of the era. Apaches, like other warring tribes of the time, liked having a lot of shots without reloading. And while isolated frontiersmen instantly appreciated the fact that its .44 would take the same cartridge as his handgun, think of its effect on people with even more erratic supplies of ammunition!

The Army continued to rely heavily on single-shot rifles and 1873 was also the year of the Springfield "Trapdoor." Infantrymen carried the heavier rifle while horse soldiers used the smaller carbine. This was the weapon of Custer's desperate fight;[21] it was also the weapon of Geronimo's equally desperate arroyo ambush, although some of the younger men had repeating rifles — Winchesters and Marlins.[22]

Officers complained that the Apaches were often better equipped. In 1876 Colonel Edward Hatch found the Apaches at Ojo Caliente "well armed with Springfield, Winchester, or Sharps rifles and carbines, Colts and Smith and Wesson Revolvers." Women and boys had muzzle-loading guns.[23] When Chato conducted his raid, traveling some 450 miles in six days and nights, his warriors carried the latest Winchesters obtained in raids or purchased from "white scoundrels who made a business of selling arms, ammunition, and whiskey to Indians." The soldiers and scouts in pursuit were stuck with single-shot Springfields.[24] And Geronimo's warriors meeting with General George Crook were also well equipped, according to Bourke: "Each was armed with a breech-loading Winchester; most had nickel-plated revolvers of the latest pattern, and a few had also bows and lances."[25]

"I got a Winchester this side of Casas Grandes," said Daklugie. "Had bullets made of silver. No good. When it was getting daylight we hunted cave to hide 'til night. My brother [Daklegon] put that gun in there. He had had two and I asked, 'What you do with the other?'

"'I put it away for safekeeping. Some time we might be chased up here by Mexicans and we will have something to go to if we need it.'

"He had a big canvas bag of ammunition, heavy and tied at the top. Could pull a string and shut it. The ammunition fitted both six-shooter and rifle. They were .44s.

"He had got that gun in the Black Range, east of the mountain [Cook's Peak] and Fort Cummings. That rifle was too heavy.

"We got attacked from the top early in the morning near Fort Cummings. . . . The troops were traveling and we could see them at the foot of the mountain. I think they were hunting black-tailed deer for they got scattered. You ought to see those deer pile out of the mesquite brush down in the flat. The troops kill some deer and be butchering. That's when my brother kill soldiers and get their guns when they were coming back to camp with a deer.

"Daklegon had hidden them in that cave and he told me where it was so if I need guns I can get them, and bullets too. And I got a rifle and two six-shooters and a big sack of ammunition."[26]

"I got one [six-shooter] in the Black Range at a hardware store. It was near Fort Cummings. . . . We broke in this hardware store and in a glass case there were six-shooters and shotguns standing up. Here was a little one. We took four or five Colt .38s. Got a shotgun too, about 12 gauge. Not much good. Shot all scatter. They tell us not to touch those guns with two barrels. The Winchester had just come out—a new gun—along about '82. They had a revolver that shot the same shell. We were going to have a war of our own. They wanted to know what that two-barreled shotgun going to do . . .

"Indian say that [shotgun] just a play toy for childs. It not good to hunt humans with. We don't know anything about buckshot. We would pick a cartridge up and rattle it. They think maybe it's a marble."[27]

Sam Kenoi said, "This gun belonged to Noche since 1886. He had it with him when Captain Crawford was killed down in Mexico. It is a Springfield 45–70, sixty-eight years old, maybe more. I keep it clean. It shoots good yet. Noche was sergeant major when Crawford was killed. He gave me the gun. He was my mother-in-law's father."[28]

Anglos described Apache camps as bristling with weapons, but no matter how many guns they had, ammunition was always a problem and even influenced how Apaches fought. "They never fight at night. They could not see to fight and waste ammunition. They not have anything to waste. Geronimo traveled in the day then when he could."[29]

Because nobody had a bullet to waste, their aim was usually true.

"So Charlie [Smith] is very old[30] but still mentally alert," Eve wrote in a letter. "The last time I saw him I told him that the officers reported that the Apaches were poor shots. He thought a few seconds and then burst into hearty laughter. Even at his age Charlie is considered the best shot on the reservation."[31]

Running

Running was a critical part of training, warfare, and communications.

"That hill right there, every morning they make you carry a heavy load and run up that hill," said Eustace Fatty. "And break the ice and go in every day. If you not do it they whip them, boys and girls both."[32]

Said Kanseah, "If the Indians want to communicate, they sent a runner—they always have one way ahead. They send a scout way ahead. If the first one saw soldiers he let the second man know and he called the rest. That's one way to get away early. They always have two men at least ahead."[33]

Eve wrote, "When they were young men, [Dan] Nicholas and his cousin Kedizinne left Victorio at El Paso del Norte at four in the morning and at midnight delivered a message to Nana, on the Rinconada, one hundred and thirty miles away."[34]

"Dan told me that one time many years ago he and [his cousin, Nelson Kedizinne] were stranded in El Paso. Upon failing to find either work or anyone who would haul them to the reservation, they decided to duplicate their fathers' return to Mescalero. 'We're as good men as they were,' said Dan. 'Why don't we run as they did.'

"'But we weren't trained runners. We hadn't been practicing all our lives as they did. Then, too, we were encumbered with clothes. However, if we'd been in breech clouts and moccasins, we still couldn't have made it. We got into Oro Grande at midnight—just half the distance—and we were nearly dead of hunger and fatigue. . . . The only light in the village was at a house in the outskirts. We went to it and saw through the window an elderly Mexican lady. . . . We waited, but needed water so badly that we finally knocked at the back door.

"'We're Indians,' I told her, 'but you need not be afraid of us. We are very tired and thirsty. If you would, please give us a drink of water.'

"Do you know what that lady did? She invited us in, gave us water and some food. Then she lent us blankets. We spread them on the porch and went to sleep. Not all White Eyes are cruel."[35]

Even in captivity, the Apaches were impressive runners.

"There was a man at Fort Sill who ran races with a race horse—a fast one too," said Sam Kenoi. "A bunch of men at Fort Sill saw it, several times. He would run against a horse. The rider had his racehorse turned with its tail to the finish line. The runner faced the line. So the rider had to turn his horse in order to race to the line. . . . When he turn his horse around, Sam is on his way and almost there. They ran a hundred yards. Sam can't keep that pace up for a long run—not like a horse can.

"Sam Haozous,[36] that was the runner's name, and he was a Chiricahua, of course. . . . He used to train me in running. He never went to school but is a very fine all-around athlete.[37]

Eve wrote, "Paul Blazer recalled having left La Luz on horseback and overtaken a Mescalero jog-trotting toward the village, about twelve miles away. The runner was followed by a little dog. Blazer passed both, but before he made the grade to the village, they outdistanced him, with the Apache carrying his dog. They beat him to the agency by about fifteen minutes."[38]

War Bonnets

"In the old days Apache chief wore war bonnets, but nobody but the chief wore them," said George Martine. "Medicine men had hats but not war bonnets. Sometimes the chief was both and had both. Some war bonnets had buffalo horns and they were worn for fighting. Those with eagle feathers were for ceremonials. They had, like Asa, long buckskin straps with eagle plumes on them falling clear to the ground. No chief even got to wear a war bonnet unless he had proved his courage. The bonnet meant he was a very brave man. Cochise had one, so did Geronimo; he wasn't a chief but was a great war leader and fighter and wore the bonnet. Juh did too. Geronimo had three. I've seen them many times. I knew him well. One had pointed ears like a coyote. He had one made of feathers too. They did not make feather ones much. Took too many eagle plumes. I've seen many war bonnets made by Mescaleros. Percy Big Mouth made them. The Mescaleros were good at making them. Most of them were made by women but men made them too."[39]

"When the Mescaleros went on the warpath they wore war bonnets. But when they got back they wore crown hats like Bernard [Second]'s."[40]

Eloise Shield refers to a beaver hat that Eve described as "fashioned somewhat like a turban with upright crown about three-and-a-half inches high. . . . Spaced at intervals around the crown are beaded designs about two inches in diameter. Sometimes other skins were used but beaver was preferred. There are still beaver on the upper Ruidoso, on the reservation."[41]

Customs of Warfare

"War paint told them who was friend or foe," said Bernard Second. "They looked much alike so it was hard to tell who was which. When Indians went into battle they unbraided their hair and let it hang free. The Mescaleros painted the lower half of their faces, usually white or yellow. That identified them to each other. Their clothes were similar and they had to make sure from a distance."[42]

"In the old days they did not cover the moccasins with beads," said Eloise Shield. "They used hard thorns for the sewing. They tied moccasins and soles to their belts with thongs. . . . If you go on the warpath you have to take an extra pair of soles and buckskin. . . . When the men went hunting they tied their hair with a long thong. If they went on the warpath . . . everything was loose, but if you killed [a man] it was tied down.

"They sat up to sleep, leaning forward with their knees on the ground and might have to be pushed over to wake them. They were dressed and ready to fight. And a long time ago they tied the rifle to their wrist so they couldn't lose it. The shield too was fastened. And the eagle feather and *hoddentin* [cattail pollen] must always be taken with them. I carry a buckskin pouch and a very little hoddentin with me all the time. Must never forget it."[43]

TWENTY SIX

Bear Tales and
Other Animal Stories

Before bears, like Apaches, were hunted to near extermination, they were a frequent presence—and threat. Women and girls picking berries, children swimming in water holes, the lone warrior returning from hunting—all might encounter a bear (shash in Apache).

Chiricahuas generally believed that evil people, including witches, might come back as bears. They also thought departed relatives could return in the form of a bear.[1] Apaches call the bear My Uncle or My Aunt, said Amelia Naiche. "And they have a respect for it. And that's why they don't eat the meat."[2] At the same time, they believed bears could be allies and protectors to those who had bear Power or those they chose to help.[3]

"All Apaches talk to the animals," said Eugene Chihuahua. "Bear is my medicine too so I talk to them. . . . No, they don't answer back but they understand and they don't hurt me. When one stands and holds his hands up he is trying to tell you he is a friend."[4]

Because of their strong beliefs, Apaches didn't hunt bears. A man might kill a bear in self-defense (Loco's scarred face and drooping eye were the Warm Springs chief's lifelong reminder of his fight with a bear), but he wouldn't touch the meat or use its skin.[5]

"[Around 1882] one of the Indians got caught by a big grizzly bear—a silver tip," said Asa Daklugie. "His name was Botillo. He went hunting alone following the river. . . . He saw something dark against the water, [but] thought he would get a drink and go back. He put his gun down and knelt to drink. That old Indian lay down to drink and there was a bear in the willows. Before he got up here is the bear holding his hands over the man's head, just like that.

"Well, he had his gun pretty close but he could not reach it. The bear was holding him by the shoulders. He tried to grab the bear by his ear—that's the weakest spot. He got a butcher knife too. But he was cornered. Old bear lift his paws off him . . .

"They wrestled a long ways, leaving the gun behind. Depend on butcher knife. He . . . went back to the water going across and stab that old bear two or three times over his ribs, trying to cut them down. Old bear began to growl, losing the air, and he said to the bear, 'Get up there. You got good meat to eat over here.

"'Why don't you come get it?'"

"When Botillo returned, he was scratched all over. He told Juh's brother the bear was dead. They returned on horseback and found the dead bear—plus another. They shot at it and it retreated.

"You're lucky," they told him. "Bear is powerful."[6]

Gladys Scott Cojo, a Mescalero, tells the story of her former sister-in-law, a San Carlos woman whose parents married her to a Tonto Apache at Camp Verde. He beat her and treated her badly, so his family helped her escape. But her husband returned from hunting sooner than expected and started in pursuit. From the top of a ridge she could see him and knew she had to move faster.

"Suddenly she heard a sort of snort and saw a grizzly bear on the trail below her. It stood by a high rock where the path was very narrow. She remembered that her grandmother had told her that bears may have the spirit of one's ancestors within their bodies and she began talking to the bear.

"'You might be my grandfather or his sister. I am in trouble with that man. He is bad to me. He is very cruel. He beats me. He makes me a prisoner in the tipi. Please don't let that man get me. Catch him, please. Don't kill him—just stop him from following me.'

"The bear turned away and went out of sight around a sharp turn. She followed and saw that it had crowded into a crack between two big rocks. She had to pass so close that it could have reached her but it did not move.

"She ran as fast as she could to the little stream in the bottom of the canyon and crossed it on the stones. Then she climbed up the steep bank, clinging to bushes and rocks as she pulled herself up the trail. When she had reached a ledge she heard a cry and looked back. It came again. She shuddered and hurried up the mountain and over the crest.

"Three days later she reached San Carlos and her people. They asked about her husband and she told them. She did not know what had happened to him but felt sure he had not been killed.

"Later some people came to San Carlos from his place. They told her that her husband had come home with both hands mangled. His fingers were broken, his gun was broken and his spirit was broken. He told them that the bear took his rifle in its hands and broke it as one does a stick. It would not let him pass. When he attempted it the bear grabbed his hands and broke them too."[7]

"I almost got caught by a bear one time," Kanseah said. He had untied his moccasin string and a bear started to chase him. "One time a bear get after me. There were two pine trees close together. Man call to me to run between the trees. And they shoot the bear just as I ran between the trees."[8]

Daklugie describes how his father, Juh, was working with his arrows when he heard a child scream and saw Kanseah running from the trees with a bear at his heels.[9] Juh couldn't shoot because the boy was between them, so he yelled for Kanseah to run between two trees growing close together.

"Someone said, 'Run between those trees.' I did and then the gun said boom! and kill the bear."[10]

"There were lots of bear in Mexico and they were pretty mean. They did hang around the water and came when the children went to water. Children like to go to water holes and swim."[11]

Kanseah and Kaywaykla told another story about a bear saving a woman's life:

"There was a woman who was a captive and she escaped from the Mexicans and was trying to find her way back home. She climbed a mountain and she got near the top of a ridge and a big bear stood up in her way. She tried to go the other way, but he blocked her path and she tried to go to the right and he stopped her again. She made a long detour. When she got to the crest she could see a big encampment of soldiers down below. If she had gone on the way she started they would have captured her. So the bear saved her life."[12]

Leroy and Darlene Enjady said, "[Dahteste] told us of a grizzly bear [in northern Mexico] that killed many of her people. He bit the ends of her mother's fingers off. Bears understand when Apaches talk to them." Once at a zoo, the aged Dahteste told a bear, "You have killed nearly all of my relatives. That's why you are a prisoner now. You are a prisoner of the White Eyes. . . . The bear got mad and growled."[13]

Eustace Fatty told another story: A woman and her two children were out picking juniper berries when a bear came up and killed the woman. Her children escaped by climbing a tree. The children cried for their mother and made their way toward a hill. "And the clown in white pants came up to them and ask, 'What you crying about?'

"The oldest say, 'Well, we are picking berries and my mother got killed by a bear and that's why we cry.'

"The clown say, 'I carry the small one and you hold my hand.' They go toward a big bluff and there was a little trail on the bluff.

"'Oh, we will fall.'

"'Don't be afraid. You will not fall.'

"Finally they go to the main place. He had a little stick and the door open and you see all kind of animals—panther, mean lion. Another room, bears facing each other. Then they see rocks clash. 'Just come follow me. You will not be hurt.'

"They go four places, dangerous. Then they see a big chief, old, white-haired. 'You come here.'

"'Tell him you come for help, you lost your mother.' So they told the old man, 'We will starve.'

"'Ask for long life.'

"'All right, you go way over there.' Old man sit there with his old lady. Clown told him the same thing.

"'No people from outside allowed.'

"They ask the same thing. 'We lost our mother. Hungry.'

"They saw the bear that killed their mother. They had a big chain around his neck. 'That is the fellow that kill your mother. Now we give you food and you can go back to your people. The clown will take you back and we will do whatever you like to this bear.'

"The clown took them back out again and gave them one ear of corn. And they ate the corn. It be like a big meal. And they go back to the Warm Springs. It took them four days to go over there. There the clown say, 'There are your people and I will watch you go back to them.' And the clown sat and watched 'til they joined their people and then he turned back . . .

"When they left that cave it filled up with rock and they never could find it again. . . . Before Fatty died he went with them and they camped and stayed three nights but did not find it."[14]

Eve Ball wrote, "Fred Peso had no very close neighbors, but his children did not complain for lack of playmates. When asked what they had been doing, the oldest, a boy, replied that they had been playing with their friends.

"'What friends?' asked their father. 'There are no children living close.'

"The oldest squirmed and replied, 'Well, anyway, they are our friends and we are not afraid of them.'

"'Not afraid of who?' demanded their father.

"Again his son hesitated but an admonition from his father brought him to terms.

"'Bears,' was the answer."[15]

Bobcat and Lion

"Ol' Bobcat, he mean," said Leroy Big Rope.[16] "He don't have no respect for nobody. He think he own this whole reservation and maybe all the world. He got claws like knives and he rip you to pieces if you get in his way. So you better get far 'way as you can but not turn your back on him. He treacherous.

"Mountain Lion, he got more sense. You don't hurt him, he don't hurt you. Maybe so you walkin' through woods at night he follow you. He circle you to find out what you doin' and keep it up for long ways.

"One dark night I could feel somethin' watchin' me but nothin' bother me. Next day I go back and find mountain lion tracks and they go in circles around me for maybe half mile. But he don't try to hurt me. He don't hurt peoples."[17]

"These folks were raising little deer," said Percy Big Mouth. "Every spring they hunt little fawns and keep them around their camp—lots of deer. One day they told a man that some[thing] was killing [their] deer but [they] couldn't get close enough to catch [it].

"'Stop right here. You see that hill? We three can go away and make a drive and it ought to run past you.'

"He got bows and arrows. These people went to timber and they yell and make lots of noise. This fellow stood up on a big rock and he heard something talking to him: 'This place is a good place right here.' He look around and don't [see] anything. Pretty soon he hear a loud [noise] back in the timber and he saw something jump toward him. He don't know what it is. He got on top of the rock and got his bow and arrow ready. Pretty soon that animal came and saw him. He could see the hair standing up on its back and its teeth sticking out. This rock stand up way high and the lion coming right here jump at him but could not reach him. He shot it right in the throat and killed that animal . . .

"Four times in succession he went over there and killed four different animals and then the man and woman let that man have their daughter for his wife. Now the wild animals did not come down any more and kill their deer."[18]

Eagles

Apaches respected eagles for their strength but didn't eat them because eagles catch snakes and lizards, which Apaches despised. They did, however, trap them to obtain feathers, usually by setting snares around a carcass, or taking eaglets from nests.[19]

"They hunted eagles for the feathers," said George Martine. "They knew where the eagles roosted. They hid and got them after they got on the roost. . . . How many feathers they get from one eagle? In old days just six from the tail. Takes lots of eagles to make a war bonnet. Now they use all the tail feathers and wings too.

"When Apache wanted feathers bad he dig a hole and get in it with a hide over him with meaty side up. When the eagle lit on it he grabbed its legs through the skin and tied them. Pretty dangerous, for it peck your eyes out if it can. Sometimes he pull out the six feathers and turn him loose. Sometimes have to kill eagle because he put up a fight. Capturing an eagle that lights on a hide is a pretty dangerous job. Takes a brave man to do that."[20]

Part IV.

Eve Ball

TWENTY SEVEN

Eve Ball

◈

Talking to survivors of an event to get their stories is a basic for writers today. But when Eve Ball began talking to Apaches living on the Mescalero Reservation, the legitimacy—and popularity—of oral history was decades away, and Indian people were still, in the eyes of the dominant society, second-class citizens.

She once said, "If nothing else is said about me, I want people to know of my long struggle to get my books published. . . . Ph.D.s never accepted the intrinsic value of oral history until the last few years. Now that it has come of age, most of the old ones who experienced the history are gone."[1]

Considering her contributions and her importance among Western historians, I was surprised at how sketchy the accounts are of Eve Ball's life. Busy and modest, she may not have considered herself a fitting subject to write or talk about. Eve deserves a book about her life, a task I'll leave to writers who knew her. However, a voluminous correspondence with fellow historians and friends reveals a generous, caring, and energetic woman and a writer who was passionate about making history accessible and readable for everyone.

◈

Katherine Evelyn Daly was born 14 March 1890, in Clarksville, Tennessee.[2] The family moved to a cattle ranch in Kansas when she was a toddler. Her mother, Gazelle Gibbs Daly, was the first woman to practice medicine in Kansas and instilled in her daughter a sense of independence and the value of education.[3]

As a child, Eve read Hawthorne and Scott. "I had read practically every-thing Scott had written before I was twelve years old," she once said. She also admitted learning a lot from Dickens.[4] She loved Kipling and was an avid Sherlock Holmes reader.

The family spent time in Arizona, and this may have been Eve's first exposure to Indian people and Southwest culture. She said she'd lived in Phoenix several years and stayed in the summer because of her mother's arthritis.[5]

In 1918, Eve received her bachelor of science degree in education from Kansas State Teachers' College. She earned her master's in education at Kansas State University in 1934 and lacked a year of having her doctorate from the University of Kansas when she married.[6] Eve's husband died a few years later, and she never remarried.[7] She became an elementary and sec-ondary teacher and college instructor in Kansas, Texas, and New Mexico,[8] teaching history and literature at Kansas City Junior College and the Col-lege of Artesia.[9]

During World War II, Eve was living in Hobbs, in the southeastern New Mexico oil patch. Hobbs in those days had an airfield and every three months a new crop of graduates drew relatives and friends, mostly from the East. With help from the local banker, Eve opened an Indian jewelry shop next to the biggest restaurant in town. "And I just cleaned up," she said. Her employees were Al and Natachie Momaday, parents of Scott N. Momaday.[10]

In 1942, she moved to Ruidoso, a resort town in southeastern New Mexico.[11] "When I came to Ruidoso, I thought I was ready to write a book," she said.[12]

Six years later, she bought an entire block near Ruidoso Downs, the fa-mous horse-racing track, for $2,250,[13] and several Hispanic residents built an adobe house for her, beginning a long friendship. She furnished her house Southwest style, and her garden was her pride and joy.[14] She also enjoyed making preserves and applesauce from the apples of her own or-chard.[15] From the beginning, she was interested in the histories of Anglo, Hispanic, and Indian residents.[16] And happily for her (and history), her house was a mile from the Mescalero Apache Reservation.

"When I came here, I was way out in the country; the road was not paved way up here. June is a hot, dry month, and my house and grape arbor were a haven. The Apache women wore long skirts dragging the ground, and they had cradles on their backs and babies in the cradles and maybe two or three little children hanging on to their skirts. Nobody in a car ever picked one up. They would have walked ten or twelve miles by the time they got here and would be exhausted. Well, they would walk up this hill, and they'd stop

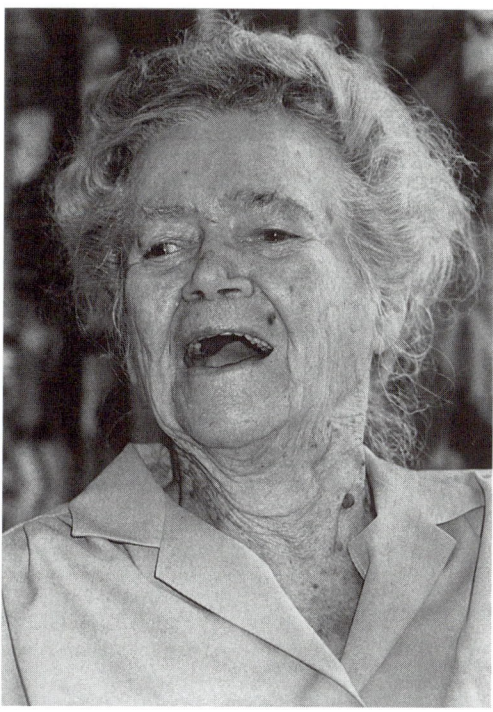

Fig. 22. Eve Ball (1890-1984) was a woman ahead of her time. (Albuquerque Tribune.)

out there and send a child to the door. They would ask very timidly if they might have a drink of water. I had a table and chairs out in the yard under the tree, and I would fix them a pitcher of ice water. Sometimes I would make iced tea or lemonade. I would go out and sit and ask questions, and I would get answers 'yes' or 'no,' but that was about the only response. They all looked alike to me then. I couldn't tell the difference in them.

"I said to a woman, 'You've been here before, haven't you?' She said, 'Five times.' She said, 'I'm going to bring my husband the next time.' I said, 'Well, fine. I'd like to meet him.' I think there were five or six old broken-down cars on the reservation; there may have been more. But most of the Indians had wagons and teams, and they just got to coming here, but nobody would come into this house. They had heard about white women. They weren't going to take any risks.

"They finally began coming in and talking pretty freely, and I learned a little bit about the situation over there from them. I found that the fewer questions asked, the more they would tell me. And I was trying to find out who the king pin was up there and, of course, I expect it was two years or so before I discovered that Asa Daklugie was in charge."[17]

"At first my object in attempting to become acquainted and get their accounts of their history and customs was entirely selfish: I wanted this information for writing.

"But the Apaches are people and many of them very fine people. They are a proud and sensitive folk, and when they do give their friendship, it is amazing and touching to find the extent of their confidence. . . . Some of these people I have known for twenty years. They come to me with their troubles and sorrows, and they ask me to share in many of their social affairs."[18]

The visits became interviews, with Eve taking verbatim notes in Gregg shorthand. One day her visitor was James Kaywaykla, nephew of Victorio and grandson of Nana. He was visiting Mescalero from Oklahoma to be on hand for the July puberty ceremony. It took Eve four years to get the first interview with Ace Daklugie, with much help from his wife Ramona and daughter Maude Geronimo, who were good friends of Eve's. Daklugie hated white people. When she didn't understand him and asked what he meant, he'd say, "White Eyes! Everything in book; nothing in head." A week before he died in 1955 he brought her his papers.[19] As her network of trust and friendship expanded, Eve eventually interviewed sixty-seven elderly Apaches.[20]

She learned to speak a bit of Apache. "No, I do not speak Apache fluently. . . . Eugene and Ace tried hard to teach me, and I have a vocabulary of perhaps 500 words. By waving my arms and speaking very slowly I can make some things understood. . . . However, my little knowledge serves me very well. If I take someone to see an Apache I can tell him whether or not that person is a friend to the Indians, or merely a curiosity seeker."[21]

Eve found that no matter how well she knew Apache people, they could still be inscrutable. She once sent a Navajo rug to friends that she had obtained from Ralph Shanta Sr. He and his wife Lydia (Daklugie's daughter) had come by one day for a visit and Eve walked out to the truck with them. They had the rug wrapped around some metal parts they were taking to the welding shop. "I asked if they'd sell and got a very negative reply. Ralph took it from around the iron rods, folded it, tucked it under his arm, started the pickup and drove off. I was stunned at the reaction, but even more so when he turned around, drove past me, and threw the rug at my feet."[22]

The more Eve got to know Apaches, the more she came to dislike Wendell Chino, then president of the tribe's business committee, which ran the reservation, and later the multi-term president of the Mescalero Apache Tribal Council.

Half Chiricahua and half Mescalero, Chino was born in 1925 on the reservation, the fifth of eleven children. His great, great-grandfather on his

Fig. 23.   Wendell Chino (1925-1998) was the Mescaleros' leader in modern times. (Albuquerque Tribune.)

mother's side was the Mescalero chief San Juan. On his father's side, Geronimo is his great granduncle. In 1951, Chino graduated from the Western Theological Seminary at Holland, Michigan, and became an ordained minister of the Dutch Reformed Church. Two years later, he became president of the business committee and when the tribe established a tribal council in 1965, he became president of that too. He led the tribe until his death in 1998, except for a four-year period, and cultivated a reputation both for improving the tribe's economic situation and for political ruthlessness.

In the winter of 1956, Eve visited Chino's father, Sam Chino,[23] to do an interview and was so outraged at his living conditions that she left this note in big, black letters on the outside of the folder containing his transcript:

"I found him living in a cave with a tarpaulin covering the south opening. His wife was dragging a dead log down the mountain to cut into wood. Wendell Chino, his son, was living in luxury in the best house in Mescalero."[24]

Sam Chino and his wife weren't the only Apaches living in desperate poverty at Mescalero. As word of this spread, Eve became a conduit for charitable activities. In 1957, the Senate conducted an investigation of poverty on the reservation, and Walker Air Force Base in Roswell sent a truckload of food.[25] For her trouble, Eve didn't exactly bask in the gratitude of tribal officials. "I have been the target of criticism (along with Vic Lamb, the editor of the *Ruidoso News*) for making known the destitution on the reservation. We've both been the recipients of clothing, food and money for relief."

New York artist Henry Schnautz began sending Eve blankets, clothing, and shoes for the Apaches. Initially, she took the boxes to the tribal government and the churches for distribution.

"I found that at least one of the ministers is charging them for garments given through the church, so that is out. The Tribal Council is accused of giving the food to relatives, friends, etc. rather than to the actually needy."[26]

"We found that the chairman of the council was using the things sent to supply either his relatives or secure votes for the coming election."[27]

"The express packages have arrived and I shall try to get them to Father Hubert and Eugene Chihuahua today or tomorrow. Both will distribute them fairly to the needy. If I turn them over to the Welfare Committee they'll be used to buy votes for Chino, chairman of the council. He is up for re-election in December. The only hope I can see on this reservation is to beat him. He's clever and unscrupulous; the Apaches think he can practice witchcraft against those who oppose him."[28]

Although Eve tried to stay out of tribal politics, she couldn't help what her Apache friends told her during their visits. And her good friend Del Barton, a Seneca woman living in El Paso, was heavily involved in trying to improve conditions for the Mescaleros and had taken a hand in Mescalero politics. That December the tribe elected five people to the tribal council. Chino won re-election by one vote, and that one challenged. But he suffered his first, and only, defeat as tribal leader.

"In the election last Saturday he was defeated and Virginia Klinecole, a Mescalero, elected Chairman. She is intelligent and well-educated; and her friends say she cannot be intimidated.... Many have been here and all feel this is the beginning of a wholesome change."[29]

"While in general conditions on the reservation are better than they were last year there's still much destitution. The range was good, the cattle fat, and the prices good. But many do not own any cattle and a great many are out of work. But Chino is out, and they have renewed hope . . .

"Members of the council come to me openly since he was defeated. They no longer fear his revenge to their opposition. They have him whipped— temporarily."[30]

Chino was then assistant pastor of the Dutch Reformed Church. He once said that "a sad experience with the church" moved him to give up the ministry and focus on tribal government. This is probably the sad experience:

"Strangely enough, when I got back from the post office Solon Sombrero and George Martine (son of the famous scout) were awaiting my return. They came by to tell me that Chino has been called into New York by the Dutch Reformed Church, in which he is an ordained minister, to refute charges that [the] ministry is of secondary importance to him, being chairman of the tribal council meaning much more to him financially. He is the most cunning person I've ever known. For years I defended him to his own people, but they finally convinced me that his religion is a blind to further his ambitions."[31]

Chino wasn't overly fond of Eve Ball either.

"The Rev. Mr. Chino . . . is opposed to having the Apaches know their history and traditions and had records destroyed and forbade members of the tribe to give interviews. Fortunately I had secured much of the material I needed previous to this action."[32]

From remarks Chino made in Eugene Chihuahua's eulogy, knowing well that Eugene and Eve were good friends, Chino made it clear that he wanted the tribe to stop telling stories about the old days and think about the future. "This chapter of history has closed upon the old Apache life. A new chapter has been opened. Eugene's days of difficulty and challenge are over; ours has just begun," the Reverend Chino said.[33]

In this period Eve became a one-person distribution center for donations to the Mescalero poor. From one shipment she filled a box for each of twenty-seven needy families.

"I think you would have to see these people open one of these boxes to know what a warm garment means to them . . .

"The down comforter I'm taking to Isabel Enjady, who is a tubercular patient, very emaciated, and unable to be comfortably warm. It will give warmth without weight. I'm having it cleaned first. The other blankets and quilts went to each of three families where there are six, nine, and eleven children respectively. These children sleep on the floor and have insufficient cover."[34]

"Then all the Indians who could came over and tried on clothes and shoes until very little remained but high heeled shoes." Those went to the Catholic Church to give away or sell in the thrift shop.

"I am sorry you could not see the happiness people exhibited at having a pair of shoes or a dress."[35]

The same names that appear in her books as the tellers of heroic tales appear in her letters in another context. A Mexican blanket went to Christian Naiche "who is also in pitiful position and is seventy-one. The grandson of Cochise!"[36]

"Yesterday May Second, daughter of Peso, last Mescalero chief, came, and the beautiful blue boucle coat fitted her. A dress, too, was right. She was so happy she cried."[37]

Eve told Schnautz that the Mescaleros appreciated his donations but probably wouldn't write him. "They get me or Father Solanus to write their business letters or fill out any forms, make income tax reports, etc. But they tell me they go to the mountain to pray to Ussen for your happiness and health. Prosperity, in their opinion, is not a fit subject for prayer."

Despite her modest circumstances, Eve's personal charity was substantial. She bought firewood for Eugene Chihuahua. She bought cortisone for Isabel Enjady, daughter of Geronimo's warrior, Perico. "She's about seventy, and badly crippled with arthritis." She obtained a wood cookstove for a family whose house burned. Alberta Begay, daughter of Massai, she wrote, "is almost blind; had cataract operations but is not greatly improved. So I gave her the money I got for the story." When Schnautz donated artwork, Eve sold it and used the money to buy medicine woman Catherine Cojo, then nearly eighty, a bed, blankets, and a cookstove. "The aged get $17.50 a month from the tribe. They manage to eat, but can buy little clothing or blankets."[38]

By 1961, conditions had begun to improve a bit. Mescaleros were getting eighty-five percent of the cattle sale money "that somebody else pocketed heretofore." And old people living in chicken houses had moved into small houses that the tribe had built at the direction of Virginia Klinecole.[39]

Eve also had quite a head for business. As she was helping and interviewing Apaches, she had figured out her own way of making money from Ruidoso's horse track without betting a dime. In 1959, Eve borrowed money to move four houses from Hobbs, then suffering an oil bust, to her three-acre property. She had them set on new foundations and re-plumbed. Then approaching seventy, Eve painted them inside and out, made draperies, and even refinished furniture and made slipcovers. She rented her units to horse people—racing commissioners, stewards, and horsemen.[40] By the next year, she had twelve rental units. And she had sold an eighteen-acre parcel near the track, purchased in 1954, to hotel developers, and was planning to use the proceeds to finish her own little empire, which by then included an antique shop.[41] It took twelve years to pay off the bank but by the early 1970s, she was earning a comfortable income.[42]

Many a visitor enjoyed Eve's "cozy adobe white house chugged full of Southwestern and Indian furnishings" and met many of her Apache friends. She entertained guests on a patio that looked out to her flower garden and was decorated with saddles. "Like the Apaches, Eve had a lively sense of humor," wrote LaVerne Harrell Clark.[43]

Eve loved gardening. "I have bulbs blooming in profusion, especially daffodils. Tulips are beginning to come out."[44] To maintain her writing and her garden, she rose at 5 A.M. and worked until 8 A.M., when she turned to her duties as a landlady and business proprietor. It was a schedule she maintained for years.[45] And she spent four hours a night reading.[46]

In her business and home, Eve employed Apache helpers, which gave her access, reference checks, and translators as she worked. "Ace's granddaughter has worked for me about twenty years, part time, and was here today. Having an original source on the place is a great help."[47]

Her tourist season was 17 May to 17 September, which allowed her to pursue her writing in fall and winter, an arrangement many writers would envy. "You saw what a Bedlam this place is in summer. But I have about three months in winter when I build a log fire, move my typewriter before it, and work eight to ten hours a day . . ."

Not only could she make a living from her apartments, she could entertain out-of-town guests, including James Kaywaykla, who spent weeks at a stretch. It's an idea she got from artist Henriette Wyeth, with whom she was friendly.[48]

Despite her intense involvement with the Apaches, Eve's first books were on other western subjects: *Ruidoso, The Last Frontier*, in 1963; *Bob Crosby, World Champion Cowboy*, 1966; and *Ma'am Jones of the Pecos*, 1969. After *Victorio* in 1970, she published *My Girlhood Among Outlaws* in 1972. *Indeh*, in 1980, was her final book. Most of her books were oral history; *Girlhood* was based on a diary. One book went unpublished.

"I wrote a book about Clell Lee, hunter of predators, who lives in the canyon of the Blue and has a hunting lodge below Hannegan's. . . . I have been unable, however, to get this book accepted, largely because (so editors say) the sympathy of the public at present is with the hunted, rather than the reverse."[49]

She also wrote, beginning in 1955, scores of stories for western magazines, usually *True West* or *Frontier Times*. One of those stories won her a Golden Spur Award from Western Writers of America in 1975. "I collected material and took typewritten interviews (via shorthand) for twenty years before submitting even one article to a magazine."[50]

By 1956 she had begun her first book on the Apaches and finished it in 1960. It wasn't to be another book on the Apache campaigns. "I plan limiting mine to events upon which Apache tradition—and memory—disagree with the accepted versions. I have enough of them to make a book."[51]

Kaywaykla was her leading source. He wrote, "I have been thinking about our attempts to write a book of the life of Chief Victorio and his people. I have learned, or [been] told, to write a book of the war days of our people could not [be] done."[52]

In the time they worked together, Eve and Kaywaykla became quite close, but they maintained the formality of their era in addressing each other. It was always "Mrs. Ball" and "Mr. Kaywaykla." In a letter following a month-long stay, he wrote, "Thanking you Mrs. Ball for being so good. I shall never forget all your kindness."[53]

Although they had the same goals, they had occasional disagreements over content. Regarding the story of how Geronimo witched his daughter, Kaywaykla wrote, "Mrs. Ball, I object. . . . I or no one else can prove he really did such a thing. Truth is what we want."[54]

The two nearly parted ways over the title of the book, with Eve wanting to call it "White Eye Justice" and Kaywaykla in vigorous disagreement. "I did not like the title 'The White Eye Justice.' It don't sound familiar to me, sound like Asa D. suggested or interpreted our people, called people pale eyes. . . ."[55] It nearly ended their collaboration, but they patched things up and went on.

At the time Eve wrote, "I know you do not understand, for if you did you would be as eager as I to see a publication made that may have lasting value to your people. I have hoped that the publication of my book on the Warm Spring[s] Apaches might create public interest in the wrongs they have suffered that might bring about the payment for the reservations taken from them and the Chiricahuas."[56]

Kaywaykla wrote, "But I do appreciate everything you done for me while we were writing the book. I know you have great respect for me. Which also, I have great respect for you."[57] Kaywaykla died in his sleep on 27 June 1963, without seeing his book published.

As Eve was overcoming resistance from within, she was hurdling obstacles from without. Publishers balked at this new version of events that didn't jibe with existing military histories. Oral history wasn't well accepted. And they didn't like the first-person, conversational history told by Kaywaykla and somewhat fictionalized by Eve. She defended the Apaches and their accounts, along with her presentation of them, with passion, but it would take ten years to get the book in print.

"The next three months I plan to use for rewriting the Kaywaykla story, omitting the criticisms of the governmental policies that seem to be a deterrent to publishers. There's not much use until Mr. K. gets here, for I am trying to get this approved by him as well as by publishers."[58]

"You cannot feel more strongly than I the necessity for submitting the manuscript to an expert for judgment," she wrote an editor.

"He will find many discrepancies: I am telling the Apache version of their history. So far as I know it has not even been attempted except by Jason Betzinez. I am fully aware that it does not coincide with the accounts submitted to the Secretary of War by officers participating in the campaigns. There are many particulars in which the Indians differ from their white antagonists . . .

"[Kaywaykla] is wise in the lore of his people. And he has read widely mostly at my suggestion. He has stayed here three weeks at a time, read and commented on my books, and given me his account, either as told him by Nana, Kaytennae, or as personal experience. When he does not know he says so. He is a fine and conscientious person, and does not deviate from the accounts of his family and people. That he really memorized these stories as our children do their literature I have no doubt. Many of the older Apaches did . . .

"Of course I wrote the book. He had the information, but not the academic background for it. I explained to him that to have a good saddle one has to have good hides. Also that there is much work involved in making those hides into a saddle. And after five years of reading and revising, he understands . . .

"I am so disgusted with the dishonesty of people who do not credit their writing to its actual source that I want Kaywaykla to have the credit—if there is any—for his material. I am also interested in the recognition I feel my due for the five years of research and hard work involved . . .

"Mr. Lottinville wanted it rewritten in conventional thesis style, with copious footnotes. And being of the academic type, he questioned any statement not hitherto published. Now those are the things that I hope to prove most valuable. I have done primary research. I do not minimize secondary sources, but where first-hand experiences are available I think some of the eminent Ph.D.s overlook a bet by not investigating them. I know of one, a very scholarly man, who boasted that he could not 'spend three days among the savages' and write a best seller. I do not value that kind of research," she wrote Dan Thrapp.[59]

"I am quite aware of the fact that memory may fail and that bias may enter into these accounts, but I am thoroughly sold on the idea that nobody can judge an individual as accurately as the people among whom he lives."[60]

"Why do historians resent having anyone come up with facts that they have ignored or overlooked? And why is not the testimony of an Indian as valid as that of the young officer ambitious for promotion or some agent or newspaper man with his center of interest purely selfish? . . . I must anticipate some unfavorable appraisal for it is a departure from some of the accepted versions of occurrences. But why write a book if one has nothing new to offer? The Chiricahua book will have several accounts that vary in some respects from those of historians, mostly in motivation and the effects of the Apache religion. I know only too well that these will be attacked. But if either or both books give the general reading public—not the scholarly ones—better understanding and some degree of sympathy with the Apaches I shall be well paid for the years of work I've put into writing them."[61]

Eve maintained a prodigious correspondence with a number of historians, particularly fellow Apache scholars Dan Thrapp and Angie Debo.[62] Besides sharing information and ruminating together on research questions of mutual interest, the three also commiserated about publishers, reviewers, and the writing life. Clearly, the friendship was important to all of them.

"You have been so generous in sharing all your specialized knowledge with me—even sometime in the 1950s when I stopped by, a stranger, you gave me your time," wrote Debo. "I still have the notes of our conversation. And after I got back home you wrote me a long letter giving some more information. So it started early and has continued."[63]

Born in the same year as Eve, Debo was then working on her own classic work, *Geronimo: The Man, His Time, His Place*. The two women were great friends; they also had some spirited disagreements. There was even a bit of competition, with each convinced her sources were the best.

"I love Angie, but she is so completely sold on [Jason] Betzinez that I fear not her decisions but those in which she accepted his accounts. And she, I think, would be correspondingly critical of Daklugie. The Apaches I know, including many in Oklahoma, were contemptuous of Jason, unjustly at times. Or so I think and have told some of them I do. As you know Apaches are contemptuous of cowardice, and because Jason never was accepted as a warrior, disliked him. They were also contemptuous of him because he married a white woman and was (they say) dominated by Anna."[64]

After Debo's *Geronimo* book was published in 1976, Eve wrote, "I too think Angie's book is excellent. And she is a fine person."[65] "Of course, there is no one else capable of having written it. . . . She did, perhaps unintentionally, attempt to some extent to whitewash Geronimo."[66] This latter is an interesting criticism because Eve, to some extent, also whitewashed Geronimo. Her primary sources were all adamant supporters and Daklugie in particular wouldn't brook any criticism of his uncle.

With Dan Thrapp, who was younger, Eve had a different relationship:

"I'm a designing woman. I want to be sure that if I am unable to complete my writing on the Apaches that somebody who knows the subject may do so. And I'm hoping you may be interested in so doing."[67]

Eve and Thrapp wrote often, but he didn't care for Eve's old-school formality. "Please don't address me as 'Mr. Thrapp.' It makes me feel as though I have a foot in the grave, which I'm sure I don't—not yet, anyway. The first name is 'Dan,' and the last name is 'Thrapp,' and use either you wish to, but that 'Mister' throws me."[68]

When Thrapp was at work on his book about Victorio, Eve wrote that she knew it would be well researched and written. "Moreover, you have ability, rare (I think) in historians, of being both scholarly and interesting."[69] Thrapp, a newspaperman, also knew the value of first-person accounts:

"[Y]our work . . . ought to be published for precisely what it is—a version from the 'other side.' There are almost none of those, because you didn't come along a generation ago with your willingness to talk with the Apaches, and your patience and ability to sort and sift what they had to say, and almost no one else did, either."[70]

While some fellow historians valued Eve's work, the style and presentation gave them pause.

"Dr. Sonnichsen[71] very generously offered to help me with my Apache book. He suggests rewriting it in the third person, observing academic requirements, and quoting copiously from the Apaches. I've rewritten part of it, but it doesn't ring true."[72]

"Like yourself, Dr. Debo disapproves my type of writing, and urges that I use the formal prescribed one acceptable to historians. I have no doubt that she is right. I know only too well what this has cost me. Still, though I think I could do it, I feel that my method of presenting the Apache accounts is fitting for my subject. Moreover, they [Apaches] can read and understand it."[73]

At one point, Eve relented and began rewriting Kaywaykla's book in the third person at the suggestion of an editor, who later rejected the manuscript. A second publisher, who thought oral history was bunk, wouldn't even look at it. Eve ended up publishing *Victorio* with an academic press that required her to pay publication costs.[74] When the book finally emerged, Eve won kudos from the most important people to her: "I had tried hard to do something to make the Apaches comprehensible to white people and ameliorate their lot a bit. Greatly to my happiness, they do approve of *Victorio*."[75] Thrapp wrote her, "The book is a good job, plows new fields, and is a genuine contribution. You can well be proud of it."[76]

"I had a letter from Dr. Angie Debo that is very gratifying. Despite the fact that she greatly dislikes use of conversation in a book of this type, she is enthusiastic about *Victorio*." Eve acknowledged her departure from convention and said she was thinking about rewriting the Chiricahua book to conform.[77]

Reviews were mixed. In the *Library Journal* a reviewer wrote that Eve's "conversational style" detracted from the book's serious message. In *Arizona and the West*, a reviewer criticized Kaywaykla's "rambling and often confusing" account and the scarcity of explanatory footnotes, but applauded the Apache spirit "shining through every page."[78] Even Thrapp, in *The Journal of Arizona History*, observed "a lack of precision" and explanation but said that the book "is meant to help balance the record, and it will do this."[79] He concluded that it was a valuable addition to Southwestern history.

Eve wasn't without opinions of others' works. She was disappointed in the chapters on Apaches in Dee Brown's *Bury My Heart at Wounded Knee*. "From my point of view he has attempted to cover too much territory. And much of his information on Apaches seems to me to lack substantiation."[80] C. L. Sonnichsen was a friend, but she hinted that the paucity of oral accounts weakens his Mescalero book.[81]

When the Santa Fe *New Mexican* sent Eve a book on the Jicarilla Apaches to review, she sent it back and asked the newspaper to find another reviewer for that volume. "It is seldom that I find a book so dull that it is work to read it, but this one is."[82]

Publication also brought seekers and hangers-on. Eve tried to help everyone who came to her for information but by the mid-1970s, the trickle had become a flow.

"I think you are right in curbing your ever present helpfulness to everybody who comes to you for help. . . . I think you are too generous," Debo wrote. "I help people too but not as much as you do."[83]

"Now that there are [just] two old Apaches left who could give authentic accounts, the academic world is beating a path to Mescalero. Chino won't admit [them] to his office, and they don't know how to get an interview with the old Apaches. They come here. . . . They don't want help, for that matter, they want me to give days of time and what I've learned by thirty years of intensive research."[84]

As *Victorio* emerged, Eve was well along with the book that would become *Indeh*.

"Now I'm hard at work on the book on the Chiricahua. I'm making Ace [Asa] Daklugie the principal narrator in it; but Chihuahua [Eugene], [Jasper] Kanseah, and Johsannie [Richard, son of Johsannie] will give their accounts of occurrences as told by their fathers. Johsannie and Chihuahua were full brothers and so Eugene and Richard are cousins. Eugene was very cooperative, liked to relate the stories he had from his father, and was a very friendly person. He was, incidentally, the Beau Brummel of the Apaches at Fort Sill. Richard, on the contrary, is very reserved, and I had great difficulty in even getting an interview with him. Not until Evans Istee, grandson of Victorio, married his daughter did I succeed . . .

"I decided to use the spelling preferred by the Indians, since all that early recorders could do was spell names phonetically." Naiche, she wrote, is pronounced with a long "i."[85]

Publishing this book was no easier than the first. One publisher with an eighteen-month contract sat on the manuscript for six years until Eve threatened to sue. Then she began the publishing rounds again. This time, Brigham Young University Press was interested.[86]

In 1974, Eve began having trouble with her vision and the following year had the first of several surgeries to remove cataracts. Months after the operation, she wrote, "I can't see a word I write." She had stopped typing, but by writing in large script with a felt-tip pen, she could make out her own words.[87]

Undeterred, she plunged ahead, completing what she thought would be the first of three books on the Chiricahuas, as well as a book on Bert Judia. Using a powerful magnifying glass, she worked about an hour at a time, several times a day. When she overworked her eyes, the punishment was headaches, dizziness, and rising blood pressure.[88]

To keep up her momentum, Eve hired two women, Lynda Sánchez and Nora Henn, to type for her. The two in time became more than typists, helping Eve more and more with the manuscript as her health deteriorated.[89]

Eve had hoped to publish three books but yielded to her advancing age and agreed to one with BYU. After some heated disagreements over editing changes, the book was completed, with BYU's editor visiting her home to read the final manuscript aloud to her.[90]

When *Indeh* finally appeared in 1980, the reviews were more enthusiastic, marking a sea change in attitudes toward oral history. "Mrs. Ball has wisely chosen to allow the Apaches to speak for themselves with a minimum of editorial comment," said a reviewer for *The Journal of Arizona History*, who also observed that the book could be enjoyed by general readers and scholars.[91] *Publishers Weekly* called it "a masterpiece of oral history."[92] A reviewer for the *Utah Historical Quarterly* praised the "wealth of details regarding the lives and careers of individual Indians."[93] Said a reviewer for the *Journal of the West*, "That so much could be gathered at all is a monumental tribute to the author, Eve Ball, and reflective of the respect with which she is regarded by the Apache people."[94]

Don Worcester, a friend of Eve's, wrote in *Arizona and the West*, "But for Eve Ball, these sincere and graphic accounts of the Apaches' side of the story would have been lost forever."[95]

Indeh had its critics for the usual reasons. "A particular difficulty with *Indeh* is that it is solely based upon oral accounts. . . . *Indeh* also suffers from several stylistic problems," opined the reviewer for the *New Mexico Historical Review*, including lack of coherent organization, unifying narrative thread, and references to time.[96] Even the reviewer for the *Utah* periodical, who otherwise praised the book, found fault with "a lack of continuity" and "disjointed" depiction of incidents.[97]

From her friends, she got high praise: "It's a classic, Eve," wrote Will Henry. "We all yearn to write that one book which will truly rate that classification. Very few of us succeed. You have."[98]

With publication of *Indeh* came overdue recognition. In 1980, she was the subject of a public television documentary, "Eve Ball: The White Apache." In 1981, she was nominated for the Governor's Award for Excellence in the Arts, received the Zia Award from New Mexico Press Women, and membership in Who's Who of American Women. In 1982, she was inducted into the Cowgirl Hall of Fame and Western Heritage Center in Hereford, Texas. And New Mexico's two U.S. senators introduced a resolution commending Eve Ball as a historian of the Southwest, adopted on 7 October 1983. The most gratifying award was the Saddleman's Award in 1981 from Western Writers of America.

While the applause of her peers must have been satisfying after enduring years of their criticism, Eve at this time was struggling mightily with her health. She had another cataract operation in 1982. "Having lived in dread of total blindness for five years, this was the only chance and a very remote one. But am very thankful that it was successful. I can hardly wait to be able to read but of course must do so and patiently."[99]

The operation was less successful than she'd hoped and she was also troubled by bursitis and a torn ligament in her right shoulder from a second fall, all of which made writing difficult and painful.[100] A nurse's aide staying in one of Eve's guest apartments was caring for her.[101] Despite doctor's advice against even sending Christmas cards because of the strain to her eyes, she pressed on.

By 1981 she had two books nearly complete. One book, with her assistant, Lynda Sánchez, was about the "lost Apaches," 450 to 500 who disappeared into Mexico in 1886, around the time the government sent Geronimo and Naiche and their people to Florida. The second book, with an unnamed helper, was about the Choctaw-Chickasaw Nation before Oklahoma's statehood. At this writing, neither one has been published.

Eve never gave up. In one of her last letters, she wrote, "And I plug out a good many magazine articles. I can't read what am writing but hope you can. . . . Believe it or not I am considering an attempt at a novel. I've never written any fiction and may not get it published. Everybody likes good fiction and comparatively few read much history."[102] She continued writing until her death on the morning of Christmas Eve 1984 at age ninety-four. Her memorial service was held at Mescalero's St. Joseph's Mission, which she once described as "a magnificent stone edifice" built by her good friend Father Albert Braun.

Her friend Joe Welch wrote, "Eve Ball has made tracks during her life which will be here a long time. Maybe forever."[103]

Notes

CHAPTER 1

1. Carolyn Niethammer, *Daughters of the Earth: The Lives and Legends of American Indian Women* (New York: Collier Books/Macmillan Publishing Co., 1977), 167.

2. Eve Ball, draft manuscript, undated, Eve Ball Manuscripts, Papers, and Letters, Provo Special Collections & Manuscripts, Harold B. Lee Library, Brigham Young University (hereafter cited as Ball MSS).

3. Ball to Elizabeth Shaw, 3 January 1970, Ball MSS.

4. Fellow Apache scholar Dan Thrapp, trying to help, wrote to Eve: "With regard to Lozen, I have found something that will be of help in explaining her, I think, in a footnote or otherwise. Goodwin, in his *Social Organization* (a very careful, honest work, as you know), says p. 537: 'In very rare instances women even went to war and helped fight and kill the enemy. Such women were not ridiculed for doing as men did, for they were not trying to be masculine but merely participating as a brave woman.' I think it might be worthwhile mentioning that reference somewhere, if you can, because it would ease the doubts of some." (Thrapp to Ball, 20 January 1970, Ball MSS.)

5. Ball, *In the Days of Victorio: Recollections of a Warm Springs Apache* (Tucson: University of Arizona Press, 1970), 21. In this comment attributed to James Kaywaykla, the first part is faithful to Kaywaykla's statements; the second could be an exaggeration.

6. Henrietta H. Stockel, *Women of the Apache Nation: Voices of Truth* (Las Vegas: University of Nevada Press), 42.

7. Ruth McDonald Boyer and Narcissus Duffy Gayton, *Apache Mothers and Daughters: Four Generations of a Family* (Norman: University of Oklahoma Press, 1992), xix.

8. Boyer and Gayton, 24.

9. Ball, draft manuscript, undated.

10. Stephen H. Lekson, *Nana's Raid, Apache Warfare in Southern New Mexico, 1881* (El Paso: University of Texas at El Paso, 1987), 5.

11. Morris Opler, *An Apache Life-Way, The Economic, Social and Religious Institutions of the Chiricahua Indians* (Chicago: University of Chicago Press, 1941), 75–76.

12. D. C. Cole, *The Chiricahua Apache, 1846–1876: From War to Reservation* (Albuquerque: University of New Mexico Press, 1988), 61–63. Cole says that for this reason, Chiricahua women formed a warrior society, which during times of war numbered about a dozen. I found no other references in Apache accounts to such a society, but include the reference as an interesting possibility. According to Cole, the female warrior society had a war priest(ess), a leader for young warriors and designated novices. And a female warrior was eligible for membership in any man's war society. Many women trained with women's society members even though they didn't plan to join.

13. Ball, *Victorio*, 115.

14. Ibid., 11.

15. Ibid., 14.

16. Ball and Linda Sánchez, "Legendary Apache Women," *Frontier Times* (October–November 1980): 8.

17. Ball, *Victorio*, 14.

18. Ball and Sánchez, 9.

19. Del Barton, *A Good Day To Die* (Garden City: Doubleday & Company, 1980).

20. Ball to Shaw.

21. Ball and Sánchez, 9.

22. Arthur Caswell Parker, *The History of the Seneca Indians* (Port Washington, New York: I. J. Friedman, 1967), 151.

23. Boyer and Gayton, 24.

24. Ibid., 54.

25. James Kaywaykla, transcript of interview by Ball, undated, Ball MSS.

26. Ball and Sánchez, 10.

27. Ball, *Victorio*, 15. Clearly, this statement is dramatized, but I believe it reflects the spirit of Kaywaykla's recollection.

28. Ball to Shaw.

29. Dan Thrapp, *The Conquest of Apacheria* (Norman: University of Oklahoma Press, 1974), 201.

30. Eustace Fatty, transcript of interview by Ball, 12 July 1955, Ball MSS.

31. Stockel, 21.

32. Ball, *Victorio*, 21.

33. Boyer and Gayton, 54.

34. Kaywaykla, interview, undated.

35. Ball, *Victorio*, 115–19.

36. Ibid., 11.

37. Ball and Sánchez, 11.

38. Ball, manuscript, undated, Ball MSS.

39. John C. Cremony, *Life Among the Apaches* (San Francisco: A. Roman & Company, 1868), 142.

40. Ibid., 243.

41. Ball, *Victorio*, 73.

42. Boyer and Gayton, 54.

43. Eve wrote that this was Lozen's role during the Cibicu outbreak. In June 1881, a charismatic medicine man named Noche-del-klinne was gaining influence among reservation Apaches. During an aborted attempt to bring him to the San Carlos agent, shooting broke out and the medicine man was killed. According to Eve, Lozen and Nana's brother Sanchez made off with a herd of soldiers' pack mules. [See Ball, "Cibicu: An Apache Interpretation," in *Troopers West: Military & Indian Affairs on the American Frontier*, edited by Ray Brandes (San Diego: Frontier Heritage Press, 1970), 129–30.] Other historians maintain that only a few Chiricahuas were present at Cibicu and that Lozen would have been in Mexico with Nana. (See Ed Sweeney, Reviewer's Report of *Apache Voices*, 22 October 1998.)

44. Ball, *Victorio*, 150.

45. Ball to Shaw.

46. Ball, *Victorio*, 150.

47. Ball, draft manuscript.

48. Ball and Sánchez, 12.

49. Ball, unpublished manuscript based on interviews with Dahteste, undated, Ball MSS.

50. Eve interviewed Dahteste, who married the scout Coonie. Her stepdaughter, Eliza Coonie, brought Dahteste, by then a tiny, delicate old lady, to Eve's home and translated. Eve wrote, "She also gave me this account of the trips she and Lozen made for Geronimo." (Ball, manuscript, undated, and interview transcripts, 4 and 10 October 1955, Ball MSS.)

51. Martine and Kayitah, transcript of interview by O. M. Boggess, 29 September 1925, Ball MSS.

52. Eugene Chihuahua, transcript of interview by Ball, undated, Ball MSS.

53. Ball with Henn and Sánchez, *Indeh: An Apache Odyssey* (Norman: University of Oklahoma Press, 1980), 111.

54. Angie Debo, *Geronimo: The Man, His Time, His Place* (Norman: University of Oklahoma Press, 1976), 307.

55. Debo to Ball, 20 April [1973?], Ball MSS.

56. James Kaywaykla to Ball, 20 June 1958, Ball MSS.

57. Jasper Kanseah, transcript of interview by Ball, 31 May 1955, Ball MSS.

58. Ball, draft footnotes, undated, Ball MSS.

59. Ball and Sánchez, 11.

60. Bessie Big Rope, transcript of interview by Ball, 7 December 1973.

61. Ball and Sánchez, 12.

62. Ball, "Appendix B," unpublished, [late 1960s?], Ball MSS.

63. Ball to Henry Schnautz, 28 May 1959; 20 June 1958; 14 July 1958; 14 January 1959; 11 July 1959; 4 November 1959; and 28 November 1960.

CHAPTER 2

1. Ojo Caliente refers to the Warm Springs Reservation in southern New Mexico Territory.

2. James Kaywaykla's father, a member of the Warm Springs band whose name wasn't recalled, was killed in battle about 1879 south of Deming during the Victorio wars when attacked by American soldiers and Apache Yuma Scouts. Kaywaykla's mother, Gouyen, was a Warm Springs-Nednhi, related on the Nednhi side to Geronimo's sixth wife, Zi-yeh.

3. Loco was chief of another Warm Springs band, then living on the San Carlos reservation. Ojo Caliente was the Warm Springs homeland near present-day Truth or Consequences, New Mexico.

4. Kaywaykla, transcript of interview by Eve Ball, 12 October 1955, Ball MSS.

5. Victorio's wife, son Charlie, and daughter Dilth-cley-ih were safely hidden in the Black Range, near present-day Ladder Ranch. (Eugene Chihuahua, transcript of interview by Ball, 26 May 1969, Ball MSS.)

6. Tissnolthos, a Chiricahua, was a close relative of Chihuahua and one of his warriors. When Chihuahua surrendered, he joined Geronimo's group. His daughter Aggie married Charlie Smith.

7. Blanco died in a skirmish with black cavalrymen from Fort Cummings. [Dan L. Thrapp, *Victorio and the Mimbres Apaches* (Norman: University of Oklahoma Press, 1974), 108–09.]

8. Because the west end of Cook's Pass was guarded, the leaders decided to escape to the south, but three tents stood in the way. Suldeen and Kaytennae decided to send the party around while they rode for the tents. (Thrapp, *Victorio*, 110.)

9. This wasn't the Lost Adams Diggings. Adams and his miners encountered Nana's group, but the year was 1864.

10. For the story of her escape, see chapter 3, "Captives," this volume.

11. James Kaywaykla, transcripts of interviews by Ball, 12 October 1955, 11 November [1955?], 8 and 12 June 1956, and 20 July 1961; and Kaywaykla to Ball, 20 January 1958, Ball MSS.

12. Ball to Thrapp, 4 January 1970, Ball MSS.

13. Thrapp to Ball, 20 January 1970, Ball MSS.

14. Ball to Thrapp, 23 January 1970, Ball MSS.

15. Thrapp, *Victorio*, 308.

CHAPTER 3

1. Eve Ball, draft manuscript, undated, Ball MSS.

2. In *Indeh: An Apache Odyssey* (Norman: University of Oklahoma Press, 1980), Eve wrote that Francesca and James Kaywaykla's cousin Ski were captured together (p. 45), but Siki and Kaywaykla's grandmother were captured at Tres Castillos in 1880.

3. S. M. Barrett, ed., *Geronimo: His Own Story* (New York: E. P. Dutton & Co., 1970), 98–99.

4. Ball, manuscript, undated, Ball MSS.

5. Eugene Chihuahua, transcript of interview by Ball, 9 October 1963, Ball MSS.

6. Eve wrote in *Indeh* (46) that they also bound wounds with a split nopal leaf, but this is questionable. See chapter 23, "The Apache Pharmacy."

7. Barrett, 98–99.

8. Chihuahua, interview.

9. Barrett, 98–99.

10. Angie Debo to Ball, 31 August 1971, Ball MSS.

11. Ball, manuscript.

12. Chihuahua, interview.

13. In 1884 General Crook began trying to secure the release of Chiricahua captives held in Mexico. In the spring of 1885 the Mexicans released thirteen women from Mexico City. Along the way they divided into two parties of six and seven. The latter group reached Monticello on 4 July. Of the other group, two reached Fort Bowie, three died, and one stayed in Chihuahua. (Ed Sweeney, letter to author, 7 March 1999.) This account conflicts with James Kaywaykla's description of an escape. He could be mistaken or Siki could have been with another group.

14. Kaywaykla, transcript of interview by Ball, 12 October 1955, Ball MSS.

15. Evelyn Gaines, transcript of interview by Ball, 2 April 1957, Ball MSS.

16. Isabel Enjady, transcript of interview by Ball, 17 October 1955, Ball MSS.

17. Frances E. Totty, "Loot Cached Years Ago Is Discovered," *Silver City Independent*, 11 May 1915.

18. George Martine, transcript of interview by Ball, 7 October 1974, Ball MSS.

19. Jennie Parks Ringgold, *Frontier Days in the Southwest* (San Antonio: The Naylor Company, 1952), 79.

20. Ibid., 80.

21. George Martine, transcript of interview with Ball, undated, Ball MSS.

22. A second explanation is this: "The strap which bound the tsach to her forehead broke and it fell, and warriors would not permit her to dismount and rescue her baby. . . . Bert Judia, about whom I'm writing a book, knew [Doubtful Adams] well." (Ball to Dan Thrapp, 23 December 1969, Ball MSS.)

23. Gaines, interview.

24. Sweeney, letter to author.

25. Ringgold, 80–83.

26. Gaines, interview.

27. George Martine, transcript of interview by Ball, 17 January 1966, Ball MSS.

CHAPTER 4

1. James Kaywaykla, transcript of interview by Eve Ball, 16 November 1956, Ball MSS.

2. Historian Dan Thrapp insists that only Juh was strategist enough to pull off such a difficult and brazen feat. Daklugie also said his father had led this raid.

[Thrapp, *Juh: An Incredible Indian* (El Paso: Texas Western Press, 1973), i–ii.] At some point, Juh and his men left the larger group, possibly assuming them to be out of harm's way, and headed for the Sierra Madre (Thrapp, 30).

3. Angie Debo, *Geronimo: The Man, His Time, His Place* (Norman: University of Oklahoma Press, 1976), 137–44.

4. Ibid., 146–49.

5. Thrapp, *Al Sieber, Chief of Scouts* (Norman: University of Oklahoma Press, 1964), 238.

6. Thrapp, *The Conquest of Apacheria* (Norman: University of Oklahoma Press, 1967), 249.

7. James Kaywaykla to Ball, undated, Ball MSS.

8. Kaywaykla, note on Ball draft manuscript, undated, Ball MSS.

9. Kaywaykla to Ball.

10. Ball, manuscript, undated, Ball MSS.

11. Jason Betzinez with Wilbert Sturtevant Nye, *I Fought With Geronimo* (New York: Bonanza Books, 1959), 72.

12. Debo, 150.

13. Kaywaykla, interview.

14. Kaywaykla to Ball.

15. Betzinez, 73.

16. Kaywaykla, transcript of interview by Ball, 24–25 December 1955, Ball MSS.

17. Kaywaykla, transcript of interview by Ball, undated, Ball MSS.

18. Kaywaykla, transcript of interview by Ball, 12 October 1955, Ball MSS.

19. Debo, 135.

20. Kaywaykla, interview, undated.

21. Kaywaykla, interview, November 1956.

22. Kaywaykla, interview, December 1955.

23. Kaywaykla, interview, November 1956.

24. Kaywaykla, December 1955.

25. Eugene Chihuahua, transcripts of interviews by Ball, 31 October 1951 and 27 September 1961, Ball MSS.

26. Chihuahua, interview, October 1951.

27. Ball, *In the Days of Victorio: Recollections of a Warm Springs Apache* (Tucson: University of Arizona Press, 1970), 143.

28. Kaywaykla note in Ball manuscript.

29. Ball, draft manuscript, undated, Ball MSS.

30. Kaywaykla, interview, November 1956.

31. Debo, 152.

32. Ball, manuscript.

33. Kaywaykla, interview, November 1956.

34. Barrett, *Geronimo: His Own Story* (New York: E. P. Dutton, 1970), 117.

35. Betzinez, 74.

36. Ball, *Victorio*, 145.

37. Ball, manuscript.

38. Thrapp, *Al Sieber*, 239.

39. Debo, 153.

40. Sixteen children under age ten were given to Mexican families at Bavispe, Bacerac, Granadas, Guasabas, Arispe, and Hermosillo. (Ed Sweeney, letter to author, 7 March 1999.)

41. Debo, 191.

42. Betzinez, 75.

43. Debo, 155.

44. Ball, *Victorio*, 155.

45. Ball, manuscript.

46. Debo to Ball, 19 May [?].

47. George Martine, transcript of interview by Ball, 10 June 1963, Ball MSS.

48. Morris Opler, "A Chiricahua Apache's Account of the Geronimo Campaign of 1886," *New Mexico Historical Review* 4, no. 4 (October 1938), 367–68.

49. Solon Sombrero, transcript of interview by Ball, 20 October 1954, Ball MSS.

50. Barrett, 116.

51. Ibid., 117.

52. Jasper Kanseah, transcript of interview by Ball, 31 May 1955, Ball MSS.

53. Asa Daklugie, transcript of interview by Ball, 16 December 1954, Ball MSS.

CHAPTER 5

1. Streeter was also probably confused with a brother living in Silver City.

2. Dan Thrapp, Encyclopedia of Frontier Biography (Glendale, California: A. H. Clark Co., 1988), 1378.

3. Thrapp, *Juh: An Incredible Indian* (El Paso: Texas Western Press, 1973), iii.

4. Thrapp, *Encyclopedia*, 1378.

5. Thrapp, *The Conquest of Apacheria* (Norman: University of Oklahoma Press, 1967), 280.

6. Thrapp, *Juh*, iii.

7. Thrapp, *Encyclopedia*, 1378.

8. James Kaywaykla expresses Apache sentiments on the subject in another context. Describing a Mexican captive who grew up as an Apache, he said, "Jose had been captured. Even he would not have married a white woman. They would marry with Mexicans but Mexicans are really other Indians." (Kaywaykla, transcript of interview with Eve Ball, 20 July 1961.)

9. Ball to Thrapp, undated, Ball MSS.

10. Ball, manuscript, undated, Ball MSS.

11. Kaywaykla and Jasper Kanseah, transcript of interview by Ball, 12 June 1956, Ball MSS.

12. Angie Debo, *Geronimo: The Man, His Time, His Place* (Norman: University of Oklahoma Press, 1976), 125.

13. Dohn-say is known to have married a young warrior named Dahkeya. She was captured by Captain Wirt Davis's scouts in 1885 and died at Fort Sill. (Ibid., 244–45.)

14. Ibid., 158.

15. Kaywaykla to Ball, 20 January 1958, Ball MSS.

16. Another white man among the Apaches was Pine Pitch House, captured as a boy and raised by the White Mountain Apache. He married a Chiricahua woman and lived with her people. He was involved in the negotiations between General Crook and the Chiricahuas in Sonora in 1883. [Keith H. Basso, ed., *Western Apache Raiding and Warfare: From the Notes of Grenville Goodwin* (Tucson: University of Arizona Press, 1971), 308.]

17. Ball to Thrapp, 3 September 1965, Ball MSS.

18. Edmund W. Wells, *Argonaut Tales: Stories of the Gold Seekers and the Indian Scouts of Early Arizona* (New York: F. H. Hitchcock, 1927), 328–30.

19. Thrapp, *Conquest*, 279.

20. Ibid.

21. Ibid., 280.

22. *Silver City Enterprise*, 20 April 1883.

23. *Silver City Enterprise*, 23 January 1885.

24. Thrapp, *Encyclopedia*, 1379.

25. Thrapp, *Conquest*, 280.

26. Thrapp, *Encyclopedia*, 1379.

CHAPTER 6

1. Three of Kayitah and Mary's children died at Fort Sill. Son Kent married Eloise Perico, and their daughter was Nancy. Kayitah's daughter Rachel married Kanesewah.

2. Eve Ball, "Martine and Kayitah Scout for General Miles," manuscript, undated, Ball MSS.

3. The Chiricahuas knew the Animas Mountains in southwestern New Mexico as "Round Mountain." (Ed Sweeney, Reviewer's Report of *Apache Voices*, 22 October 1998.)

4. George Martine, transcript of interview by Ball, 25 September 1957, Ball MSS.

5. Sam Kenoi told Morris Opler that Martine lagged behind Kayitah because he was afraid. [Opler, "A Chiricahua Apache's Account of the Geronimo Campaign of 1886," *New Mexico Historical Review* 13, no. 4 (October 1938): 375.] Apache scholar Angie Debo wrote that Kenoi's account of the surrender was accurate "except for a spiteful charge of cowardice against Martine, which is plainly untrue." [*Geronimo: The Man, His Time, His Place* (Norman: University of Oklahoma Press, 1976), 283n.] Debo wrote to Eve that she considered Kenoi a reliable source but said, "Oh, I do not take seriously his charge that one of the two who went with Gatewood after the hide-outs was a coward and followed far behind the other. . . . But I think his account of the conference [between Miles and Geronimo] is accurate. It fits other things I know." (Debo to Ball, 29 February 1972, Ball MSS.)

6. Kayitah was Yanosha's first cousin. (Debo, 280.) Yanosha was brother-in-law to Kayitah's wife.

7. Jasper Kanseah, transcript of interview by Ball, [mid-1950s?], Ball MSS.

8. Kanseah, transcript of interview by Ball, 12 June 1956, Ball MSS.

9. Ulzanna, also known as Johlsannie, was Chihuahua's older brother and his lieutenant. [Ball, *Indeh: An Apache Odyssey* (Norman: University of Oklahoma Press, 1980), 45.]

10. Eugene Chihuahua, transcripts of interviews by Ball, undated and 1960, Ball MSS.

11. Ball, manuscript, undated, Ball MSS.

12. Kanseah, transcript of interview by Ball, 20 October 1954, Ball MSS.

13. Ball, manuscript.

14. Kanseah, transcript of interview by Ball, 18 November [1954?], Ball MSS.

15. Kanseah, interview, October 1954.

16. Ball, manuscript.

17. Kanseah, interview, November [1954?].

18. Yanosha's sister, a Chiricahua-Nednhi woman named She-gha, was a close relative of Cochise. (Debo, 63.)

19. Eve wrote to Dan Thrapp that "while I can give no proof, I can cite Daklugie's insistence that his father led the force that killed Cushing. Until this time editors have refused to accept the statement of the old Apaches as to occurrences." (Ball to Thrapp, 5 October 1967, Ball MSS.)

20. Ball, manuscript.

21. Kanseah, interview, November [1954?].

22. Ball, manuscript.

23. Asa Daklugie, transcript of interview by Ball, 16 December 1954, Ball MSS.

24. Daklugie, transcript of interview by Ball, undated, Ball MSS.

25. Yanosha and his wife had a daughter, Winona Magoosh, and a son, Homer.

26. Debo to Ball, 20 April [1973?], Ball MSS.

27. Daklugie, interview, undated.

28. Kanseah and Lucy Gonoltsis had three sons (Jasper Jr., Lee, and Wilson) and two daughters (Velma Chee and Abbie Gaines).

CHAPTER 7

1. Morris Opler, "A Chiricahua Apache's Account of the Geronimo Campaign of 1886," *New Mexico Historical Review* 13, no. 4 (October 1938), 367–68.

2. Istee lived with his own fears: "So long as he lived Charles Istee told that the white people might kill him cause he was Victorio's son." (Charlie Smith, transcript of interview by Eve Ball, 8 June 1955, Ball MSS.)

3. Sam Kenoi, transcript of interview by Ball, undated, Ball MSS.

4. Jasper Kanseah, transcript of interview by Ball, 8 June 1955, Ball MSS.

5. Asa Daklugie, transcript of interview by Ball, 16 December 1954, Ball MSS.

6. Daklugie, transcript of interview by Ball, August 20, 1954, Ball MSS.

7. Daklugie, interview, December 1954.

8. In a letter to Dan Thrapp (3 June 1966, Ball MSS), Eve wrote: "Christian Naiche, grandson of Cochise, spent the entire day here yesterday, and I wrote shorthand for hours." While Anglos believe the great chief died of cancer, Christian insisted, as other Apaches did, that Cochise was witched. "To the Apaches witchcraft is real and to be feared."

9. Daklugie, interview, August 1954.

10. Kanseah, transcript of interview by Ball, 12 June 1956, Ball MSS.

11. Amelia Naiche, transcript of interview by Ball, undated, Ball MSS.

12. Ball to Henry Schnautz, 25 July 1957, Ball MSS.

13. Naiche's daughter Dorothy married James Kaywaykla; their son was Harold.

14. Ball to Schnautz, 30 June 1957, Ball MSS.

15. Amelia Naiche, interview.

16. Kanseah, interview, June 1956; and James Kaywaykla, transcript of interview by Ball, 12 June 1956, Ball MSS.

17. Ball to Schnautz, 25 July.

18. Amelia Naiche, interview.

19. Amelia Naiche, transcript of interview by Ball, 28 January 1954, Ball MSS.

20. Amelia Naiche, transcript of interview by Ball, 7 August 1969, Ball MSS.

21. Ball to Schnautz, 25 July.

22. Daklugie, interview, December 1954.

23. Amelia Naiche, interview, January 1954.

24. Christian Naiche, transcript of interview by Ball, 21 September 1958, Ball MSS.

25. Ball to Schnautz, 25 July.

26. Ball to Schnautz, 1 February 1960, Ball MSS.

27. Ball to Don Worcester, 13 January 1981, Ball MSS.

28. Ball, manuscript, undated, Ball MSS.

Chapter 8

1. Eve Ball to Henry Schnautz, 15 June 1960.

2. Joseph Evans, Letter to editor, *True West* (November–December 1959): 4.

3. Joseph Evans, Letter to editor, *True West* (January–February 1960): 56.

4. Christian Naiche, transcript of interview by Eve Ball, 21 September 1958, Ball MSS.

5. Ibid.

6. Angie Debo, *Geronimo: The Man, His Time, His Place* (Norman: University of Oklahoma Press, 1976), 251–52, 327, 448.

7. Ball, "Notes," undated, Ball MSS.

8. Niño Cochise and A. Kinney Griffith, "Apache Tears," *Old West* (Winter 1967): 2–14.

9. Cochise and Griffith, *The First Hundred Years of Niño Cochise: The Untold Story of an Apache Indian Chief* (New York: Abelard Schuman, 1971).

10. Ball, "Notes."

11. Ball to Dan Thrapp, 13 April 1968, Ball MSS.

12. The story referred to here is Cochise and Griffith, "Apache Tears."

13. Herman Lehmann, "Nine Years Among the Indians, 1870–1879," parts 1 and 2, *Frontier Times* (March 1963): 7; (May 1963): 8.

14. Ball to Thrapp, 8 October 1967, Ball MSS.

15. Ball to Thrapp, 8 April 1968, Ball MSS.

16. Debo to Ball, 29 February 1972, Ball MSS.

17. Peter Farb, review of *The First Hundred Years of Niño Cochise: The Untold Story of an Apache Indian Chief*, by Ciye Niño Cochise and A. Kinney Griffith, *New York Review of Books* 17 (16 December 1972): 36.

18. Leroy Yarbrough to Ball, 6 June 1962 and 11 January 1965, Ball MSS.

19. Ball to Thrapp, 5 October 1967.

Chapter 9

1. Britton Davis, *The Truth About Geronimo* (New Haven: Yale University Press, 1929), 61.

2. Dan Thrapp, *The Conquest of Apacheria* (Norman: University of Oklahoma Press, 1967), 80.

3. Ibid., 82.

4. Diana Hadley, Peter Marshall, and Don Bufkin, "Environmental Change in Aravaipa, 1870–1970: An Ethnoecological Survey" (Phoenix: Arizona State Office of the U.S. Bureau of Land Management, September 1991), 35, 37, 40.

5. Ibid., 46.

6. Davis, 61.

7. Royal E. Whitman to Vincent Colyer, 17 May 1871, in Vincent Colyer, "Peace with the Apaches of New Mexico and Arizona" (Washington, D.C.: Government Printing Office, 1872), 31; and Thrapp, *Conquest*, 80.

8. Woodworth Clum, *Apache Agent: The Story of John P. Clum* (Boston: Houghton, Mifflin Co., 1936), 57–63.

9. Whitman to Colyer.

10. Ibid., 31–32.

11. Thrapp, *Conquest*, 85, 87, 90.

12. Colyer, "Peace with the Apaches," 15, 17.

13. John Clum, "Es-kim-in-zin," *New Mexico Historical Review*, part 1, 3 (October 1928): 403.

14. Thrapp, *Conquest*, 92.

15. Woodworth Clum, *Apache Agent*, 75–76.

16. Colyer, 38.

17. Davis, 61.

18. John Upton Terrell, *Apache Chronicle* (New York: World Publishing/Times Mirror, 1972), 280, 294.

19. Thrapp, *Conquest*, 94.

20. Terrell, 286.

21. Colyer, 16–17.

22. Terrell, 294–95.

23. Thrapp, *Conquest*, 111.

24. Terrell.

25. John Clum, 406.

26. Terrell, 306–07.

27. Helga Danielsen, "Over-kill in Apache Land," *Frontier Times* (June–July 1971): 61.

28. Thrapp, *Conquest*, 156.

29. Terrell, 309–11, and Thrapp, 159.

30. John Clum, "Es-kim-in-zin," *New Mexico Historical Review*, part 1, 3 (October 1928): 403; part 2, 4 (January 1929): 20.

31. Ibid., part 1, 399, 413.

32. Ibid., 414.

33. Ibid., part 2, 4.

34. Woodworth Clum, 141–42.

35. John Clum, "Es-kim-in-zin," part 2, 5.

36. Woodworth Clum, 154.

37. John Clum, part 2, 6.

38. Woodworth Clum, 187.

39. Ibid., 171–72.

40. Ball to Thrapp, 14 February 1970, Ball MSS.

41. Ball, *Indeh: An Apache Odyssey* (Norman: University of Oklahoma Press, 1980), 39–40.

42. Ball, manuscript, undated, Ball MSS.

43. Asa Daklugie, transcript of interview by Ball, 27 November 1954, Ball MSS.

44. Ball, *Indeh*, 39–40.

45. Ball, manuscript.

46. John Clum, "Geronimo," *New Mexico Historical Review* 3, no. 3 (July 1928): 218.

47. Ibid., 246.

48. Ball to Thrapp, 1 March 1977, Ball MSS.

49. Ball to Thrapp, 8 April 1974, Ball MSS.

50. Ball to Thrapp, 22 March 1977, Ball MSS.

51. Woodworth Clum, 255–56.

52. John Clum, "Es-kim-in-zin," part 2, 13.

53. Davis, 62–63.

54. John Clum, part 2, 15.

55. Ibid., 21–23.

56. U.S. Department of the Interior, "Annual Report of the Commissioner of Indian Affairs to the Secretary of the Interior," 1890, in collection of reports, 1870–1896 (Washington, D.C.: Government Printing Office, 1890).

57. Earle Robert Forrest, *Lone War Trail of Apache Kid* (Pasadena: Trail's End Publishing Co., 1947), 105–06.

58. John Clum, "Es-kim-in-zin," part 2, 21–23.

59. Ball, manuscript.

60. John Clum, part 2, 23.

61. U.S. War Department, "Case of Apache Indian Eskimenzin," (Washington, D.C., 11 April 1893).

62. Thrapp, *Al Sieber, Chief of Scouts* (Norman: University of Oklahoma Press, 1964), 364.

63. "Case of Apache Indian Eskimenzin."

64. Ibid.

65. John Clum, "Es-kim-in-zin," part 2, 14–15, 17–18, 20–21, 26.

66. Hugh Lenox Scott, *Some Memories of a Soldier* (New York: The Century Co., 1928), 183–84.

67. Thomas M. Vincent to Headquarters of the Army Adjutant General's Office, 14 September 1894, Ball MSS.

68. Scott, 189–90.

69. Hadley, et al., 50.

Chapter 10

1. Thrapp, *Al Sieber, Chief of Scouts* (Norman: University of Oklahoma Press, 1964), 320.

2. Ibid., 322.

3. Phyllis de la Garza, *The Apache Kid* (Tucson: Westernlore Press, 1995), 1.

4. Ibid., 6–7.

5. Ibid., 15.

6. Ibid., 15–17.

7. Thrapp, 323.

8. Dan R. Williamson, "The Apache Kid: Red Renegade of the West," *Arizona Highways* (May 1939): 14.

9. Garza, 16, 21–25.

10. Thrapp, 326.

11. Garza, 28–30.

12. Thrapp, 332.

13. Williamson, 15.

14. Thrapp, 332.

15. George Ester, transcript of interview by Eve Ball, 13 July [?], Ball MSS.

16. Asa Daklugie, transcript of interview by Ball, 18 February 1953, Ball MSS.

17. Thrapp, 332–33.

18. Garza, 63–64, 75.

19. Jess Hayes, *Apache Vengeance: True Story of Apache Kid* (Albuquerque: University of New Mexico Press, 1954), 53.

20. Garza, 87–99.

21. Hayes, 147.

22. Ibid., 153.

23. Garza, 136.

24. *Alamogordo News*, 4 March 1926.

25. Thrapp, 346–48.

26. Williamson, 31.

27. Gladys Scott Cojo, transcript of interview by Ball, undated, Ball MSS.

28. Daklugie, interview.

29. Diana Hadley, Peter Marshall, and Don Bufkin, "Environmental Change in Aravaipa 1870–1970: An Ethnoecological Survey" (Phoenix: Arizona State Office of the U.S. Bureau of Land Management, September 1991), 50.

30. Daklugie, transcript of interview by Ball, 14 February 1955, Ball MSS.

31. Bert Judia, "The Apache Kid," as told to Ball, manuscript, undated, Ball MSS. A note on the manuscript says that the story was "published but impossible to collect from him." Attempts to locate the published version were unsuccessful.

32. Ibid.

33. Jennie Parks Ringgold tells a similar story, but in her version the Kid escaped to the Sierra Madre. [Ringgold, *Frontier Days in the Southwest* (San Antonio: The Naylor Company, 1952), 112–15.]

34. Garza, 154.

35. Eugene Chihuahua, transcript of interview by Ball, undated, Ball MSS.

36. Daklugie, transcript of interview by Ball, 18 February 1955, Ball MSS.

37. Jess Hayes to Ball, 1 April 1965.

38. Gladys Scott Cojo, quoted in Judia manuscript.

39. Cojo, interview.

40. Earle Robert Forrest, *Lone War Trail of Apache Kid* (Pasadena: Trail's End Publishing Co., 1947), 86–87.

41. Garza, 162.

42. Ross Santee, "Apache Kid," *Arizona Highways* (February 1948): 9.

43. Garza, 162.

44. Forrest, 88.

45. Thrapp, 400–01.

46. Judia.

CHAPTER 11

1. Alberta Begay as told to Eve Ball, "Massai—Broncho Apache," *True West* (July–August 1959). Begay's statements cited in the chapter derive from a transcript of an interview by Ball, 21 July 1955, Ball MSS.

2. "When Alberta read *Broncho Apache* [a novel written by Paul Iselin Wellman in 1936], she was both pleased and offended with the account of her father. No Apache, she said indignantly, would have eaten snake, especially rattlesnake. And her father escaped from the train with Grey Lizard, a Tonkawa, not east of the Mississippi, but in Missouri." [Ball, "Appendix B," [late 1960s?], Ball MSS.]

3. Eugene Chihuahua, transcript of interview by Ball, undated, Ball MSS.

4. Jasper Kanseah, transcript of interview by Ball, 18 November [?], Ball MSS.

5. James Kaywaykla, transcript of interview by Ball, 24 November [?], Ball MSS.

6. Jason Betzinez with Wilbert Sturtevant Nye, *I Fought with Geronimo* (New York: Bonanza Books, 1959), 143–44.

7. Kaywaykla, interview.

8. Betzinez, 144.

9. Kanseah, interview.

10. Nelson A. Miles, *Personal Recollections and Observations of General Nelson A. Miles* (Chicago: The Werner Co., 1896), 529.

11. In the *True West* story, Ball describes Massai spying on women bathing in a spring. This makes a racy yarn, but it's dubious. It would have been highly out of character for the prudish Apaches, and the penalty if caught was death.

12. Mrs. Jake Cojo, transcript of interview by Ball, 19 June 1956, Ball MSS.

13. Jess Hayes, *Apache Vengeance: True Story of Apache Kid* (Albuquerque: University of New Mexico Press, 1954), 34.

14. Ibid., 35–36.

15. Thrapp, 344.

16. Hayes, 158.

17. Ball, Indeh*: An Apache Odyssey* (Norman: University of Oklahoma Press, 1980), 248–60.

18. Walter Hearn, *Killing of the Apache Kid* (n.p., n.d.), 17–22, in Zimmerman Library Collections, University of New Mexico, Albuquerque, New Mexico.

19. Evelyn Dahl to Ball, 2 April 1957, Ball MSS.

20. Clay W. Vaden, "The Apache Kid," manuscript, 24 October 1936, New Mexico Records Center & Archives, Santa Fe, New Mexico.

21. Phyllis de la Garza, *The Apache Kid* (Tucson: Westernlore Press, 1995), 171–72.

22. Hearn, 22–23.

23. Irving McNeil, "The Indian Way," *New Mexico Magazine* (July 1952).

24. Vaden.

25. Ibid.

26. Begay, interview.

CHAPTER 12

1. Asa Daklugie, transcript of interview by Eve Ball, 16 December 1954, Ball MSS.

2. James Kaywaykla, transcript of interview by Ball, 4 March 1961, Ball MSS.

3. Eustace Fatty, transcript of interview by Ball, 10 July 1954, Ball MSS.

4. Dan Thrapp, *The Conquest of Apacheria* (Norman: University of Oklahoma Press, 1974), 126, 363.

5. Ball to Thrapp, 14 February 1970, Ball MSS.

6. Percy Big Mouth, transcript of interview by Ball, 27 October 1954, Ball MSS.

7. Gordo was born around 1830 and lived in the Mogollon and Burro Mountains in western New Mexico. In 1870 he joined the Warm Springs Apaches in trying to make peace with the Americans and lived with that group on a newly created reser-

vation at Tularosa, but the Warm Springs Apaches were unhappy and wanted to return to Ojo Caliente, their traditional home. Gordo moved his band in 1873 to the Chiricahua reservation at Fort Bowie, which he vacated in 1874 in favor of Mexico, only to return to the reservation. When the Chiricahua reservation closed, Gordo rejoined the Warm Springs at Ojo Caliente. (Ed Sweeney to author, 1 May 1999.)

8. Marion Cojo, transcript of interview by Ball, undated, Ball MSS.

9. Fatty, interview.

10. Sam Kenoi, transcript of interview by Ball, 6 October 1954, Ball MSS; and Opler, "A Chiricahua Apache's Account of the Geronimo Campaign of 1886," *New Mexico Historical Review* 3, no. 4 (October 1938): 363.

11. Fatty, interview.

12. Thrapp, *Victorio and the Mimbres Apaches* (Norman: University of Oklahoma Press, 1974), 259.

13. Kenoi, interview.

14. Fatty, interview.

15. Kenoi, interview. There is some confusion here. Eve refers to Gordo as "Gordo" (Fatty), while Eustace Fatty said his father was David Fatty.

16. Fatty, interview.

17. Kenoi, transcript of interview by Ball, 12 October 1954, Ball MSS.

18. Ball to Thrapp, 29 November 1973, Ball MSS.

19. Daklugie, interview.

20. Fatty, interview.

21. Daklugie, interview.

22. There may have been another daughter, Cheuleh; nothing is known of her. Juh's sister was the first wife of Victorio's second, Kaytennae. (Daklugie, transcript of interview by Ball, 23 March [?], Ball MSS.)

23. Jasper Kanseah, transcript of interview by Ball, 12 June 1956, Ball MSS.

24. Daklugie, interview, 23 March.

25. Daklugie, transcript of interview by Ball, undated, Ball MSS.

26. Opler, 360.

27. Kenoi, interview, 6 October 1954.

28. Opler, 362–63.

29. Ball, "Notes," undated, Ball MSS.

30. Ibid.; and Ball and Lynda Sánchez, "Daklugie, Son of Juh," *New Mexico Magazine* (April 1981): 10.

31. Opler, 381–82.

32. Ball, "Notes"; and Kenoi, interview, 12 October 1954.

33. Kenoi, interview, 12 October.

34. Ball, manuscript, undated, Ball MSS; and Kenoi, interview, 6 October 1954.

35. Kenoi, interview, 6 October.

36. Ball, "Notes."

37. Eve wrote incorrectly that Chato was made tribal secretary because of his fine penmanship. See Ball, *Indeh: An Apache Odyssey* (Norman: University of Oklahoma Press, 1980), 282.

38. Ball, manuscript.

39. Kenoi, interview, 12 October 1954.

40. Ball, "Notes."

41. Dan Nicholas, transcript of interview by Ball, 12 October 1968, Ball MSS.

42. C. L. Sonnichsen, *The Mescalero Apaches* (Norman: University of Oklahoma Press, 1958), 266.

43. Kenoi, transcript of statement, 25 March 1951, Ball MSS.

44. Kenoi, interview, 6 October 1954.

CHAPTER 13

1. Charlie Smith, transcript of interview by Eve Ball, 5 December 1967, Ball MSS.

2. Ball, "Apache Customs," manuscript, undated, Ball MSS.

3. Ball, *Indeh: An Apache Odyssey* (Norman: University of Oklahoma Press, 1980), 300–01.

4. Isabel Enjady, transcript of interview by Ball, 17 October 1955, Ball MSS.

5. Darlene Enjady, transcript of interview by Ball, 7 December 1973, Ball MSS.

6. George Martine, transcript of interview by Ball, 2 August 1966, Ball MSS.

7. Ball, manuscript, undated, Ball MSS.

8. Sam Chino, transcript of interview by Ball, 28 March 1956, Ball MSS.

9. Asa Daklugie, transcript of interview by Ball, undated, Ball MSS.

10. Eustace Fatty, transcript of interview by Ball, 10 July 1954, Ball MSS.

11. Woodrow Wilson, transcript of interview by Ball, 15 October 1958.

12. Daklugie, interview.

13. Leroy and Darlene Enjady, transcript of interview by Ball, 7 December 1973, Ball MSS.

14. Angie Debo, *Geronimo: The Man, His Time, His Place* (Norman: University of Oklahoma Press, 1976), 125.

15. Ibid., 135.

16. Ibid., 221, 237.

17. Ibid., 125.

18. Ibid., 245–46.

19. Perico and Bi–ya-neta had two daughters, Dolly and Isabel, and a son, Harry. Isabel married Clarence Enjady, a Mescalero. Their daughters are Darlene Enjady and Cecelia, and sons Wallace and Wayne. (Eve Ball, notes, undated.)

20. Debo, 286–90.

21. Isabel Enjady, transcript of interview, 16 October 1955, Ball MSS.

22. Debo, 304.

23. Isabel Enjady, interview, 16 October.

24. Debo, 448.

CHAPTER 14

1. "The Mescaleros seldom had but one wife. Sometimes when a man was killed, somebody, usually the man's brothers, must take the widow and children for they

could not live without men to protect and feed them." (Percy Big Mouth, transcript of interview by Ball, 27 October 1954, Ball MSS.)

"A man was obligated to look after his brother's widow or his wife's sister if her husband died. You are obligated to your brother's wife. If your brother went to the Happy Land the wife would become the property of the in-laws.

"For mourning the women mutilated themselves, not only cut their hair but mutilated their faces sometimes. That was also a Plains custom." (Bernard Second, transcript of interview by Ball, 9 February 1972, Ball MSS.)

2. C. L. Sonnichsen, *The Mescalero Apaches* (Norman, University of Oklahoma Press, 1958), 142.

3. Eve Ball, manuscript, undated, Ball MSS; and Sonnichsen, 91, 142.

4. Sonnichsen, 92.

5. Ball, manuscript.

6. Sonnichsen, 113.

7. Ball, manuscript.

8. Sonnichsen, 8–9.

9. Ball, manuscript.

10. Sonnichsen, 134.

11. Ball, manuscript.

12. Sonnichsen, 151–52.

13. Ball, manuscript.

14. *The New Mexican*, 3 December 1872.

15. Ball, manuscript.

16. *The New Mexican*.

17. *The New Mexican*, 10 December 1872.

18. Sonnichsen, 149.

19. Unknown source (probably Bernard Second), transcript of interview by Ball, undated, Ball MSS.

20. Second, interview; and Eloise Shield, transcript of interview by Ball, 14 December 1973, Ball MSS.

21. Second, interview.

22. U.S. Department of the Interior, "Annual Report of the Commissioner of Indian Affairs to the Secretary of the Interior," 1882, in collection of reports, 1870–1896 (Washington, D.C.: Government Printing Office, 1882), 124.

CHAPTER 15

1. C. L. Sonnichsen, *The Mescalero Apaches* (Norman: University of Oklahoma Press, 1958), 110–13.

2. Eve Ball, manuscript, undated, Ball MSS.

3. Sonnichsen, 114.

4. Big Mouth, translated by his son Percy Big Mouth, transcript of interview by Ball, 16 November 1951, Ball MSS.

5. Ball, "Big Mouth, Last Apache Scout," manuscript, undated, Ball MSS.

6. Bernard Second, transcript of interview by Ball, 9 February 1972, Ball MSS.

7. Sonnichsen, 114–17.

8. Percy Big Mouth, transcript of interview by Ball, 10 November 1954, Ball MSS.

9. Solon Sombrero, grandson of Natzili, transcript of interview by Ball, 20 October 1954, Ball MSS.

10. Big Mouth, interview.

11. Ball, "Big Mouth, Last Apache Scout."

12. Big Mouth, interview.

13. Sonnichsen, 134–35.

14. May Peso Second, transcript of interview by Ball, undated, Ball MSS.

CHAPTER 16

1. C. L. Sonnichsen, *The Mescalero Apaches* (Norman: University of Oklahoma Press, 1958), 147.

2. Percy Big Mouth, transcript of interview by Eve Ball, 10 November 1954, Ball MSS.

3. Eliza [?] Coonie, transcript of interview by Ball, undated, Ball MSS.

4. Sonnichsen, 150–52, 158–76.

5. Big Mouth, transcript of interview by Ball, 27 October 1954, Ball MSS.

6. Big Mouth, transcript of interview by Ball, 16 November 1951, Ball MSS.

7. Big Mouth, interview, November 1954.

8. Coonie, interview.

9. Solon Sombrero, transcript of interview by Ball, 20 October 1954.

10. "At one time we had three chiefs—Roman Grande, Natzili and Gregorio; then Magoosh, San Juan, Sans Peur and Peso. [Sans Peur was San Juan's son. Peso succeeded Natzili after his death in 1898.]

" . . . When we wanted to appoint a chief they would look at the family, if he were a good-talking man. Then they elected him a chief." (Big Mouth, translated by his son Percy Big Mouth, transcript of interview by Ball, 15 October 1950, Ball MSS.)

11. Woodrow Wilson, transcript of interview by Ball, 30 September 1958, Ball MSS.

12. Bears and mountain lions were considered dangerous, and Apaches did not eat turkey.

13. Gregorio once performed a ceremony to relieve pain in Dr. Blazer's back. The pain left and never returned. (Ball, manuscript, undated, Ball MSS.)

14. Big Mouth, interview, November 1954.

15. Ibid.

16. Big Mouth, interview, November 1951.

CHAPTER 17

1. Bernard Second, transcript of interview by Eve Ball, 9 February 1972, Ball MSS.

2. Apparently another little-known band, the Blue Mountain Band, was closely related to the Lipans. A splinter group of the Warm Springs Apaches, they lived between Mescalero and the Rio Grande, from Socorro to El Paso.

"I don't know what became of them but Spanish came in from the south, tie them up and march them south. Three times they took them and made slaves of them, march them south. The few left joined the Lipans." (Percy Big Mouth, transcript of interview by Ball, 10 November 1954, Ball MSS.)

3. Harry W. Basehart, *Apache Indians XII: Mescalero Apache Subsistence Patterns and Socio-Political Organization: Commission Finds on the Apache* (New York: Garland Publishing Inc., 1974), 12–13.

4. Ibid., 183.

5. Sonnichsen, 4.

6. Big Mouth, transcript of interview by Ball, 16 November 1951, Ball MSS.

7. Woodrow Wilson, transcript of interview by Ball, 30 September 1958, Ball MSS.

8. Stanley Noyes, *Los Comanches: The Horse People, 1751–1845* (Albuquerque: University of New Mexico Press, 1993), xxii–xxiii.

9. Ernest Wallace and E. Adamson Hoebel, *The Comanches, Lords of the South Plains* (Norman: University of Oklahoma Press, 1952), 17.

10. "When we pick up a bunch of ranch horses we ride one and let the rest follow. Sometimes they rode one and all the rest follow because they know that horse. It is kin to them and they take care of them." (Asa Daklugie, transcript of interview by Ball, 16 December 1954, Ball MSS.)

11. Wallace, 46.

12. Second, interview.

13. Big Mouth, interview, November 1954.

14. Noyes, xxii–xxiii, 3, 24.

15. Wallace, 7–8.

16. F. Stanley, *The Apaches of New Mexico, 1540–1940* (Pampa, Texas: Pampa Print Shop, 1962), 78.

17. Wallace, 288.

18. Noyes, 158.

19. Alton Peso, transcript of interview by Ball, 14 November 1954, Ball MSS.

20. Noyes, 285.

21. Basehart, 28–29.

22. Ibid., 39, 46–48.

23. Richard Magoosh, transcript of interview by Ball, 29 September 1963, Ball MSS.

24. Basehart, 76, 105, 111, 125–26, 142–43.

25. Sonnichsen, 55, 65, 79–80.

26. Sonnichsen, 49–55.

27. A. N. Blazer, "Blazer's Mill," *New Mexico Magazine* (January 1938): 2, 20, 48–49.

28. U.S. Department of the Interior, "Annual Report of the Commissioner of

Indian Affairs to the Secretary of the Interior," 1871, in collection of reports, 1870–1896 (Washington, D.C.: Government Printing Office, 1871), 401–02.

29. Ibid., 1872 report, 53–54.

30. Ball, *Indeh* (Norman: University of Oklahoma Press, 1980), 281.

31. Magoosh, transcript of interview by Ball, August 1954, Ball MSS.

32. U.S. Department of the Interior, "Annual Report," 1872, in collection of reports, 1870–1896 (Washington, D.C.: Government Printing Office, 1872), 263.

33. Natzili's son was Sombrero and his grandson was Solon Sombrero. (Percy Big Mouth, transcript of interview by Ball, 15 October 1950, Ball MSS.) For unknown reasons, soldiers jailed the old chief in an adobe building. He managed to remove enough iron bars to escape, and falling snow covered his tracks. Three weeks later hunters found his frozen body near a spring. (Ball, *Indeh*, 214.) "Natzili froze to death near Camp Geronimo." (Byron Treas, transcript of interview by Ball, 11 December 1973, Ball MSS.) Natzili died in 1898.

34. U.S. Department of the Interior, "Annual Report," 1877, part by Agent F. C. Godfroy, in collection of reports, 1870–1896 (Washington, D.C.: Government Printing Office, 1877), 154–56.

35. Solon Sombrero, transcript of interview, 20 October 1954, Ball MSS.

36. Ball, *Indeh*, 211–12.

37. Sombrero, transcript of interview by Ball, 22 June 1962, Ball MSS.

38. U.S. Department of the Interior, 1877, 156.

39. Ball, *Indeh*, 267–71.

40. Eric Tortilla, transcript of interview by Ball, 11 February 1955, Ball MSS.

41. Sonnichsen, 135.

42. Sonnichsen, 187.

43. U.S. Department of the Interior, "Annual Report," 1883, part by William H. H. Llewellyn, in collection of reports, 1870–1896 (Washington, D.C.: Government Printing Office, 1883), 117.

44. Unknown source, transcript of interview by Ball, undated, Ball MSS.

45. Magoosh, interview, September 1963.

46. Magoosh, interview, August 1954.

47. May Peso Second, transcript of interview by Ball, 17 December 1964, Ball MSS.

48. Big Mouth, transcript of interview by Ball, undated, Ball MSS.

49. U.S. Department of the Interior, "Annual Report," 1886, in collection of reports, 1870–1886 (Washington, D.C.: Government Printing Office, 1886), 199–200.

50. Ball, *Indeh*, 267–71, and Sonnichsen, 255.

51. Sam Chino, transcript of interview by Ball, 28 March 1956, Ball MSS.

52. Sombrero, interview, October 1954.

53. Sombrero, transcript of interview by Ball, 15 December 1954, Ball MSS.

54. Peso Second, transcript of interview by Ball, 30 January 1967, Ball MSS.

Chapter 18

1. May Peso Second, transcript of interview by Eve Ball, 30 August 1965, Ball MSS.

2. Ball, *Indeh* (Norman: University of Oklahoma Press, 1980), 204–10.

3. The story related in *Indeh* (p. 205) attributes her motives to avenging the death of her husband. In this account she is more concerned with earning her own freedom.

4. In the version in *Indeh* (p. 208), it was the girl who made advances toward the chief, which encouraged him to lead her into the brush.

5. Peso Second, transcript of interview by Ball, 2 September 1964, Ball MSS.

6. Ball, *Indeh*, 210.

7. Peso Second, transcript of interview by Ball, 17 December 1964, Ball MSS.

8. Big Mouth, translated by Percy Big Mouth, transcript of interview by Ball, 15 October 1950, Ball MSS.

9. Percy Big Mouth, transcript of interview by Ball, undated, Ball MSS.

10. Percy Big Mouth, transcript of interview by Ball, 10 November 1954, Ball MSS.

11. Peso Second, interview, September 1964; and transcript of interview by Ball, 10 November 1954, Ball MSS.

12. Percy Big Mouth, transcript of interview by Ball, 30 January 1967, Ball MSS.

13. Forest L. Williams to Eve Ball, 7 May 1965, Ball MSS.

14. Ralph Shanta, transcript of interview by Ball, 13 August 1963, Ball MSS.

15. Percy Big Mouth, transcript of interview by Ball, 16 November 1951[?], Ball MSS.

16. Ball, manuscript, undated, Ball MSS.

17. Ball to Henry Schnautz, 14 January 1959, Ball MSS.

CHAPTER 19

1. "Victorio usually wore beaded buckskin, a magnificent *bayetta* blanket—scarlet background with white and black stripes—and was well groomed." (Eve Ball to Henry Schnautz, 16 May 1957, Ball MSS.) "It was said that Nana wore watch chains dangling from his ears, which were pierced." (Eve Ball, notes from Bernard Second interview, 9 February 1972, Ball MSS.)

2. James Kaywaykla apparently doubted the much-told story of Victorio's episode with Russell. In a handwritten note to Eve Ball, he said, "Victorio's appeal to agent Russell for admittance to the Mescalero Reservation could not be true, for he determined to fight for his home, Ojo Caliente, to the last." (Note in Ball MSS.)

3. C. L. Sonnichsen, *The Mescalero Apaches* (Norman: University of Oklahoma Press, 1958), 179–206.

4. Sam Chino, transcript of interview by Ball, 28 March 1956, Ball MSS.

5. Percy Big Mouth, transcript of interview by Ball, 27 October 1954, Ball MSS.

6. Paul Blazer, transcript of interview by Ball, 15 August 1954, Ball MSS.

7. Big Mouth, transcript of interview by Ball, 10 November 1954, Ball MSS.

8. Big Mouth, transcript of interview by Ball, 15 October 1950, Ball MSS.

9. Sonnichsen, 214–18.

10. Muchacho Negro was later jailed in Santa Fe with a ball and chain fastened to his ankle. "He escaped and walked back to Mescalero carrying the ball and chain

still attached to him. He had no food on all that walk but had found a barrel cactus and got water." (Bessie Big Rope and Leroy and Darlene Enjady, transcripts of interviews by Ball, 7 December 1973, Ball MSS.)

11. Ralph Shanta, transcript of interview by Ball, 20 September 1971, Ball MSS.

12. Ball, manuscript, undated, Ball MSS.

13. Sonnichsen, 179–206.

14. Dan Thrapp, *Victorio and the Mimbres Apaches* (Norman: University of Oklahoma Press, 1974), 266–70.

15. Sonnichsen, 179–206.

16. Big Mouth, interview, October 1950.

17. Solon Sombrero, transcript of interview by Ball, 22 June 1962, Ball MSS.

18. Big Mouth, transcript of interview by Ball, 27 October 1954, Ball MSS.

19. Thrapp, 291.

20. Isabel Enjady, transcript of interview by Ball, 17 October 1955, Ball MSS.

21. Thrapp, 309.

22. George Martine, transcript of interview by Ball, 2 August 1966, Ball MSS.

23. Big Mouth, interview, October 1954.

24. Ball, *Indeh* (Norman: University of Oklahoma Press, 1980), 26.

25. Sonnichsen, 214–18.

26. Thrapp, 309.

27. Sonnichsen, 179–206.

28. Big Mouth, interview, October 1954.

29. Chino, interview.

30. Thrapp, 273.

31. Big Mouth, interview, October 1954.

CHAPTER 20

1. Percy Big Mouth, transcript of interview by Eve Ball, 27 October 1954, Ball MSS.

2. C. L. Sonnichsen, *The Mescalero Apaches* (Norman: University of Oklahoma Press, 1958), 143–47.

3. Big Mouth, transcript of interview by Ball, undated, Ball MSS.

4. Sonnichsen cites another story from Percy Big Mouth in which a medicine woman relayed a message from the Mountain Spirits. (Sonnichsen, 145–46.)

5. Big Mouth, interview, October 1954.

6. Dah-eh-wol was a medicine man. His sons were Joe and Henry Treas, who lived at Three Rivers. Joe Treas met an untimely end, allegedly shot by other Apaches.

Treas had killed a man in self-defense when a drunk shot at him while he was inside his tent. "He pulled on his belt and six-shooter, stepped outside and the drunk shot at him again. Joe fired only one shot [with a six-shooter at about 150 yards] and hit him."

Some time later, Treas was on his way to a feast, when he was ambushed.

"Joe Treas was killed pretty close to where Camp Geronimo is now. There were lots of tall sunflowers around there. He was riding toward them when a friend called to him and warned him that somebody was hidden in those sunflowers and might ambush him. There were three men in those bushes and they ran toward the Peñasco. The police never caught them. . . . Joe was on his way to the feast when he was killed." (Byron Treas, transcript of interview by Ball, 11 December 1973, Ball MSS.)

7. Ibid.

8. Eric Tortilla, transcript of interview by Ball, 11 February 1955, Ball MSS.

9. Alton Peso, transcript of interview by Ball, 14 November 1954, Ball MSS.

10. Sonnichsen, 144, 147.

11. May Peso Second, transcript of interview by Ball, 4 January 1964, Ball MSS.

12. Alton Peso, interview.

13. "Old Man" Peso had at least one brother. "Peso's older brother was very blond. After they were grown they were making a raid on the army and the soldiers thought he was a white man. Some other Indians killed him, thinking he was a white man." (May Peso Second, transcript of interview by Ball, 30 January 1967, Ball MSS.)

14. Unknown source, probably Alton Peso or May Peso Second, transcript of interview by Ball, undated, Ball MSS.

15. Alton Peso, interview.

16. May Peso Second, transcript of interview by Ball, 4 January 1964, Ball MSS.

17. Alton Peso, interview.

18. U.S. Department of the Interior, "Annual Report of the Commissioner of Indian Affairs to the Secretary of the Interior," 1885, in collection of reports, 1870–1896 (Washington, D.C.: Government Printing Office, 1885), 151.

19. May Peso Second, interview, January 1964.

20. U.S. Department of the Interior, "Annual Report," 1878, part by Agent F. C. Godfroy, in collection of reports, 1870–1896 (Washington, D.C.: Government Printing Office, 1878), 107.

21. Paul Blazer, transcript of interview by Ball, undated, Ball MSS.

22. Alton Peso, interview.

CHAPTER 21

1. Carisso Gallerito, transcript of interview by Eve Ball, 14 October 1954, Ball MSS.

2. Percy Big Mouth, transcript of interview by Ball, 10 November 1954, Ball MSS.

3. Robert Marshall Utley, *Billy the Kid: A Short and Violent Life* (Lincoln: University of Nebraska Press, 1989), 113–14.

4. Leroy and Darlene Enjady, transcript of interview by Ball, 7 December 1973, Ball MSS.

5. Big Mouth, interview.

6. Bessie Big Rope, transcript of interview by Ball, 7 December 1973, Ball MSS.

7. Big Mouth, transcript of interview by Ball, 27 October 1954, Ball MSS.

8. Ball, manuscript, undated, Ball MSS.

9. Eric Tortilla, transcript of interview by Ball, 11 February 1955, Ball MSS.

CHAPTER 22

1. Edward Franklin Castetter and Morris Opler, *The Ethnobiology of the Chiricahua and Mescalero Apache* (Albuquerque: University of New Mexico Press, 1936), 10–11.

2. Paul Blazer, transcript of interview by Eve Ball, 23 September 1954, Ball MSS.

3. Castetter and Opler, 36.

4. James Kaywaykla, transcript of interview by Ball, 12 October 1955, Ball MSS.

5. Castetter and Opler, 38.

6. Ibid., 40.

7. Ball, *In the Days of Victorio: Recollections of a Warm Springs Apache* (Tucson: University of Arizona Press, 1970).

8. Asa Daklugie, transcript of interview by Ball, 20 August 1954, Ball MSS.

9. Castetter and Opler, 40.

10. Daklugie, interview.

11. Castetter and Opler, 40.

12. Jasper Kanseah, transcript of interview by Ball, 20 October 1954, Ball MSS.

13. Castetter and Opler, 41–42.

14. Dahteste, transcript of interview by Ball, translated by Eliza Cooney, 12 July 1951, Ball MSS.

15. Daklugie, transcript of interview by Ball, 27 November 1954, Ball MSS.

16. James Kaywaykla, transcript of interview by Ball, 4 March 1961, Ball MSS.

17. Castetter and Opler, 43, 47.

18. Eustace Fatty, transcript of interview by Ball, 10 July 1954, Ball MSS.

19. Castetter and Opler, 42.

20. Ball, *Days of Victorio*, 19.

21. Castetter and Opler, 48.

22. Lawrence Clayton, "An Interview with Eve Ball," *The Journal of Big Bend Studies* 3 (1991): 133.

23. Dahteste, interview.

24. Fatty, transcript of interview by Ball, 12 July 1954, Ball MSS.

25. Charlie Smith, transcript of interview by Ball, 5 December 1967, Ball MSS.

26. Clayton, 133.

27. Castetter, 25–26.

28. "Our men were serving as scouts at Fort Stanton. At the agency the Indians went for rations and reported. Enjady and many of his [illegible] were scouts. He was the chief hunter for the soldiers and his name means "mighty hunter." (Solon Sombrero, transcript of interview by Ball, 22 June 1962, Ball MSS.)

29. Leroy and Darlene Enjady, transcripts of interviews by Ball, 7 December 1973, Ball MSS.

30. Donald C. Cole, "An Ethnohistory of the Chiricahua Apache Indian Reservation, 1872–1876" (Ph.D. diss., University of New Mexico, 1981), 140–42.

31. Daklugie, transcript of interview by Ball, 22 August 1954, Ball MSS.

32. Angie Debo, *Geronimo: The Man, His Time, His Place* (Norman: University of Oklahoma Press, 1976), 23.

33. Cole, 144.

34. Percy Big Mouth, transcript of interview by Ball, 16 November 1951, Ball MSS.

35. Daklugie, transcript of interview by Ball, undated, Ball MSS.

36. Evelyn Gaines, transcript of interview by Ball, 2 April 1957, Ball MSS.

37. Daklugie, interview, 22 August 1954.

38. Daklugie, interview, November 1954.

39. Kaywaykla, transcript of interview by Ball, 24 November [?], Ball MSS.

40. Fatty, interview, 10 July 1954.

41. Big Mouth, interview, November 1951.

42. George Martine, transcript of interview by Ball, 7 October 1974, Ball MSS.

43. Big Mouth, transcript of interview by Ball, 10 November 1954, Ball MSS.

44. Big Mouth, transcript of interview by Ball, 27 October 1954, Ball MSS.

45. Kanseah, transcript of interview by Ball, undated, Ball MSS.

46. Kaywaykla to Ball, 20 January 1958, Ball MSS.

47. Ball, manuscript, [1970?], Ball MSS.

48. Daklugie, interview, undated.

49. Ball, manuscript, undated, Ball MSS.

50. Kaywaykla, quoted in Ball, manuscript.

51. Daklugie, interview, 24 August 1954.

52. Fatty, interview, 12 July 1954.

53. Unknown source, transcript of interview by Ball, undated, Ball MSS.

54. Darlene Enjady, interview.

55. Dahteste, interview.

56. Daklugie, interview, undated.

57. Ball, notes from interview with Bernard Second, 9 February 1972, Ball MSS.

58. Ibid.

59. Kanseah, transcript of interview by Ball, 8 June 1955, Ball MSS.

60. Daklugie, interview, 24 August 1954.

61. Kanseah and Kaywaykla, transcripts of interviews by Ball, 12 June 1956, Ball MSS.

62. Eugene Chihuahua, transcript of interview by Ball, undated, Ball MSS.

63. Big Mouth, interview, November 1951.

CHAPTER 23

1. Christian Naiche, transcript of interview by Eve Ball, 21 September 1958, Ball MSS.

2. Eve Ball, manuscript, undated, Ball MSS.

3. Morris E. Opler, *An Apache Life-Way: The Economic, Social, and Religious Institutions of the Chiricahua Indians* (Chicago: University of Chicago Press, 1941), 217.

4. Naiche, interview.

5. Solon Sombrero, transcript of interview by Ball, 15 December 1954, Ball MSS.

6. Asa Daklugie, transcript of interview by Ball, 23 March [?], Ball MSS.

7. Ales Hrdlicka, "Physiological and Medical Observations among the Indians of the Southwestern United States and Northern Mexico," Bulletin 34 (Washington, D.C.: Bureau of American Ethnology, 1908), 231.

8. Naiche, interview.

9. Hrdlicka, 234, 238; Walter Ebeling, *Handbook of Indian Foods and Fibers of Arid America* (Berkeley: University of California Press, 1986), 129; and William Dunmire and Gail Tierney, *Wild Plants and Native Peoples of the Four Corners* (Santa Fe: Museum of New Mexico Press, 1997), 261–63.

10. Eustace Fatty, transcript of interview by Ball, 10 July 1954, Ball MSS.

11. Hrdlicka, 238.

12. Opler, 223.

13. Daklugie, interview.

14. Virgil J. Vogel, *American Indian Medicine* (Norman: University of Oklahoma Press, 1970), 166.

15. Fatty, interview.

16. Hrdlicka, 235.

17. Opler, 220.

18. Woodrow Wilson, transcript of interview, 30 September 1958, Ball MSS.

19. L. S. M. Curtin, *Healing Herbs of the Upper Rio Grande* (Los Angeles: Southwest Museum, 1965), 97–98; and Hrdlicka, 233.

20. Opler, 221.

21. Hrdlicka, 235.

22. Ball, notes, undated, Ball MSS.

23. Eugene Chihuahua, transcript of interview by Ball, undated, Ball MSS.

CHAPTER 24

1. Eve Ball, notes for speech, "Apache Medicine and Medicine Man," Las Cruces, New Mexico, undated, Ball MSS.

2. Eugene Chihuahua, transcript of interview by Ball, 14 December 1964, Ball MSS.

3. Eustace Fatty, transcript of interview by Ball, 10 July 1954, Ball MSS.

4. Dan Nicholas, transcript of interview by Ball, 9 June 1966, Ball MSS.

5. Asa Daklugie, transcript of interview by Ball, 16 December 1954, Ball MSS.

6. Fatty, interview.

7. Unknown source (probably Kanseah or Charlie Smith), transcript of interview by Ball, undated, Ball MSS.

8. Daklugie, interview.

9. James Kaywaykla, transcript of interview by Ball, 24–25 December 1955, Ball MSS.

10. Sam Kenoi, transcript of interview by Ball, 6 October 1954, Ball MSS.

11. Eugene Chihuahua, transcript of interview by Ball, undated, Ball MSS.

12. Ball to Henry Schnautz, 3 October 1959, Ball MSS.

13. Ball to Schnautz, 4 November 1959, Ball MSS.

14. Kenoi, transcript of interview by Ball, 6 October 1954, Ball MSS.

15. Ball, manuscript, undated, Ball MSS.

16. Ibid.

17. Ibid.

18. Ibid.

19. Eloise Shield, transcript of interview by Ball, 14 December 1973, Ball MSS.

20. Shield, interview.

21. Ball, manuscript, [1972], Ball MSS.

22. Ball to Dan Thrapp, 19 May 1973, Ball MSS.

CHAPTER 25

1. Jasper Kanseah and James Kaywaykla, transcripts of interviews by Ball, 12 June 1956, Ball MSS.

2. Percy Big Mouth, transcript of interview by Ball, 16 November 1951, Ball MSS.

3. Eustace Fatty, transcript of interview by Ball, 12 July 1954, Ball MSS.

4. Paul Blazer, transcript of interview by Ball, 23 September 1954, Ball MSS.

5. Big Mouth, interview.

6. Eve Ball, manuscript, undated, Ball MSS.

7. Fatty, interview.

8. Echos's name means "fine feather." His daughter Helen married Chato.

9. Eugene Chihuahua, transcript of interview by Ball, 14 December 1964, Ball MSS.

10. Frank C. Lockwood, *The Apache Indians* (Lincoln: University of Nebraska Press, 1938), 59.

11. Kaywaykla, transcript of interview by Ball, 24 November [?]Ball MSS.

12. Chihuahua, transcript of interview by Ball, 27 September 1961, Ball MSS.

13. Kanseah, transcript of interview by Ball, 20 October 1954, Ball MSS.

14. Asa Daklugie, transcript of interview by Ball, undated, Ball MSS.

15. Big Mouth, interview.

16. John C. Cremony, *Life Among the Apaches* (San Francisco: A. Roman & Company, 1868), 189.

17. Jason Betzinez with Wilbert Sturtevant Nye, *I Fought with Geronimo* (New York: Bonanza Books, 1959), 85.

18. Fatty, interview.

19. Ball, manuscript, undated, Ball MSS.

20. Sam Chino, transcript of interview by Ball, 28 March 1956, Ball MSS.

21. R. C. House, "Symbols of Destiny: The Guns That Rode West," *Roundup Magazine* (April 1996): 7–10.

22. Betzinez, 77.

23. Dan Thrapp, *Victorio and the Mimbres Apaches* (Norman: University of Oklahoma Press, 1974), 175.

24. Britton Davis, *The Truth About Geronimo* (New Haven: Yale University Press, 1929), 59.

25. Thrapp, *Al Sieber, Chief of Scouts* (Norman: University of Oklahoma Press, 1964), 280.

26. Daklugie, transcript of interview by Ball, 22 March 1954, Ball MSS.

27. Daklugie, interview, undated.

28. Sam Kenoi, transcript of interview by Ball, 4 November 1954, Ball MSS.

29. Daklugie, transcript of interview by Ball, 16 December 1954, Ball MSS.

30. At that writing Charlie Smith was about ninety-three.

31. Ball to Thrapp, 4 January 1970, Ball MSS.

32. Fatty, interview.

33. Kanseah, transcript of interview by Ball, 8 June 1955, Ball MSS.

34. Ball, "Appendix B" manuscript, [late 1960s?], Ball MSS.

35. Ball, "Dan Nicholas," draft chapter manuscript, undated, Ball MSS.

36. Sam Haozous was a great-great-grandson of Mahko and grandson of Mangas Coloradas. [Angie Debo, *Geronimo: The Man, His Time, His Place* (Norman: University of Oklahoma Press, 1976), 110.] His mother was Nah-ke-de-sah, daughter of Mangas, and his father Gonah-hleenah. In 1913 he chose to stay in Oklahoma, where he married Blossom, the half-Apache daughter of George Wratten. They had four children, including the artist Allan Houser. Sam Haozous died in 1957.

37. Kenoi, interview.

38. Ball, "Dan Nicholas."

39. George Martine, transcript of interview by Ball, 14 February 1974, Ball MSS.

40. Eloise Shield, transcript of interview by Ball, 14 December 1973, Ball MSS.

41. Ball, notes from interview with Bernard Second, 9 February 1972, Ball MSS.

42. Bernard Second, transcript of interview by Ball, 9 February 1972, Ball MSS.

43. Shield, interview.

CHAPTER 26

1. Eve Ball, *Indeh: An Apache Odyssey* (Norman: University of Oklahoma Press, 1980), 63.

2. Amelia Naiche, transcript of interview by Ball, 2 April 1957, Ball MSS.

3. D.C. Cole, *The Chiricahua Apache, 1846–1876: From War to Reservation* (Albuquerque: University of New Mexico Press, 1988), 45.

4. Ball, manuscript, undated, Ball MSS.

5. Ball, *Indeh*, 63, 87, 269.

6. Asa Daklugie, transcript of interview by Ball, undated, Ball MSS.

7. Ball, manuscript, undated, Ball MSS.

8. Jasper Kanseah, transcript of interview by Ball, 20 October 1954, Ball MSS.

9. Ball, *Indeh*, 14.

10. Kanseah, transcript of interview by Ball, 18 November [?], Ball MSS.

11. Kanseah, transcript of interview by Ball, 8 June 1955, Ball MSS.

12. Kanseah and James Kaywaykla, transcripts of interviews by Ball, 12 June 1956, Ball MSS. This story is retold, although not word for word, in Kaywaykla as told to Ball, "Witchcraft," *Frontier Times* (February–March, 1965).

13. Leroy and Darlene Enjady, transcript of interview by Ball, 7 December 1973, Ball MSS.

14. Eustace Fatty, transcript of interview by Ball, 12 July 1954, Ball MSS.

15. Ball, "Fearless Apaches," manuscript, undated, Ball MSS.

16. Leroy Big Rope was the son of Lawrence Big Rope and grandson of Big Rope. Leroy's grandmother, Bessie Big Rope, was a medicine woman.

17. Eve Ball, "Count His Toes," manuscript, undated, Ball MSS.

18. Percy Big Mouth, transcript of interview by Ball, 16 November 1951, Ball MSS.

19. Morris E. Opler, *An Apache Life-Way, The Economic, Social and Religious Institutions of the Chiricahua Indians* (Chicago: University of Chicago Press, 1941), 238–239, 329–330.

20. George Martine, transcript of interview by Ball, 14 February 1974, Ball MSS.

CHAPTER 27

1. Lynda A. Sánchez, "Eve Ball," *New Mexico Magazine* (April 1981): 33.

2. In the foreword to Ball's *Indeh* (Norman: University of Oklahoma Press, 1980), Dan Thrapp writes that Eve was born in Kentucky on her grandfather's plantation (p. xiii). Clarksville is just over the Kentucky-Tennessee state line.

3. Kimberly Moore Buchanan, "Eve Ball," in John R. Wunder, ed., *Historians of the American Frontier*, 46.

4. Lawrence Clayton, "An Interview with Eve Ball," *The Journal of Big Bend Studies* 3 (1991): 126.

5. Ball to Henry Schnautz, 16 May 1957, Ball MSS.

6. Ball to Evelyn King, 15 May 1961, Ball MSS.

7. *Ruidoso News* (New Mexico), 24 December 1984.

8. Buchanan, 46.

9. Lela Waltrip, "The Quiet Lady of Noisy River," *The Roundup* (August 1974): 10–11.

10. Clayton, 127–28.

11. *Indeh*, xiii.

12. Clayton, 128.

13. Ball to Schnautz, 3 October 1959.

14. Sánchez, 26.

15. Waltrip, 10–11.

16. Sánchez, 26.

17. Clayton, 130–31.

18. Eve Ball, "Appendix B," [late 1960s?], Ball MSS.

19. Ball to Thrapp, 5 January 1977, Ball MSS.

20. Ball to Elizabeth Shaw, 3 January 1970, Ball MSS.

21. Ball to Thrapp, 4 April 1968, Ball MSS.

22. Ball to Don Worcester, 24 April 1980, Ball MSS.

23. Sam Chino said his father was a Chiricahua named José Mario and his mother

was Juh's sister. They had two sons, Sam and John Chino. Sam and John "were not exiled but when they refused to fight for their people, [they were] driven out by their unpopularity. They took refuge at Mescalero and are numerous now." (Ball to Thrapp, 17 November 1967, Ball MSS.)

"Those who did not volunteer to fight were not banished, except as the disapproval of their people might constitute that punishment. But many who did not wish to fight left their tribe and took refuge with others, as did several Chiricahua who came to their brothers, the Mescaleros. Among them were Sam and John Chino. These, who corresponded to the modern conscientious objector, adjusted easily to reservation life." (Dan Nicholas, transcript of interview by Ball, 17 July 1961, Ball MSS.)

"I thought of one thing I should not have written in Victorio. I said that Sam Chino and his brother were not banished by the council of the Chiricahua but left because of their unpopularity owing to their refusal to join in any raid undertaken by the tribe. That is true but I need not have said it. . . . If the two left to escape military service, which the older Chiricahua say they did, undoubtedly the statement would have antagonized Wendell. He loves publicity if favorable, and is adept at getting it." (Ball to Thrapp, 13 April 1974, Ball MSS.)

At Mescalero, Sam Chino resisted the temptation of riding with Victorio and instead joined the Indian police force in the early 1880s. He died in 1958[?] at about 102. [C. L. Sonnichsen, *The Mescalero Apaches* (Norman: University of Oklahoma Press, 1958), 191–92.]

Sam married a Mescalero woman, which made him and his son Mescalero. (Sam Chino, with Amelia Naiche translating, transcripts of interviews by Ball, 28 March 1956 and 28 January 1956, Ball MSS; and Carisso Gallerito, transcript of interview by Ball, 14 October 1954, Ball MSS.)

24. Ball, note, 28 March 1956, Ball MSS.

25. Ball to Schnautz, 25 July 1957, Ball MSS.

26. Ball to Schnautz, 5 August 1957, Ball MSS.

27. Ball to Schnautz, 26 April 1958, Ball MSS.

28. Ball to Schnautz, 10 September 1958, Ball MSS.

29. Ball to Schnautz, 14 January 1959, Ball MSS.

30. Ball to Schnautz, 21 January 1959, Ball MSS.

31. Ball to Schnautz, 4 November 1959, Ball MSS.

32. Ball, "Anglo Files on Apaches," notes, undated, Ball MSS.

33. Bill McGaw, "Eugene Chihuahua, 97, Last Apache Chief Laid to Rest at Mescalero," *The Southwesterner* (May 1963): 10.

34. Ball to Schnautz, 9 February 1959, Ball MSS.

35. Ball to Schnautz, 1 February 1960, Ball MSS.

36. Ball to Schnautz, 3 February 1961, Ball MSS.

37. Ball to Schnautz, 12 February 1961, Ball MSS.

38. Ball to Schnautz, 15 June 1960, Ball MSS.

39. Ball to Schnautz, 16 March 1961, Ball MSS.

40. Ball to Schnautz, 3 October 1959, Ball MSS.

41. Ball to Schnautz, 17 May and 17 October 1960, Ball MSS.
42. Ball to Schnautz, 21 December 1971, Ball MSS.
43. LaVerne Harrell Clark to Dennis Rowley, 4 September 1992, Ball MSS.
44. Ball to Schnautz, 16 March 1961, Ball MSS.
45. Ball to Schnautz, 25 July 1957, and Ball to Thrapp, 22 April 1977, Ball MSS.
46. Ball to Thrapp, 5 October 1967, Ball MSS.
47. Ball to Thrapp, 1 September 1970, Ball MSS.
48. Ball to Thrapp, 22 November 1965, and 7 December 1967, Ball MSS.
49. Ball to Thrapp, 21 September 1970, Ball MSS.
50. Ball to Thrapp, 27 January 1967, Ball MSS.
51. Ball to Thrapp, 17 November 1967, Ball MSS.
52. James Kaywaykla to Ball, 21 May 1956, Ball MSS.
53. Kaywaykla to Ball, 11 July 1956, Ball MSS.
54. Kaywaykla, note on Ball letter to him, undated, Ball MSS.
55. Kaywaykla to Ball, 22 November 1962, Ball MSS.
56. Ball to Kaywaykla, 17 March 1962, Ball MSS.
57. Kaywaykla to Ball, 18 September 1962, Ball MSS.
58. Ball to Schnautz, 28 November 1960, Ball MSS.
59. Ball to King, 15 May 1961, Ball MSS.
60. Ball to Thrapp, 16 May 1968, Ball MSS.
61. Ball to Thrapp, 1 September 1970, Ball MSS.
62. Thrapp is author of *Al Sieber, Chief of Scouts*; *The Conquest of Apacheria*; *General Crook and the Sierra Madre Adventure*; and *Victorio and the Mimbres Apaches*. Angie Debo wrote a number of histories, including *Geronimo: The Man, His Time, His Place*.
63. Debo to Eve Ball, 3 July [1973?], Ball MSS.
64. Ball to Thrapp, 1 March 1977, Ball MSS.
65. Ball to Thrapp, 2 February 1977, Ball MSS.
66. Ball to Thrapp, 11 April 1977, Ball MSS.
67. Ball to Thrapp, 31 January 1970, Ball MSS.
68. Thrapp to Ball, 4 April 1974, Ball MSS.
69. Ball to Thrapp, 8 April 1974, Ball MSS.
70. Thrapp to Ball, 20 January 1970, Ball MSS.
71. Historian C. L. Sonnichsen wrote *The Mescalero Apaches*, among other books.
72. Ball to Thrapp, 7 December 1967, Ball MSS.
73. Ball to Thrapp, 28 December 1970, Ball MSS.
74. Ball to Schnautz, 11 July 1959, and 21 December 1971, Ball MSS; Ball to Worcester, 24 November 1978, Ball MSS; and Ball to Thrapp, 1 September 1970, Ball MSS.
75. Ball to Schnautz, 21 December 1971, Ball MSS.
76. Thrapp to Ball, 7 January 1971, Ball MSS.
77. Ball to Thrapp, 10 January 1971, Ball MSS.
78. Richard E. Oglesby, review of *In the Days of Victorio: Recollections of a Warm Springs Apache*, by Eve Ball, *Arizona and the West* (1971): 93–94.

79. Thrapp, review of *In the Days of Victorio: Recollections of a Warm Springs Apache*, by Eve Ball, *The Journal of Arizona History* 12 (Summer 1971): 145–46.

80. Ball to Thrapp, 14 June 1971, Ball MSS.

81. Ball to Thrapp, 8 April 1974, Ball MSS.

82. Ball to Thrapp, 25 April 1974, Ball MSS. She doesn't name the book, but it could have been *The Jicarilla Apache Indians: A History, 1598–1888* (New York: Garland, 1974) by Alfred Barnaby Thomas.

83. Debo to Ball, 28 May 1975, Ball MSS.

84. Ball to Thrapp, 14 December 1977, Ball MSS.

85. Ball to Thrapp, 14 February 1970, Ball MSS.

86. Ball to Schnautz, 22 December 1978, Ball MSS.

87. Ball to Thrapp, 10 and 23 January 1974, and 2 December 1975, Ball MSS.

88. Ball to Thrapp, 5 January and 2 February 1977, Ball MSS; Ball to Will Henry, 14 March 1980, Ball MSS.

89. Ball to Thrapp, 1 March 1977, Ball MSS; Ball to Worcester, 26 March 1979, Ball MSS.

90. Ball to Schnautz, 22 December 1978, Ball MSS; Ball to Worcester, 27 January 1980, Ball MSS.

91. Lori Davisson, review of *Indeh: An Apache Odyssey*, by Eve Ball, *The Journal of Arizona History* 22 (Spring 1981): 154–55.

92. *Publishers Weekly*, review of *Indeh: An Apache Odyssey*, by Eve Ball, 217 (16 May 1980): 205.

93. R. David Edmunds, review of *Indeh: An Apache Odyssey*, by Eve Ball, *Utah Historical Quarterly* 49 (Winter 1981): 98–99.

94. Robert L. Munkres, review of *Indeh: An Apache Odyssey*, by Eve Ball, *Journal of the West* 20 (July 1981): 92–93.

95. Donald E. Worcester, review of *Indeh: An Apache Odyssey*, by Eve Ball, *Arizona and the West* 23 (Summer 1981): 177–78.

96. John Anthony Turcheneske, Jr., review of *Indeh: An Apache Odyssey*, by Eve Ball, *New Mexico Historical Review* 57 (July 1982): 297.

97. Edmunds.

98. Will Henry to Ball, 19 February 1981, Ball MSS.

99. Ball to Henry, 17 January 1982, Ball MSS.

100. Lynda Sánchez to Worcester, 27 October 1982, Ball MSS; Ball to Worcester, undated, Ball MSS; Ball to Will Henry, undated, Ball MSS.

101. Ball to Henry, 29 December 1981, Ball MSS.

102. Ball to Henry, 8 January 1983, Ball MSS.

103. *Ruidoso News* (New Mexico), 27 December 1984.

Bibliography

Alamogordo News, 4 March 1926.

Ball, Eve. "Cibicu: An Apache Interpretation." In *Troopers West: Military & Indian Affairs on the American Frontier*, edited by Ray Brandes. San Diego: Frontier Heritage Press, 1970.

___ and Lynda Sánchez. "Daklugie, Son of Juh." *New Mexico Magazine* (April 1981): 10–11.

Ball, Eve. "Early Days at Blazer's Mill." *Frontier Times* (June–July 1979): 28–31, 50–51.

___. "Flight from the Bosque Redondo." *True West* (July–August 1971): 36–37, 52, 54.

___. *In the Days of Victorio: Recollections of a Warm Springs Apache*. Tucson: the University of Arizona Press, 1970.

___ with Nora Henn and Lynda A. Sánchez. *Indeh: An Apache Odyssey*. Norman: University of Oklahoma Press, 1980.

Ball, Eve. "Legendary Apache Women." *Frontier Times* (October–November 1980): 8–12.

___. Papers and Letters. Provo Special Collections & Manuscripts, Harold B. Lee Library, Brigham Young University, Provo, Utah (Ball MSS).

Barrett, S. M., ed. *Geronimo: His Own Story*. New York: E. P. Dutton & Co., 1970.

Barton, Del. *A Good Day to Die*. Garden City: Doubleday & Company, 1980.

Basehart, Harry W. *Apache Indians XII, Mescalero Apache Subsistence Patterns and Socio-Political Organization: Commission Finds on the Apache*. New York: Garland Publishing Inc., 1974.

Basso, Keith H., ed. *Western Apache Raiding and Warfare: From the Notes of Grenville Goodwin*. Tucson: University of Arizona Press, 1971.

Begay, Alberta as told to Eve Ball. "Massai-Broncho Apache." *True West* (July–August 1959): 2–5, 8–11.

Betzinez, Jason with Wilbert Sturtevant Nye. *I Fought with Geronimo*. New York: Bonanza Books, 1959.

Blazer, A. N. "Blazer's Mill." *New Mexico Magazine* (January 1938): 2, 20, 48–49.

Boyer, Ruth McDonald and Narcissus Duffy Gayton. *Apache Mothers and Daughters: Four Generations of a Family*. Norman: University of Oklahoma Press, 1992.

Brandes, Ray, ed. *Troopers West: Military & Indian Affairs on the American Frontier*. San Diego: Frontier Heritage Press, 1970.

Buchanan, Kimberly Moore. "Eve Ball." In John R. Wunder, ed. *Historians of the American Frontier*, pp. 46–55. New York: Greenwood Press, 1988.

Castetter, Edward Franklin and Morris Opler. *The Ethnobiology of the Chiricahua and Mescalero Apache*. Albuquerque: University of New Mexico Press, 1936.

Clayton, Lawrence. "An Interview with Eve Ball." *The Journal of Big Bend Studies* 3 (1991): 125–38.

Clum, John P. "Es-kim-in-zin." Parts 1 and 2. *New Mexico Historical Review* 3 (October 1928): 399–420; 4 (January 1929): 1–27.

___. "Geronimo." Parts 1, 2, and 3. *New Mexico Historical Review* 3, no. 1 (January 1928): 1–40; 3, no. 2 (April 1928): 121–44; 3, no. 3 (July 1928): 217–64.

___. "The San Carlos Police." *New Mexico Historical Review* 4, no. 3 (July 1929): 203–19.

___. "Victorio." *New Mexico Historical Review* 4 (April 1929): 107–27.

Clum, Woodworth. *Apache Agent: The Story of John P. Clum*. Boston, Houghton, Mifflin Co., 1936.

Cochise, Ciye Niño and A. Kinney Griffith. *The First Hundred Years of Niño Cochise: The Untold Story of an Apache Indian Chief*. New York: Abelard Schuman, 1971.

___ and A. Kinney Griffith. "Apache Tears." *Old West* (Winter 1967): 2–14.

Cole, D.C. *The Chiricahua Apache, 1846–1876: From War to Reservation*. Albuquerque: University of New Mexico Press, 1988.

___. "An Ethnohistory of the Chiricahua Apache Indian Reservation, 1872–1876." Ph.D. diss., University of New Mexico, 1981.

Colyer, Vincent. "Peace with the Apaches of New Mexico and Arizona." Washington, D.C.: Government Printing Office, 1872.

Cremony, John C. *Life Among the Apaches*. San Francisco: A. Roman & Company, 1868.

Curtin, L. S. M. *Healing Herbs of the Upper Rio Grande*. Los Angeles: Southwest Museum, 1965.

Danielsen, Helga. "Over-kill in Apache Land." *Frontier Times* (June–July 1971): 14–19, 60–66.

Davis, Britton. *The Truth About Geronimo*. New Haven: Yale University Press, 1929.

Davisson, Lori. Review of Indeh: An Apache Odyssey, by Eve Ball. *The Journal of Arizona History* 22 (Spring 1981): 154–55.

Debo, Angie. *Geronimo: The Man, His Time, His Place*. Norman: University of Oklahoma Press, 1976.

Dunmire, William and Gail Tierney. *Wild Plants and Native Peoples of the Four Corners*. Santa Fe: Museum of New Mexico Press, 1997.

Ebeling, Walter. *Handbook of Indian Foods and Fibers of Arid America*. Berkeley: University of California Press, 1986.

Edmunds, R. David. Review of Indeh: An Apache Odyssey, by Eve Ball. *Utah Historical Quarterly* 49 (Winter 1981): 98–99.

Evans, Joseph. Letter to editor. *True West* (November–December 1959): 4.

___. Letter to editor. *True West* (January–February 1960).

Farb, Peter. Review of *The First Hundred Years of Niño Cochise: The Untold Story of an Apache Indian Chief*, by Ciye Niño Cochise and A. Kinney Griffith. New York Review of Books 17 (16 December 1972): 36.

Forrest, Earle Robert. *Lone War Trail of Apache Kid*. Pasadena: Trail's End Publishing Co., 1947.

de la Garza, Phyllis. *The Apache Kid*. Tucson: Westernlore Press, 1995.

Hadley, Diana, Peter Marshall, and Don Bufkin. "Environmental Change in Aravaipa, 1870–1970: An Ethnoecological Survey." Phoenix: Arizona State Office of the U.S. Bureau of Land Management, September 1991.

Hayes, Jess G. *Apache Vengeance: True Story of Apache Kid*. Albuquerque: University of New Mexico Press, 1954.

Hearn, Walter. *Killing of the Apache Kid*. N.p., n.d. [In Zimmerman Library Collections, University of New Mexico, Albuquerque, New Mexico.]

House, R. C. "Symbols of Destiny: The Guns that Rode West," *Roundup Magazine* (April 1996): 7–10.

Hrdlicka, Ales. "Physiological and Medical Observations among the Indians of the Southwestern United States and Northern Mexico." Bulletin 34 Washington, D.C.: Bureau of American Ethnology, 1908.

Kaywaykla, James as told to Eve Ball. "Witchcraft." *Frontier Times* (February–March 1965): 26–27, 72.

Lehmann, Herman. "Nine Years Among the Indians, 1870–1879." Parts 1 and 2. *Frontier Times* (March 1963): 7; (May 1963): 8.

Lekson, Stephen H. *Nana's Raid, Apache Warfare in Southern New Mexico, 1881*. Southwestern Studies Series No. 81. El Paso: The University of Texas at El Paso, 1987.

Lockwood, Frank C. *The Apache Indians*. Lincoln: University of Nebraska Press, 1938.

McGaw, Bill. "Eugene Chihuahua, 97, Last Apache Chief Laid To Rest at Mescalero." *The Southwesterner* (May 1963): 10, 13, 14.

McNeil, Irving. "The Indian Way." *New Mexico Magazine* (July 1952): 12–14.

Miles, Nelson A. *Personal Recollections and Observations of General Nelson A. Miles*. Chicago: The Werner Co., 1896.

Munkres, Robert L. Review of Indeh: *An Apache Odyssey*, by Eve Ball. *Journal of the West* 20 (July 1981): 92–93.

The New Mexican, 3 December 1872.

Niethammer, Carolyn. *Daughters of the Earth: The Lives and Legends of American Indian Women*. New York: Collier Books/Macmillan Publishing Co., Inc., 1977.

Noyes, Stanley. *Los Comanches: The Horse People, 1751–1845*. Albuquerque: University of New Mexico Press, 1993.

Oglesby, Richard E. Review of *In the Days of Victorio: Recollections of a Warm Springs Apache*, by Eve Ball. *Arizona and the West* (1971): 93–94.

Opler, Morris E. *An Apache Life-Way: The Economic, Social, and Religious Institutions of the Chiricahua Indians*. Chicago: University of Chicago Press, 1941.

___. "A Chiricahua Apache's Account of the Geronimo Campaign of 1886." *New Mexico Historical Review* 4, no. 4 (October 1938): 360–86.

___ and Catherine H. Opler. "Mescalero Apache History in the Southwest." *New Mexico Historical Review* 25, no. 1 (January 1950): 1–36.

Parker, Arthur Caswell. *The History of the Seneca Indians*. Port Washington, New York: I. J. Friedman, 1967.

Publishers Weekly. Review of *Indeh: An Apache Odyssey*, by Eve Ball. 217 (16 May 1980): 205.

Ringgold, Jennie Parks. *Frontier Days in the Southwest*. San Antonio: The Naylor Company, 1952.

Rope, John and edited by Grenville Goodwin. "Experiences of an Indian Scout." *Arizona Historical Review* 7, no. 1 (January 1936): 31–68.

The Ruidoso News, 24 December 1984, and 27 December 1984.

Sánchez, Lynda A. "Eve Ball." *New Mexico Magazine* (April 1981): 26–27, 32–33.

Santee, Ross. "Apache Kid." *Arizona Highways* (February 1948): 4–9.

Scott, Hugh Lenox. *Some Memories of a Soldier*. New York: The Century Co., 1928.

Silver City Enterprise, 20 April 1883 and 23 January 1885.

Silver City Independent, 11 May 1915.

Sonnichsen, C. L. *The Mescalero Apaches*. Norman: University of Oklahoma Press, 1958.

Stanley, F. *The Apaches of New Mexico, 1540–1940*. Pampa, Texas: Pampa Print Shop, 1962.

Stockel, H. Henrietta. *Women of the Apache Nation*. Las Vegas: University of Nevada Press, 1993.

Sweeney, Ed. "Reviewer's Report of *Apache Voices*," 22 October 1998.

Terrell, John Upton. *Apache Chronicle*. New York: World Publishing/Times Mirror, 1972.

Thomas, Alfred Barnaby. *The Jicarilla Apache Indians: A History, 1598–1888*. New York: Garland, 1974.

Thrapp, Dan L. *Al Sieber, Chief of Scouts*. Norman: University of Oklahoma Press, 1964.

___. *The Conquest of Apacheria*. Norman: University of Oklahoma Press, 1967.

___. *Encyclopedia of Frontier Biography*. Glendale, California: A. H. Clark Co., 1988.

___. Foreword to *Indeh: An Apache Odyssey*, by Eve Ball with Nora Henn and Lynda A. Sánchez. Norman: University of Oklahoma Press, 1980.

___. *Juh: An Incredible Indian*. Southwestern Studies Monograph No. 39. El Paso: Texas Western Press, University of Texas at El Paso, 1973.

___. *General Crook and the Sierra Madre Adventure*. Norman: University of Oklahoma Press, 1971.

___. Review of *In the Days of Victorio: Recollections of a Warm Springs Apache*, by Eve Ball. The Journal of Arizona History 12 (Summer 1971): 145–46.

___. *Victorio and the Mimbres Apaches*. Norman: University of Oklahoma Press, 1974.

Turcheneske, John Anthony, Jr. Review of *Indeh: An Apache Odyssey*, by Eve Ball. New Mexico Historical Review 57 (July 1982): 297.

U.S. Department of the Interior. "Annual Report of the Commissioner of Indian Affairs to the Secretary of the Interior." Collection of reports, 1870–1896. Washington: Government Printing Office, 1870–1896.

U.S. War Department. "Case of Apache Indian Eskimenzin." Washington, D.C.: War Department, 11 April 1893.

Utley, Robert Marshall. *Billy the Kid: A Short and Violent Life*. Lincoln: University of Nebraska Press, 1989.

Vaden, Clay W. "The Apache Kid." Manuscript, 24 October 1936. New Mexico Records Center and Archives, Santa Fe, New Mexico.

Vogel, Virgil. J. *American Indian Medicine*. Norman: University of Oklahoma Press, 1970.

Wallace, Ernest and E. Adamson Hoebel. *The Comanches, Lords of the South Plains*. Norman: University of Oklahoma Press, 1952.

Waltrip, Lela. "The Quiet Lady of Noisy River." *The Roundup* (August 1974): 10–11.

Wells, Edmund W. *Argonaut Tales: Stories of the Gold Seekers and the Indian Scouts of Early Arizona*. New York: F. H. Hitchcock, 1927.

Williamson, Dan R. "The Apache Kid: Red Renegade of the West." *Arizona Highways* (May 1939): 14–15, 30–31.

Worcester, Donald E. Review of *Indeh: An Apache Odyssey*, by Eve Ball. Arizona and the West 23 (Summer 1981): 177–78.

Wunder, John R., ed. *Historians of the American Frontier*. New York: Greenwood Press, 1988.

Index

Page numbers in parentheses following note number refer to the page that has the information that the note is continuing. Italicized numbers are page references for photographs.